AF789578

IFLA

International Federation of Library Associations and Institutions
Fédération Internationale des Associations de Bibliothécaires et des Bibliothèques
Internationaler Verband der bibliothekarischen Vereine und Institutionen
Международная Федерация Библиотечных Ассоциаций и Учреждений
Federación Internacional de Asociaciones de Bibliotecarios y Bibliotecas

IFLA Publications 111

Preparing for the Worst, Planning for the Best: Protecting our Cultural Heritage from Disaster

Proceedings of a conference sponsored by
the IFLA Preservation and Conservation Section,
the IFLA Core Activity for Preservation and Conservation
and the Council on Library and Information Resources, Inc.,
with the Akademie der Wissenschaften
and the Staatsbibliothek zu Berlin.
Berlin, Germany, July 30 - August 1, 2003

Edited by
Johanna G. Wellheiser and Nancy E. Gwinn

K · G · Saur München 2005

IFLA Publications
edited by Sjoerd Koopman

Recommended catalogue entry:

Preparing for the Worst, Planning for the Best:
Protecting our Cultural Heritage from Disaster
Proceedings of a conference sponsored by the IFLA Preservation and Conservation Section,
the IFLA Core Activity for Preservation and Conservation
and the Council on Library and Information Resources, Inc.,
with the Akademie der Wissenschaften and the Staatsbibliothek zu Berlin.
Berlin, Germany, July 30 - August 1, 2003
[International Federation of Library Associations and Institutions]
– München : Saur, 2005, 192 p. 21 cm
(IFLA publications ; 111)
ISBN 3-598-21842-7

Bibliographic information published by Die Deutsche Bibliothek
Die Deutsche Bibliothek lists this publication in the Deutsche Nationalbibliografie;
detailed bibliographic data is available in the Internet at
http://dnb.ddb.de.

∞

Printed on permanent paper
The paper used in this publication meets the minimum requirements of
American National Standard – Permanence of Paper
for Publications and Documents in Libraries and Archives
ANSI/NISO Z39.48-1992 (R1997)

© 2005 by International Federation of Library Associations
and Institutions, The Hague, The Netherlands
Alle Rechte vorbehalten / All Rights Strictly Reserved
K. G. Saur Verlag GmbH, München 2005
Printed in the Federal Republic of Germany

All rights reserved. No part of this publication may be reproduced, stored in a retrieval system of any nature, or transmitted, in any form or by any means, electronic, mechanical, photocopying, recording or otherwise, without the prior written permission of the publisher.

Printed / Bound by Strauss GmbH, Mörlenbach

ISBN 3-598-21842-7
ISSN 0344-6891 (IFLA Publications)

TABLE OF CONTENTS

ACKNOWLEDGEMENTS

We wish to thank the following organizations for sponsoring the conference:

IFLA Preservation and Conservation Section

IFLA Core Activity for Preservation and Conservation

Council on Library and Information Resources, Inc.

Akademie der Wissenschaften

Staatsbibliothek zu Berlin

We also want to acknowledge the following organizations for supporting the conference:

Koninklijke Bibliotheek Den Haag

Toronto Public Library

Ashgate Publishing, Ltd.

BELFOR International GmbH

Krah & Grote Measurement Solutions

MPM Marketing GmbH

PAL PRESERVATION ACADEMY GmbH

Preservation Technologies B.V.

Conference Organizing Committee

Nancy E. Gwinn, Smithsonian Institution Libraries

John McIlwaine, University College London

Birte Timmermann, Staatsbibliothek zu Berlin

Ingeborg Verheul, Koninklijke Bibliotheek Den Haag (conference coordination)

Johanna G. Wellheiser, Toronto Public Library

Olaf Janssen, Koninklijke Bibliotheek Den Haag (conference website design)

INTRODUCTION

With a year's perspective, as we worked through the conference papers, it became even more clear that libraries, archives and other memory institutions around the world must take seriously the need for effective disaster management. This need has been further emphasized by the multiple hurricanes that struck the Caribbean region and the United States in the fall of 2004.

This IFLA (International Federation of Library Associations and Institutions) conference, held in Berlin from July 30 to August 1, 2003, resulted from discussions of the IFLA Standing Committee on Preservation and Conservation (http://www.ifla.org/VII/s19/index.htm) that recognized the increasing occurrences of disasters and conflicts worldwide and their impact on cultural heritage. Conference organizers wished to inform and enable administrators to effectively prepare for, react and respond to, and recover from disasters. The intensive 2-1/2 day program included sixteen speakers from twelve countries representing a cross-section of expertise from the library, archive and museum communities, both public and private sectors. The ninety participants from twenty-five countries also reflected this rich diversity. The program's six sessions proceeded from high-level disaster planning to the specifics of collection recovery. To complement the presentations, conferees enjoyed talking with company representatives of firms engaged in various aspects of disaster management.

The conference papers pointed to some common trends, challenges, pitfalls and achievements:

- The increasing success of cooperative efforts at all levels – local, regional, national and international;
- The value of sharing the experience of disaster plans in action;
- The critical need to understand the human factor in disaster response;
- The practical difficulties of implementing plans during major disasters;
- The consequences of ignoring human communications issues;
- The importance of building local capacities through training;
- The value of effective and integrated pre-planning – people and material resources;
- The importance of the risk assessment process that enables careful direction of scarce resources;
- The continuing need for affordable and accessible recovery techniques and technologies;
- The recognition that accepted response measures are often not possible when disaster strikes especially in the developing world; and
- The important role that libraries and archives can play in providing disaster prevention and recovery information to their own communities and the public.

This conference provided an important opportunity for participants to learn from the experience and expertise of countries worldwide. Closing discussion indicated that, in spite of the progress made toward disaster prevention and planning in recent years, there is a continued need to identify and disseminate information on suitable and effective strategies and technologies, to develop effective interdisciplinary collaborations and to build awareness of the requirements for successfully protecting and preserving our cultural heritage.

In preparing this publication, the editors wish to thank the authors, who revised their papers and patiently answered numerous queries. We also wish to thank the conference organizers, especially Ingeborg Verheul, whose adept administration made the conference work smoothly, the conference sponsors, and the trade fair participants for supporting the conference, and thus this publication. Manfred Link and Dr. Rainer Ostermann of K.G. Saur provided much assistance with the production, for which we are grateful. And finally, our thanks to IFLA's Sjoerd Koopman for his support and enthusiasm for our efforts.

Johanna G. Wellheiser
Nancy E. Gwinn

October 2004

CONFERENCE PROGRAM

Preparing for the Worst, Planning for the Best: Protecting our Cultural Heritage from Disaster

Sponsored by the
IFLA Preservation and Conservation Section and
IFLA Preservation and Conservation Core Activity and
Council on Library and Information Resources, Inc.

Akademie der Wissenschaften – Berlin, Germany
July 30-August 1, 2003

Wednesday, July 30

8:00-9:00am **Registration and Trade Fair**

9:00-9:30am **Welcome**

- Steffen Wawra, Direktor, Akadmiebibliothek, Berlin, Germany
- John McIlwaine, Chair, Standing Committee, IFLA Preservation and Conservation Section
- Marie-Thérèse Varlamoff, Director, IFLA Core Activity for Preservation and Conservation

9:30am-12:00pm **Session 1: National Policy Planning**

This session features speakers from countries that have established national planning efforts and/or national policies and strategies for handling disasters, specifically as they relate to cultural organizations, such as libraries, archives, and museums. Several countries are organizing their efforts under the direction of The International Committee of the Blue Shield, the equivalent, in the field of cultural heritage, of the Red Cross.

Moderator: *Nancy E. Gwinn, Director, Smithsonian Institution Libraries, Washington, D.C., USA, and Secretary, Standing Committee, IFLA Preservation and Conservation Section*

A Cooperative Approach to Emergency Preparedness and Response
Lawrence L. Reger, President, Heritage Preservation, Washington, D.C., USA

Disaster Prevention in Latin America and Ibero-American Countries
Celia Ribeiro Zaher, Director, National Library of Brazil, Rio de Janeiro, Brazil

Setting Up Emergency Plans: A Regional Approach for Dutch Cultural Heritage
Marja Peek, Consultant, Netherlands Institute for Cultural Heritage, Amsterdam, The Netherlands

12:00-12:45pm **Session 2: Plenary Session**

In the context of recent events worldwide, this session discusses the importance of disaster planning and the efforts of the International Blue Shield initiative to stimulate national planning to ensure protection of culture heritage within each country.

Moderator: *Marie-Thérèse Varlamoff, Director, IFLA Core Activity for Preservation and Conservation*

The Blue Shield: The Cultural Red Cross?
Ross Shimmon, Former President, International Committee of the Blue Shield and Former Secretary General, IFLA, The Hague, The Netherlands

2:00-4:00pm **Session 3: Institutional Planning**

This session focuses on disaster planning at the institutional level. While the emphasis is on the theoretical, there is a secondary focus on what has been shown to actually work, based on practical experiences in libraries and other sectors, and on what has been reported in the literature. What are the human response and resource issues? What are the training requirements? How is training best implemented? What are the trends, challenges, pitfalls and success stories?

Moderator: *Graham Matthews, Professor of Information and Library Management, School of Business Information, Faculty of Law, Liverpool John Moores University, Liverpool, UK*

Earthquake Preparedness at the Istanbul Museums
Nevra Ertuk, Research Assistant, Faculty of Art and Design, Museum Studies Program, Art Management Program, Yildiz Technical University, Istanbul, Turkey

Disaster Management and Libraries; Planning into Action: The Institutional Perspective
Graham Matthews, Professor of Information and Library Management, School of Business Information, Faculty of Business and Law, Liverpool John Moores University, Liverpool, UK

Psychological Stress and Recovery
Maj Klasson, Professor, Library and Information Science, University College of Borås, Linköping, Sweden

4:00-5:00pm **Trade Fair**

6:00-7:00pm **Exhibition Opening and Reception**
Staatsbibliothek zu Berlin

Thursday, July 31

9:00am-12:30pm **Session 4: Disaster Plans in Action**

This session presents stimulating case studies of institutions that have experienced disasters. Speakers describe their experiences, what the consequences were, and how they coped with what actually happened. If the institution had a disaster plan, what happened when disaster hit? Did it work? If the institution didn't have a plan, what happened? Would a disaster plan have helped? How were resources mobilized? What lessons were learned?

Moderator: *Johanna Wellheiser, Manager, Preservation and Digitization Services, Toronto Public Library, Canada, and Information Coordinator, Standing Committee, IFLA Preservation and Conservation Section*

The Development and Use of Library Disaster Plans: The Berlin Experience
Annette Gerlach, Head of Historical Collections, Zentral- und Landesbibliothek, Berlin, Berlin, Germany

The Prague Flood Diary
Jiři Vnouček, Head of Conservation Department, National Library of the Czech Republic, Prague, Czech Republic

Vietnamese Libraries: The Collections, Their Value, and the Protection of the Documentary Heritage from Disaster
Chu Tuyet Lan, Director, Department of Documentation and Information, The Institute of Han-Nom Studies, Hanoi, Vietnam

Hurricanes and Disaster Response: Lessons Learned in Jamaica from "Gilbert"
John Aarons, Government Archivist of Jamaica, Jamaica Archives and Records Department, Office of the Prime Minister, Spanish Town, Jamaica

2:00-4:00pm **Session 5: Assessing the Risk**

This session introduces models for assessing risk and setting priorities for salvage in libraries, archives, and museums. How does an institution arrive at decisions? Who makes the choices, and whose responsibility is it? Do politics play a role? What are the insurance considerations?

Moderator: *Helen Shenton, Head, Collection Care, British Library, London, UK and Corresponding Member, Standing Committee, IFLA Preservation and Conservation Section*

Seeking Balanced Risk Mitigation: Risk Assessment at the Canadian Museum of Nature
R. Robert Waller, Chief Conservation, Canadian Museum of Nature, Ottawa, Canada

Writing a Disaster Plan: Identifying Risk
René Teygeler, Consultant, The Netherlands

4:00-5:30pm **Vendor Presentations and Trade Fair**

Friday, August 1

9:00-11:00am **Session 6: Options for Collections Recovery**

In this session, specialists discuss options for treating various types of collection materials following a disaster. What are the options – their benefits and risks? What are the proven treatments reported in the literature? What are the promising new technologies?

What commercial services are available? Speakers will consider books and paper, photographs, and film and new media.

Moderator: *John McIlwaine, Professor Emeritus of Bibliography of Asia and Africa, School of Library, Archive & Information Studies, University College, London, UK, and Chair, IFLA Preservation and Conservation Section*

Comparison of Drying Methods
Hilary Kaplan, Senior Conservator and Kathleen Ludwig, Senior Conservator, National Archives and Records Administration, Washington, D.C., USA

Recovery of a Water-soaked Photograph Collection in The Netherlands
Clara von Waldthausen, Photograph Conservator, Amsterdam, The Netherlands

Audiovisual and Modern Information Media: Disaster Mitigation & Recovery
Léon-Bavi Vilmont, Research Engineer, Audiovisual Materials and New Media, Centre de Recherches sur la Conservation des Documents Graphiques, Paris, France

11:30-12:00pm **Discussion and Closing Remarks**

Moderators: *John McIlwaine and Nancy E. Gwinn*

SESSION 1: NATIONAL POLICY PLANNING

This session featured speakers from countries that have established national planning efforts and/or national policies and strategies for handling disasters, specifically as they relate to cultural organizations, such as libraries, archives and museums. Several countries are organizing their efforts under the direction of The International Committee of the Blue Shield, the equivalent of the Red Cross in the field of cultural heritage.

A COOPERATIVE APPROACH TO EMERGENCY PREPAREDNESS AND RESPONSE

Lawrence L. Reger

President, Heritage Preservation, Washington, D.C., USA

Abstract

The United States does not have an official national policy regarding the provision of assistance to libraries and archives, museums, historical societies, and historic sites to mitigate, prepare or respond to disasters and other kinds of emergencies. However, it does have an increasingly effective network to address these events at the national, state and local levels.

This paper focuses on the work and initiatives of the Heritage Emergency Task Force. Led by Heritage Preservation and the Federal Emergency Management Agency, a voluntary partnership of 34 non-governmental associations and U.S. government agencies established the Heritage Emergency National Task Force in 1995. The Task Force's mission is to help institutions that own collections or historic sites and make them available to the public to better protect their collections from disasters. It promotes preparedness and mitigation measures and provides expert information on response and salvage to institutions.

Best known of the Task Force's accomplishments is the Emergency Response and Salvage Wheel, a highly respected and practical tool for protecting documents, art, and artifacts from water. More than 90,000 of these wheels are in use throughout the world.

Cataclysm and Challenge is a comprehensive report of the damage and loss to cultural property that resulted from the events of September 11, 2001. It also addresses basic emergency management needs and explores what resources institutions will need to cope effectively in the future.

One of the most important efforts of the Task Force is to provide information to individuals who suffer damage to family treasures, e.g., photographs and books, in a disaster. After people secure their safety, health, shelter and food, the next thing they are most concerned about are things that they want to pass on to their children and grandchildren. When cultural institutions demonstrate that they can be of assistance to the citizens in times of need, they strengthen support for efforts to protect our nation's heritage for future generations. The latest Task Force initiative, "Alliance for Response," will bring together cultural heritage leaders and emergency management professionals, e.g., firefighters, to strengthen local response networks and develop mitigation projects for their communities.

Introduction

Many issues involving disasters are common to all information organizations. This is the basis of my remarks today – that it makes sense for all different kinds of collecting institutions to join together in common cause, while still engaging in emergency planning and preparedness for their own institution.

There are two principal threats to cultural heritage:

- The **slow but relentless,** which includes among other things inherent vice in materials and improper storage, and of course, the other is ...
- The **swift and catastrophic** which includes everything from water pipes breaking and thefts, to natural disasters and something our country has seldom experienced until recently – terrorist attacks.

This paper will cover how we have made the beginnings of developing a cooperative national heritage emergency strategy to help libraries, archives, museums and similar organizations to:

- Take steps to prevent or mitigate damage from a potential disaster;
- Prepare to respond to an emergency of whatever magnitude and, of course; and
- Provide assistance when a disaster does occur.

In our country, as I believe is the case in most countries, emergency response is the responsibility of local governments. Their citizens look to them first to provide emergency medical, police and fire personnel. We call them "first responders." They are critical to our work.

Because some emergencies affect more than just one community or are of great magnitude, our federal and state governments have developed agencies to provide both personnel and financial assistance to help citizens recover from a disaster, as well as:

- To offer and sometimes require efforts to eliminate conditions that are likely to lead to a disaster, for example, moving an entire community to above a flood plain zone; and
- To provide information, training and financial assistance to assist communities to be prepared for an emergency. An example is the proper way to board up building openings before a hurricane strikes.

Both are seen as an investment that in the long run will save lives and reduce the cost of repairs and reconstruction. Obviously, the less damage resulting from a disaster, the more money is saved in responding to one.

The National Heritage Emergency Task Force

Our work began in 1994. I would like to say that it was because we had the foresight to know how important it was, that as national and regional organizations, we ourselves needed to be prepared to help our constituents when they suffer damage from an emergency. However, it took an earthquake in California and major flooding in several states to prompt us to act.

In response to these disasters we felt we needed to take action to our help our members and others to prepare for and respond to emergencies and to ensure that they qualified for financial support from our federal government to help them recover from a disaster. There was no question that hospitals and schools, even businesses and families, qualified. However, whether libraries, archives, museums and similar organizations qualified was unclear.

How did we begin? As is usually the case in our country, with a meeting! We worked hard to ensure that there would be good news – the Director of the Federal Emergency Management Agency (FEMA) announced that its regulations had been clarified so that it was clear that collecting institutions qualified for Federal disaster assistance. This helped to put everyone in a positive frame of mind and all agreed that it was important to form an interdisciplinary program to enhance and compliment the work of each organization. As a result, the National Heritage Emergency Task Force was established.

General agreement was reached on three points:

- All of our organizations needed to better plan to help our constituents to respond to an emergency and assist them to be prepared for one.
- Since disasters often cover a large geographical area, more than one kind of collecting institution may be affected and, therefore, a joint effort made practical sense.

- Most importantly, by working together we could accomplish things our organizations could not do individually.

The two co-sponsors of the Task Force are Heritage Preservation, which is a private non-profit organization or nongovernmental organization (NGO) and FEMA.

There are 32 other members of the Task Force. They consist of:

- Associations, which are NGOs, for example, the Council on Library and Information Resources, Inc. and the American Library Association;
- National and regional conservation groups, again NGOs, including the American Institute for Conservation and the Regional Alliance for Preservation; and
- Federal government agencies that either provide financial support through grants to cultural heritage organizations or have their own collections. Examples here are the National Endowment for the Humanities, the Library of Congress, the Smithsonian Institution and the National Archives and Records Administration.

From the beginning, Task Force members have represented the broad spectrum of those concerned about the preservation of cultural and scientific heritage, (libraries, archives, museums, and historical societies) and preservation of historic buildings and sites and archeological sites and repositories, as well as, other kinds of collecting organizations, such as scientific research collections not open to the general public. For sake of brevity, I will use the term "collecting institutions" from now on when referring to the kinds of groups we seek to help in our work.

Heritage Preservation is the only organization in our country whose mission encompasses all these kinds of collecting institutions. This is one of the reasons that we are one of the Task Force's co-sponsors.

The Task Force agreed on five general areas that needed to be addressed:

- Information for collecting institutions;
- Training for conservation and preservation professionals;
- Onsite assistance;
- Promoting city and state-wide emergency task forces; and
- Information for the public.

Resources and Training

Information for collecting institutions is where we have put most of our efforts to date. Some of you may be familiar with the Emergency Response and Salvage Wheel, which we have produced in both English and Spanish. It provides information for staff about what do during the first 48 hours after an emergency. This is information that any staff member can use, not just conservators and preservation professionals. More than 100,000 of these wheels have been sold or distributed free and we know that wheels are in use in more than 40 countries. The wheel has been translated and produced in three other languages – Chinese, Dutch and French – and we hope that soon there will be a Japanese version.

Other information resources include "flood packets," that are mailed to collecting institutions after we have a nationally declared disaster. The packets contain detailed information about salvaging damaged collections and stabilizing buildings. Another is "Resources for Recovery," a guide to Federal emergency assistance that is available to collecting institutions.

In the area of training: working with the Task Force, members of the American Institute for Conservation developed, tested, and refined a disaster response curriculum, which was used in a series of six regional training workshops. There were 85 individuals trained and a number of them continue to provide training to others. This has increased our capability to provide onsite assistance.

FEMA and Heritage Preservation have established the Heritage Emergency Roster. Task Force members helped to enlist qualified persons that FEMA can quickly call upon to go on site in case of a major national disaster.

September 11, 2001, changed our country in profound ways, changes that are still evolving. Our response was to produce a report, *Cataclysm and Challenge*, on the impact of the terrorist attacks on cultural heritage. The report assessed the preparedness of collecting institutions in the area around the World Trade Center and provided recommendations for what steps should be taken to prepare for this or any other kind disaster. I don't think you will be surprised by the recommendations, but given that they come from those who experienced this terrible event first-hand they have prompted many institutions to take steps to implement them. The report received a significant amount of general media attention throughout our country, especially on the anniversary of September 11 last year. It was featured in many newspapers and on national radio and television networks.

Because of the nature of the September 11 attacks, in most cases there was little that could be done to avert the loss of cultural heritage. One example of prompt action was the Jewish Museum, which is near the epicenter of the attacks. The staff turned on the electric switch to close the ventilators. When the electricity failed, staff went to the roof to hand crank them closed. Those interviewed emphasized that:

- Emergency planning must be a priority, both preparing the plan initially and keeping it current.
- Staff should regularly practice implementing the plan and ensure that there are emergency supplies onsite or close by.
- Action should be taken to plan for contingencies to prevent damage from likely kinds of emergencies.

Other lessons we learned were to maintain an up-to-date catalog and store a copy offsite. Also, collecting institutions need to get to know their first responders – police, medical and fire personnel – so they will be knowledgeable about the institution's mission, collections and building. If first responders are familiar with cultural institutions in their community, they can often prevent destruction of cultural heritage. We call this "take a firefighter to lunch."

The report reinforced our efforts to promote city and statewide emergency task forces, through our Alliance for Response project, with special emphasis on involving first responders.

We currently are working with four cities to develop model interdisciplinary local emergency task forces. They are Boston, Cincinnati, Dallas and New York City. We hope to be able to replicate these models throughout our country.

Before turning to what I feel is one of the most important goals of the Task Force – information for the public – let me say that, if we are not prepared to prevent damage from emergencies, future generations will be the poorer for it. Emergency preparedness does not require significant amounts of personnel resources or money. Mostly it requires persistence and perseverance.

Information for the Public

Why did I say information for the public is one of our most important goals? Because the cultural heritage community can provide direct help to people who experience an emergency, and in turn, will benefit from it by building public awareness about the importance of collecting institutions preserving the cultural heritage they have for the future generations of their city, state, nation and the world. In turn, this can lead to increased financial support.

If you demonstrate that you are doing something to help your citizens and, especially if it is part of an interdisciplinary effort, we have found that government agencies and private funders will respond with financial support.

After people have secured their safety, health, shelter, food and clothing, the next thing they are most concerned about is saving the things that they cherish.

We have developed information that any citizen can use to take steps to salvage family heirlooms. This information is part of FEMA's website and in the case of a major disaster, FEMA publishes a newspaper for those in the disaster area and these recommendations are included.

Our plans call for preparing a brochure that first responders can hand out as part of the information that is provided to those who have been in a disaster. We also hope to develop short videos that can be used by television stations.

Let me reiterate again. If we are not prepared, our citizens and future generations will be the poorer for it. Now is the time to act.

References

Cataclysm and Challenge: Impact of September 11, 2001, on Our Nation's Cultural Heritage. A report by Heritage Preservation on behalf of the Heritage Emergency National Task Force. 2002.
http://www.heritagepreservation.org/NEWS/Cataclysm.htm

Emergency Response and Salvage Wheel
http://www.heritagepreservation.org/PROGRAMS/Wheel1.htm

Federal Emergency Management Agency
http://www.fema.gov/

Heritage Preservation
http://www.heritagepreservation.org

The Author

Lawrence Reger has been president of Heritage Preservation since 1988. He has served as director of the American Association of Museums and at the National Endowment for the Arts as, successively, General Counsel; Director, Planning and Management; and Director, Program Development and Coordination. He began his career as a lawyer after receiving his J.D. from Vanderbilt University in 1964.

The Joliet Public Library in Joliet, Illinois, after a firebombing on April 19, 1989.

Photo courtesy the Joliet Public Library.

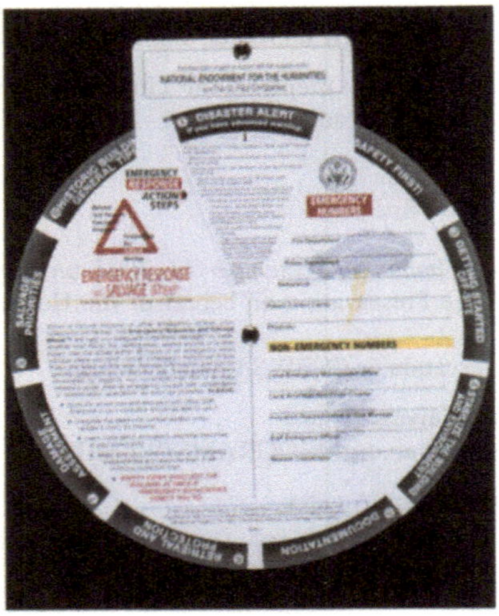

Since its publication in 1997, the Emergency Response and Salvage Wheel has become the single most recognized and respected tool for protecting documents, art, and artifacts from water damage. Wheels are in use throughout the world in more than 40 countries.

Photo courtesy Heritage Preservation.

Jennifer Castro of the U.S. Marine Corps Museums Branch examines a print in the damaged area of the Pentagon after the terrorist attack on September 11, 2001.

Photo courtesy Jennifer Castro, Marine Corps Museums Branch.

The National Summit on Emergency Response was held in December 1994 to develop a coordinated emergency response program for cultural heritage. It led to the creation of the Heritage Emergency National Task Force.

Photo courtesy Heritage Preservation.

DISASTER PREVENTION IN LATIN AMERICA AND IBERO-AMERICAN COUNTRIES

Celia Ribeiro Zaher

Director, National Library of Brazil, Rio de Janeiro, Brazil

Abstract

The Asociación de Paises Iberoamericanos para el Desarrollo de las Bibliotecas Iberoamericanas (Association of Countries of Ibero-America for the Development of Ibero-American National Libraries, or ABINIA) has as one of its objectives the preservation of collections and cultural memory in national libraries on a regional basis. With assistance from staff of the IFLA Core Activity in Preservation and Conservation (IFLA PAC), at its General Assembly in 2000, ABINIA members agreed to survey the current situation of its members and their preservation needs and programs. This paper provides the results of the questionnaire, which showed a widespread lack of clear policies relating to disaster prevention and mitigation, and many environmental and storage conditions that put collections at risk. The author recommends next steps for ABINIA and outlines a program for creating blue print plans for disaster prevention for national libraries on a regional basis, in groups with a common language and cultural heritage.

Introduction

The Asociación de Paises Iberoamericanos para el Desarrollo de las Bibliotecas Iberoamericanas (Association of Countries of Ibero-America for the Development of Ibero-American National Libraries, or ABINIA) encompasses all national libraries in the countries of the Latin American continent, as well as the Portuguese- and Spanish-speaking parts of the Ibero Peninsula. One of the major objectives of ABINIA is the preservation of collections and cultural memory in national libraries in the designated region identified by their common languages and their cultural heritage. In order to perform this task ABINIA has, since its creation in 1985, identified mechanisms that could help institutions in the countries covered by its program to create an understanding of the actions required to safeguard this heritage in the present and for future generations.

ABINIA has joined the International Federation of Library Associations and Institutions Preservation and Conservation Core Program (IFLA PAC) to create the Center for Preservation in Venezuela in collaboration with the National Library of Venezuela, which assumes costs of staff and running costs of the center and provides technical assistance to countries in the region of Spanish denomination. Among the center's main activities are staff training on preservation practices and the evaluation and analysis of the preservation needs of collections and recommendations for remedial actions. These activities are undertaken by specialists in the region and monitored by ABINIA.

In order to expand and decentralize these activities, new IFLA PAC centers have been proposed for Chile, Brazil and Trinidad and Tobago. This decentralization will provide for the necessary language distribution in Portuguese, Spanish and English and a structure that will enable more efficient response to the needs outlined by countries in the region.

ABINIA Deliberations

To determine how best to begin its work in preservation, disaster management and safeguarding of collections against all sorts of dangers, ABINIA began its deliberations at the

XI General Assembly in Cuba, held on October 16-20, 2000. After the coordinator of IFLA PAC introduced the topic, conferees agreed to send a jointly sponsored questionnaire to evaluate the current situation in national libraries, as well as in other main libraries in Latin American countries. Delegates also approved the creation of a Latin American Network for preservation of documentary material, which should reinforce programs already carried out by IFLA PAC in the region.

Although the response to the questionnaire was not 100 percent, the results showed the need to reinforce actions towards preservation of collections and buildings. At the next Assembly, held on October 17-19, 2001, in Lisbon, participants decided to distribute a manual on disaster prevention in archives and libraries prepared by the National Library of Portugal to serve as a guide for other libraries of ABINIA. More importantly, participants voted to adopt the manual for use at the national libraries in Latin America and asked the ABINIA secretariat to prepare a follow-up study. Finally, the group requested ABINIA members to study, reproduce and disseminate, at the national level, material concerning disaster prevention in order to create general national awareness of the measures needed to prevent disasters.

Part of deliberations at the Lisbon Assembly in 2001 concerning prevention of disasters to libraries focused on the vulnerability of libraries to damage because of armed conflicts. Thus, the Assembly approved a special declaration to call this to the attention of the library community in Latin America countries.

Declaration of Lisbon, October 19, 2001

The ABINIA Declaration of Lisbon, October 19, 2001, condemns acts of terrorism in whatever form, considering them as crimes against humanity and endangering cultural goods and heritage, and deplores the destruction of the eighty libraries, located at the Twin Towers in New York, which was a result of such acts. It also:

- Considers inadmissible these attempts that are against the essence of the human being and of society and which result in the loss of cultural heritage, which documents the evolution of mankind;
- Calls upon its members to intensify work towards the betterment of all people and to diffuse peace and culture among men in pursuit of peace on Earth, as proclaimed by UNESCO;
- In the face of the serious treats against cultural heritage, declares that it believes in efforts such as the Biblioteca of Alexandria, which represents the eternal symbol of culture and wisdom; and
- Declares that such thinking was expressed by the known intellectual and free thinker of the region, Jose Martí, who said "Ser cultos es el mode de ser libres, y ser buenos es el unico modo de ser dichosos" (To be cultivated is a way to be free, and to be kind is the only way to achieve happiness).

The next year, at the XIII General Assembly held in Rio de Janeiro on November 12-14, 2002, ABINIA members decided to establish new IFLA PAC Centers to operate from the national libraries of Brazil, Chile and Trinidad and Tobago. All three libraries agreed to support the centers and cover the costs of their operations. Conferees also decided to profit from the venue of the next General Assembly, to be held in Mexico in 2003, and organize training courses in Mexico, Cuba and Panama, and to plan similar activity in conjunction with the ACURIL (Association of Caribbean University and Research Libraries) meeting in Trinidad and Tobago in 2004.

One of the major issues largely debated in IFLA meetings was brought to the attention of the ABINIA members: the necessity to create National Committees of the Blue Shield, involving libraries, archives and museums. This action would permit the establishment of emergency assistance plans for national libraries and to create awareness at the national level about issues of safeguarding national collections.

Diagnosis of the Situation in Latin American Libraries

The set of decisions taken by ABINIA members in these general assemblies and the follow-up actions to the Declaration were based on information gathered by IFLA/PAC and ABINIA during 2000 on the situation of preservation of documentary heritage in national and other major libraries in Latin America. The information-gathering exercise followed the members' concern that there was no clear picture emerging from the situation in all countries that could lead to the establishment of clear-cut policies at government levels and by institutions. It was decided that a diagnosis needed to be made and that an evaluation was forthcoming to identify difficulties and needs in order to create a network of professionals. Further, a training program would expand the number of staff equipped to carry out preservation procedures, thus enabling the national libraries to apply IFLA PAC policies of prevention.

The resulting questionnaire was sent to all libraries collaborating with IFLA PAC Center in Venezuela. Analysis of the results showed a series of patterns that emerged from the lack of preservation policies or negligence and to identify actions that are necessary to plan the safeguarding of collections in areas which suffered disasters. The results were summarized as follows:

Collections

Sizes vary enormously, as well as types of collections. They vary from 114,000 to about 5 million books.

Special Collections

Photographs on negatives and plaques of glass with gelatin have special problems. An example is the collection of more than 800,000 negatives at the Public Library of Medellín, Colômbia.

Climatic Conditions

Climatic conditions among libraries vary with a contamination rate of 60 percent of the areas occupied. It should be noted that 40 percent of the libraries analyzed were located in tropical climates.

Buildings, Environmental Control Conditions

- 10 percent of the building occupied by libraries were built before 1900
- 50 percent of the buildings were built between 1900 and 1950

- 20 percent were built between 1951 and 1980
- 20 percent were built after 1980

Only libraries built after this decade were made to meet library specifications required to prevent disasters and contamination in general within good storage conditions.

Since extreme temperatures vary from 2°C (36°F) to 38°C (100°F) in libraries as result of lack of temperature control, the diagnosis is that:

- 60 percent of countries with these variations have problems of conservation.
- 70 percent of institutions control temperature and humidity but not all have air conditioning.
- Only 30 percent apply relative humidity control for the whole area. Some libraries use dehumidifiers and chemical products to control environment and temperature.
- Air-conditioning works only 30 percent of each 24-hour period in most institutions. This causes oscillating changes in temperature, which are known to endanger collections. Nevertheless, shutting off air-conditioning during nights and weekends is a common practice in libraries in developing countries. Shortage of funds for new central air-conditioning systems and for maintenance, repair or replacement of faulty appliances inhibits change to better practices.

Electricity

In most of the libraries, poor installation or maintenance of electrical wiring jeopardizes any effort concerning disaster prevention. Most cases of fire have originated from electric combustion, which is difficult to prevent. Although it can occur at any time, it mostly happens during hours when staff is not available. So risk of mechanical disasters because of bad wiring is high on the list for possible causes of disaster.

Illumination

Fifty percent of libraries use artificial lighting in the reading rooms or in storage areas. Lighting measurements showed 150 lux in storage areas and 200 lux in reading rooms.

Plagues and Insects

Destruction by rodents and insects is a permanent concern and is responsible for a large number of great losses in collections, because there is little monitoring of storage conditions. Thirty percent of libraries have suffered plagues. Very few have a policy of fumigation at regular intervals to prevent insects, nor are there disinfection procedures for large quantities of collections.

Storage Conditions

Storage problems impact significantly on the conservation of collections, since restricted budgets in libraries prevent establishment of adequate environmental conditions. Proper storage exists in only 40 percent of the libraries surveyed. All types of conservation and preservation problems derive from this situation.

In evaluating existing preservation programs, survey results showed that 60 percent of the responding libraries bind their books and 70 percent have laboratories for small repairs of collections. As to long-term preservation, only 80 percent of libraries microfilm their collections for storage and use by readers. Some offer microfilm services to users. Although the numbers are small, some libraries have started to use CD-ROM and e-mail to provide digital copies of journal articles.

Dissemination of Information

It is a general feeling that professionals and authorities lack knowledge on what to do and how to do it, in part because there is an evident lack of documentation in Spanish, nor is there easy access to what exists. In consequence, an effort should be made to make information about proper preservation practices and disaster prevention available widely through a good dissemination program, especially to the authorities that hold the preservation funds.

In summary, the questionnaire results describe the conditions in libraries in Latin American and the Caribbean. This analysis points the way to work towards solving these more common problems and shows how to deal with the more urgent problems. It is necessary to help libraries to cope with these problems of preservation and to plan to implement urgent actions to prevent everyday problems. The evaluation also showed the need to organize plans for the future to fight against disasters, which may occur as the result of bad management or natural disasters.

Disaster Prevention: How to Achieve it?

The analysis of the questionnaire showed that 30% of institutions functioning as libraries have prepared plans for disaster prevention. On the other hand, 40% of these plans have not been updated. These statistics make clear that there is no acute conscience of the need to prepare for disaster prevention, nor to evaluate the preservation status of the collection and determine those priority elements that can be responsible for starting a disaster.

Common Practices for Disaster Prevention

To start the evaluation, it is necessary to identify common practices in libraries, in order to determine those considered for long-term attention that should become routine. Expanding existing practices can help prevent disasters of all kinds, apart from those classified under the heading of natural causes and armed conflicts. Those cannot be prevented, but certain measures can diminish their disastrous effects.

To counteract floods or insect infestation, some practices are known, but a lack of policy or commitment to apply preventive measures is common. It is well-known, for example, that in case of a flood, water-soaked materials should be frozen, but libraries either ignore those steps or do not take quick action to salvage materials. There are no contracts of agreements worked out among institutions responsible for libraries and whatever facilities exist that can freeze materials, so no immediate action can be taken. Instead, the common practice following a flood is to fumigate the library, but not to send documents outside. Libraries are not thinking ahead about possible disasters and including disaster prevention measures in their procedures.

Disaster Prevention Risks

Of the major risks identified throughout libraries, the foremost one is that buildings are badly situated, with little protection from rain and minor floods resulting from poor maintenance of sewage and water installations. Other risk elements are air pollution and insects, which proliferate as a result of poor climatic conditions in storage and in photographic laboratories, where there is danger of fire combustion from acetates and nitrates. Libraries with those conditions need to take measures to prevent accidents from turning into disaster by taken preventive actions and being aware of possible risks to collections.

Recommendation for Future Action by ABINIA: A Blue Print Plan

ABINIA could develop a blue print to serve as the basis for the creation of a major regional plan to be discussed and applied for disaster prevention in national libraries in the region. This project would bring an element of planning into the region and create greater awareness of the possible risks that currently exist, as well as measures needed to prevent disasters or to salvage collections. This plan should be based on the experiences deriving from disasters that have previously occurred in national libraries, mainly the floods and hurricanes in Eastern Europe and the Caribbean.

Objectives

It is necessary to evaluate all the difficulties inherent to creating such a plan, so that responsible staff will understand the drawbacks and be willing to face potential problems with drafting ~~it~~ and planning its different stages. To facilitate the task for each library, it would be useful to first draft the portions that would be common to all the plans beforehand. In this way principles and common actions and procedures would be spelled out, as well as guidelines on how to proceed to analyze and evaluate the collections.

A new questionnaire will have to be sent to evaluate the current status of buildings and environmental conditions, since the analysis made in the present paper was based on the 2002 questionnaire, sent out prior to the ABINIA meeting in October in Lisbon.

ABINIA will have to assist the national libraries by providing an expert to help each library draft and fill in the blue print plan's template. The blue print plan must be disseminated widely to all libraries beforehand to familiarize staff with its scope and objective. However, staff involved with preparing the blue print plan must understand the basic steps required for disaster prevention. For this purpose, courses on disaster prevention must be given at the regional level to train staff in the many different phases involved in identifying problems and how to deal with them.

Obstacles

Determining the information required for the plan. Before drafting the plan, it is necessary to know who will be involved in the process and what statistics and data will be needed during the preparation of the plan, so that staff can be assigned beforehand to collect and analyze the relevant information.

Funding. It is essential to identify the sources of financing to carry out the plan, or else it cannot be implemented, since material, storage and other areas may need renovation or adjustment, and contracts with salvage companies that have large freezers must be arranged.

Execution. Timeframes have to be established and goals underlined to be achieved within the periods allotted.

Resources of intellectual and financial nature. Staff skills and expertise need to be identified so that the right people are included among the groups that will create the plan and execute the tasks assigned. If outside expertise is needed, funds must be identified to cover such expenses.

Preparing the Plan

Study the risks coming from outside the building itself. It is necessary to survey the environment in which the building is located to identify possible risks, such as location near rivers or underwater plumbing or flood possibilities.

Study the risks originating from inside the building. It is necessary to evaluate the electricity status of the building, as well as the plumbing and the sewage outlets. The situation of the ceiling and the windows must be evaluated to identify possible leaks that may occur during rainstorms. Closing windows in book stack areas is also important to avoid inundations that can damage books placed near windows.

Evaluate and identify risks coming from climatic conditions. In towns and countries prone to hurricanes and earthquakes, it is important to have ready-made plans for disaster prevention that are part and parcel of the national security plans for evacuation and disaster prevention. These libraries are under stress and duress and cannot survive if well-defined plans are not drawn up and preventive measures taken.

Study conditions appropriate for new buildings and/or adaptations of existing buildings. When the library plans for a new building or building renovation, appropriate measures should be taken to study special arrangements and plans for safeguarding precious collections. In a new building it is necessary to review all exits, storage spaces, electricity, plumbing and sewage with a view to evacuation techniques and safeguarding of collections and personnel.

Drafting the Plan

Identify responsibilities. It is essential to identify staff responsibilities, not only at the stage of thinking through and writing down the measures needed, but also when the plan is implemented, such as the responsibilities for the evacuation, safeguarding collections, fixing identified drawbacks through administrative measures, lines of command, etc.

Identify personnel. Personnel have to be identified by name, position and line of command besides the specific tasks that are assigned to them during the preparation of the plan, as well as when coping with a disaster and its aftermath.

Identify objectives. The objectives to be achieved by the plan need to be clearly specified with goals and a timeframe for the work to be accomplished. These objectives should include flow charts in case of disaster, required training for disaster prevention, training for treatment of material damaged and first aid to collections, and a full plan for salvaging collections against water or fire disasters.

Evaluating the Collections

To establish a plan, one must first evaluate the collections in order to establish priorities in case of disaster, to identify exit issues for these collections, and to pinpoint personnel to take care of the salvage, as well as the steps for the movement of institutions and people to work in this salvage unit. It should be clear which collections would undergo the first salvaging efforts, based on their economical value, as well as cultural heritage value and rarity. Irreplaceable material has priority over current collections that can be replaced. Of course, all human life has priority over material goods.

There is no doubt that actions need to be taken by librarians and other officers responsible for cultural institutions in this Region. Time is of the essence for preventive measures. It is hoped that the different forums where this plea will be made will ignite response from audiences and create the necessary impact to propel this initiative forward. The goal is that institutions accept the recommendations and participate on the Regional Plan proposed and that ABINIA will commit itself fully to the successful implementation of this program.

The Author

Celia Ribeiro Zaher is Director of the National Library of Brazil. She is an honorary president of ABINIA, an organization encompasses all national libraries in the countries of the Latin American continent, as well as the Portuguese- and Spanish-speaking parts of the Ibero Peninsula, and is a member of the Board of Directors of the Council on Library and Information Resources, Inc., a private, operating foundation headquartered in Washington, D.C., USA. She also holds a Vice-chairmanship of the International Advisory Committee of the UNESCO´s Memory of the World Program.

SETTING UP EMERGENCY PLANS: A REGIONAL APPROACH FOR DUTCH CULTURAL HERITAGE

Marja Peek[1]

Consultant, Netherlands Institute for Cultural Heritage, Amsterdam, The Netherlands

Abstract

Why, when virtually nobody questions the need for them, are emergency plans at collection-keeping institutions at best only rudimentary and at worst lacking altogether? Because there is no glamour in such a plan! But can something which is not in itself enjoyable or exciting perhaps be made a little more fun, a little more alluring? With that in mind, in 2001 The Netherlands Institute for Cultural Heritage (ICN) started a large-scale prevention project for cultural heritage institutions in The Netherlands. Entitled "Glamour for Safety and Security," this project was devised to assist museums and other keepers of cultural heritage in The Netherlands in compiling and implementing a disaster plan. Deadlines and celebrations played an important role in achieving this goal.

For the Glamour for Safety and Security project, the ICN opted to take a regional approach, so that the knowledge and experience acquired could be shared through local networks. This project did not need to prove that setting up an emergency plan is necessary and useful. Rather it showed that it can be an easy and enjoyable enterprise.

Introduction

On May 13, 2000, The Netherlands was shocked by news of a huge explosion at a fireworks depot in Enschede, a town in the east of the country. Twenty-two people were killed in the disaster and an entire residential district destroyed. The force of the blast also badly damaged the nearby Rijksmuseum Twente, one of the Dutch national museums. Part of the museum's roof collapsed onto the display cabinets below. Disasters do happen, and they can affect museums. This fireworks explosion is just one of a number of serious incidents, such as floods, fire, vandalism and theft of books, prints and paintings that cultural organizations in The Netherlands have suffered.

A report published by the State Inspectorate of Cultural Heritage in September 2000 revealed that only three of the twenty state-funded museums in The Netherlands had a detailed disaster plan in place at the time of the explosion. We can safely assume that the situation was little different in other parts of the Dutch museums sector.

At a stroke, the explosion in Enschede eliminated any lingering doubts about the need for a disaster plan at cultural heritage institutions. Keepers of collections in The Netherlands no longer have to be convinced of the importance of such a plan. Unfortunately, though, this development has not resulted in a substantial increase in the number of effective plans actually in place.

During the major Dutch prevention project, which began in 2001 and is still under way, the two most talked-about museum robberies of recent memory in our country took place: the theft of extremely valuable jewellery and diamonds from the Museon in The

---

1 I would like to thank Antoinette Visser, Head of the Consultancy Department of the ICN, and Eelke Boswijk, coordinator of the pilot project, for their contributions to this address.

Hague in December 2002, and the break-in at the Van Gogh Museum in Amsterdam just a few days later, when two paintings were stolen.

Because of these terrible events during the past few years, as well as the growing global interest in prevention in general, keepers of collections are becoming increasingly aware of the many different threats they face. The need for them to take preventive measures is growing. But ask any museum, library or archive at random about its disaster plan and you are almost sure to be told that it is nearly ready. Disaster plans are always nearly ready.

So why, when virtually nobody questions the need for them, are disaster plans at collection-keeping institutions at best only rudimentary and at worst lacking altogether? This was the question that The Netherlands Institute for Cultural Heritage (ICN) asked itself in 2001 – and came up with this answer. There is no glamour in such a plan! In other words, there is no glory to be gained and other matters always seem to take priority. Safety and security are just not sexy.

An exhibition has to be ready on time. A publication has to be sent to the printer. Loans have to be shipped, and so on. Deadlines have to be met, and when they are, there is always the reward of a party. The successes are celebrated, the initiators congratulated. But disasters have no deadlines, and they are certainly not festive occasions to be worked towards. If all goes well, they do not even happen.

Glamour for Safety and Security

But can something that is not in itself enjoyable or exciting be made a little more fun, a little more alluring? In 2001, with that in mind, the ICN had the idea for a large-scale prevention project for cultural heritage institutions in The Netherlands, to be called "Glamour for Safety and Security."

The ICN is the national center of knowledge about the preservation and management of "moveable" cultural heritage. It is unique because of the activities it combines: practical conservation science, education, consultancy and the management of the state's own collection. The institute is based at two centres, in Amsterdam and in Rijswijk near The Hague. Politically, it falls under the auspices of the Directorate of Cultural Heritage in the Ministry of Education, Culture and Science.

ICN devised the Glamour for Safety and Security project to assist museums and other keepers of cultural heritage in The Netherlands in compiling and implementing a disaster plan. Deadlines and celebrations played an important role.

Considerable attention should be paid to embedding care for the collection into the disaster plan, be this a new or an existing one. Looking after people and buildings is important, but, museums, libraries and archives also have to care for their actual collections. Keepers of collections prefer to have one single plan in place covering people, property and the collection itself. Encouraging cooperation between management departments (general and technical services, security) and those actually responsible for the collection (collection management, restoration and conservation) is therefore vital.

Beyond the confines of the institution itself, it is important to develop a network of colleagues, of government at the national, provincial and local levels, of emergency services (such as the fire brigade and the police) and of commercial recovery companies. Again, the Glamour project paid particular attention to this aspect.

A disaster plan can be defined as an organization-wide system of agreements and warnings for use in the event of an emergency or a disaster. This includes lists of the telephone numbers of internal and external contact persons, the addresses of suppliers, emergency procedures, a list of priority items in the collection, evacuation and escape instructions, plans showing escape routes and facilities like fire-extinguishing equipment, instructions for staff, and so on. The purpose of a disaster plan is to retain as much control as possible in the event of an emergency or a disaster, and so gain time. A prompt and proper response to an emergency or a disaster can prevent a great deal of damage, both at the time and later. Moreover, such a plan has a preventive effect since it encourages constant thinking about safety and security.

The Glamour for Safety and Security project opted to take a regional approach, so the knowledge and experience acquired could thus be shared through local networks. But since such an approach had not been taken before, we had to develop it from scratch. The first step was to carry out a pilot project with a group of institutions from one particular region, since once the right approach was developed, it could be applied by other institutions in other parts of The Netherlands. In this way it would be possible to ensure that every cultural heritage institution in the country would have its own disaster plan in place within a few years.

ICN launched the pilot project in the summer of 2002 with a gala reception in The Hague, the seat of the Dutch government, situated in the south-west of The Netherlands. It is home to a number of renowned art museums, the National Library and the National Archive Service and also the ICN collection.

The beautiful Old Second Chamber of the States General – the hall in which the Dutch National Assembly used to meet – served as the launch location. Here, the Mayor of The Hague, on behalf of the participating institutions, was presented with an empty folder. This symbolised the work those organizations were about to start, in order to fill it with their disaster plans. The region's Chief Fire Officer and Chief Constable also attended the event.

The ICN appointed Eelke Boswijk as coordinator to oversee the organization of the pilot project and Ton Cremers to advise and supervise the participants through the procedure. The pilot is not confined to museums, but became a cross-sector project with the participation of two archives and a library. In total, nineteen institutions are taking part, including:

- The Mauritshuis Museum
- The Communication Museum
- The Bredius Museum
- The Meermanno Museum, The Museum of the Book
- The Exposition Site 'Beelden aan zee' (Statues near the Sea)
- The Municipal Museum
- The Municipal Archives
- The National Library (Royal Library)

As keeper of the state collection, the ICN is also a participant in the pilot project, along with the State Inspectorate of Cultural Heritage. Because it sets the criteria which a good disaster plan has to meet, this organization has an important part to play. Those criteria will be further developed based upon the results of the pilot.

Another important participant is the Second Chamber of the States General. Collection management is not, of course, part of the "core business" of the lower house of the Dutch

Parliament, but it does possess an art collection. The Second Chamber's participation is providing a great deal of knowledge about safety and collection management in a non-museum environment.

Important principles underlying the pilot project are self-motivation on the part of the institutions involved and their active participation. Sharing knowledge and providing one another with professional support are key activities. To this end, working meetings are organized and "homework" assignments issued. The institutions themselves write, implement and maintain their own disaster plans. The same applies to training their staff and testing the plan.

The ICN regularly reports on the progress of the pilot project through publications and our website. The results are being made available to the entire cultural heritage sector. The Dutch media have also covered this unique project. Articles about it have appeared in the trade press and a national newspaper, and there has even been a television report on it.

The pilot project is divided into five phases. It has now reached the last of these, which ends in September 2003. Naturally, this occasion will be marked with a celebration. On this day their proud owners will symbolically present the disaster plans to the Mayor of The Hague.

Finally, a two-day congress will be held in The Hague on November 6-7, 2003. The title will be "Glamour for Safety and Security," the congress language will be Dutch, and about 200 people are expected to attend. ICN is organizing the congress in collaboration with The Netherlands Museum Association. All the results from the pilot project will be presented. The congress is open to keepers of collections from museums, libraries and archives; students and teachers from relevant courses; professional organizations; conservators-restorers; national, provincial and municipal officials; commercial recovery companies; the emergency services; financiers; the trade press and anybody else with an interest in the subject.

Project Results

First of all, there are both the brand-new disaster plans drawn up by the participating institutions and the network built in The Hague during the pilot project. The intention is that this network will continue to exist even after the project has ended, to act as a "safety net" in the event of future disasters. Several institutions have already reached specific agreements in this respect, in the form of covenants.

The pilot project will also produce several publications, such as a Dutch-language guide to writing a disaster plan. A short version of this has been published on the ICN website. The printed guide will appear during the congress in November 2003.

Another product will be model disaster plan based upon an imaginary institution. This will contain appendices that can be used as the basis for real plans or even be adopted verbatim, such as a list of priority items in the collection, a form for recording objects in the event of the collection being evacuated, a list of emergency supplies and facilities, internal and external alert lists, and so on. My own role in the project is to coordinate the various publications. As a consultant at the ICN, my duties include promoting safety and security. In this capacity, I am also involved in supervising individual institutions in the writing of their disaster plans.

A Regional Approach

One of the objectives of the pilot project has been to develop a regional approach to prevention projects and to compile written guidelines for such an approach. Those guidelines are now ready.

One of the important basic principles underlying the regional approach is that museums, archives and libraries work together when compiling and implementing disaster plans, so that knowledge and experiences are shared through networks. The regional approach is project-based. All staff of an institution must contribute to the project to the extent of their own abilities and expertise. Active involvement by senior management is of the utmost importance, for they must demonstrate that they attach great significance to the disaster plan and must ensure that that plan is actually put into effect. A number of policy decisions need to be made and a budget must be allocated. Externally, the institution should work with various organizations: fellow keepers of collections, government, the emergency services, commercial recovery companies and experts in the fields of restoration and repair.

Implementing the Regional Approach

The regional approach involves working meetings, information meetings and individual supervision. At the working meetings, the disaster plan is examined step by step. The participants learn from one another and make use of the expertise provided by the ICN, along with resources to assist in writing the plan, including a guide and examples.

The main purpose of the information meetings is to share knowledge – for example, about recent developments and events. These meetings are also used to establish contacts with external organizations, such as the emergency services. Throughout the project, specific expertise and support are available to individual institutions, including a helpdesk and site visits.

Since the pilot project began, institutions from other parts of the country have shown an interest in adopting the regional approach. Concrete plans are already in place for follow-up projects in the towns of Delft and Leiden.

The real challenge is not building up a network or writing a disaster plan, it is keeping them both alive – creating an organization that is alert, ready and trained. This pilot project did not need to prove that a disaster plan is necessary and useful. But what we have now shown in The Hague is that it can be easy and enjoyable, that it is something you simply must do.

References

Peek, Marja and Ton Cremers. 2003. *Handleiding voor het maken van een calamiteitènplan voor collectiebeherende instellingen* (a manual to make a disaster preparedness plan especially for collection-keeping institutions). Amsterdam: Instituut Collectie Nederland.

The Author

Marja Peek is a consultant in the Consultancy Department of The Netherlands Institute for Cultural Heritage (ICN), working in the fields of collections management and safety and security (disaster prevention). Previously she was coordinator of the Information Department at ICN. She holds a degree in art history and archaeology from the State University in Leiden.

SESSION 2: PLENARY SESSION

In the context of recent events worldwide, this session discussed the importance of disaster planning, the international Blue Shield initiative and the protection of cultural heritage.

THE BLUE SHIELD: THE CULTURAL RED CROSS?

Ross Shimmon

Former President, International Committee of the Blue Shield, and Former Secretary General, International Federation of Library Associations and Institution, The Hague, The Netherlands

Abstract

The International Committee of the Blue Shield (ICBS) was formed in 1996 by the four NGOs (non-governmental organizations) representing archives, libraries, monuments and sites, and museums: ICA (International Council on Archives), IFLA (International Federation of Library Associations and Institutions, ICOMOS (International Council on Monuments and Sites) and ICOM (International Council of Museums).

This presentation outlines the history of the Committee, its current work and future strategy. In light of recent disasters and tragedies, for example, the destruction of the Buddhas in Afghanistan, the floods in Prague, the war in Iraq, and the continuing conflict in the Middle East, it asks the question does the Blue Shield have the ability to make a difference?

Presentation

Those terrible images of the looting, destruction and torching of the National Museum, National Library and Archives, and other cultural institutions in Baghdad reminded us all – if indeed we needed reminding so soon after the rocket-propelled destruction of the Buddha statues in Afghanistan – of just how vulnerable our cultural heritage is.

The records of human civilizations – archives, books, manuscripts, tablets, monuments, artefacts of all kinds, historic sites, and the structures which house them – are more than the cultural property of both those particular civilizations they document and their successors. They individually help to define a people and a culture. They confer an identity upon individuals and groups. But together, they are the common inheritance of all humanity.

We need them to survive down the centuries so that we can anchor ourselves both in the past and in the present. So they need protection from disasters – those brought on by people (war, conflict, terrorism), by nature (floods, earthquake and the local environment), and accident (fire and other disasters). They also need protection from neglect, such as lack of investment in staff, equipment and maintenance.

One form of protection is the Blue Shield. The Blue Shield is the official symbol of The Hague Convention on the Protection of Cultural Property in the Event of Armed Conflict of 1954. It makes provision for the safeguarding of cultural property, paralleling the humanitarian provisions in the much better known Geneva Conventions.

The Hague Convention requires states to:

- prepare in time of peace for the safeguarding of cultural property against the effects of armed conflict;
- refrain from any act of hostility against such property;
- respect cultural property by refraining from any use of the property likely to expose it to damage or destruction in the event of armed conflict;
- prohibit, prevent and put a stop to theft, pillage, or misappropriation of, and any acts of vandalism directed against, cultural property;

- refrain from any reprisals against cultural property;
- introduce military regulations to ensure observance of the Convention and foster respect for the culture and cultural property of all peoples; and
- establish services and personnel within their armed forces to secure such respect and to co-operate with civilian authorities.

However, the provisions for enforcement and for sanctions in the event of non-compliance are "remarkably weak and rather vague," according to expert Patrick Boylan (2003, 11).

In 1999, a Second Protocol to The Hague Convention was adopted. It greatly limited the circumstances in which an attack on cultural property could be mounted on the grounds of "military necessity." It also made provision for "exceptional protection" for the most important sites and institutions. Perhaps most important of all, it introduced the concept of a "cultural war crime."

For the first time, once the Protocol comes into effect, there will be permanent institutional arrangements to oversee the application of the Convention. The States Parties, that is, the member states which have signed and ratified the Convention and its Protocol, will meet every two years. There will also be a twelve-member Committee for the Protection of Cultural Property in the Event of Armed Conflict, which will meet at least once a year.

The International Committee of the Blue Shield (ICBS) is formally recognised in the Protocol as an advisory body to the Committee and to the States Parties.

When will the Protocol come into effect?

When a minimum of twenty states have signed and ratified the Protocol. Fifteen have done so at present. We know that several (including the United Kingdom) have announced their intention to do so shortly. We hope that sufficient states will do so in time for it to come into effect in the year of the fiftieth anniversary of The Hague Convention in 2004.

Why is it important?

Apart from the enhanced protection it will give to designated sites, the concept of a war crime is important. It will mean that those responsible for the deliberate damage to and destruction of cultural institutions and collections can be prosecuted. This should act as a stronger deterrent compared with the current sanctions.

What is the International Committee of the Blue Shield?

It is a small body with large ambitions. It was founded in 1996 by the four international non-governmental organizations (NGOs) representing the interests of archives, libraries, monuments and sites, and museums: The International Council on Archives (ICA); the International Council on Monuments and Sites (ICOMOS); the International Council of Museums (ICOM) and IFLA. It works closely with United Nations Educational, Scientific and Cultural Organization (UNESCO), whose representatives attend its meetings, and a representative of the International Centre for the Study of the Preservation and Restoration of Cultural Property (ICCROM) is an observer. We have also recently decided to invite a representative of the International Committee of the Red Cross (ICRC).

Our remit is to:

- facilitate international responses to threats or emergencies threatening cultural property;

- encourage safeguarding and respect for cultural property, especially by promoting risk preparedness;
- train experts at national and regional level to prevent, control and recover from disasters;
- act in an advisory capacity for the protection of endangered heritage; and
- consult and co-operate with other bodies including UNESCO, ICCROM and ICRC.

I think that you will agree that, for an organization without a penny to its name, it is demanding list.

What do we do?

Perhaps I can best answer this by a case study. Each of the four founding organizations is represented by one, or sometimes two, people. One representative is usually the Secretary General of the organization. We meet three or four times a year. Each of the four NGOs takes it in turns to host the meetings, usually in Paris. When it is IFLA's turn, Marie-Thérèse Varlamoff (who is one of IFLA's regular representatives) arranges for us to meet at the Bibliothèque nationale de France. We discuss current issues. Recent examples have included the floods in Eastern Europe, the war in Afghanistan, the conflict in Israel and Palestine and, of course, the war in Iraq.

At our meeting in February this year, we decided to issue statements, raising our concerns about:

- the lack of progress in restoring cultural institutions in Afghanistan;
- the impact of the continuing conflict in Israel and Palestine; and
- the potential damage to cultural property in Iraq, if war broke out.

We issued these as press releases. As the current President of ICBS, I wrote to Presidents George Bush, Saddam Hussein and Prime Minister Tony Blair, urging them to "take all necessary steps to protect cultural property in the event of war breaking out." (Shimmon 2003) I sent copies of these letters to the ambassadors of the three countries in The Hague and their representatives at UNESCO. I wrote a letter to the London *Guardian* newspaper raising the same concerns, which was published.

In the immediate aftermath of the war in Iraq, we issued a further statement expressing our horror at the reports of looting, destruction and loss of material at the archives, libraries and museums. We urged the coalition forces to protect the collections, institutions and sites. We also urged the governments of the USA and the UK to ratify the Second Protocol. I wrote again to George Bush and Tony Blair along the same lines.

UNESCO called an emergency meeting in Paris on April 17. We were fully represented. We fought hard to ensure that archives and libraries were included in the report of that meeting and that one of the recommendations should be that a multi-disciplinary mission would be sent to Iraq to investigate the situation and make recommendations. This was agreed. We were also represented at a meeting in early May, called by INTERPOL in Lyon, to discuss measures to be taken to prevent illicit trade in cultural goods illegally exported from Iraq.

A mission was sent in June. Although a librarian had been identified by UNESCO to take part – Jean-Marie Arnoult (the predecessor of Marie-Thérèse Varlamoff as Director of IFLA/PAC) – he was prevented from going. The official reason was that the size of the mission had to be reduced on security grounds. We protested strongly about this and gained a great deal of publicity.

We posted on the Blue Shield pages on IFLANET reports of the situation in Iraq as we received them.

UNESCO sent a second mission on June 30, returning on July 6. Jean-Marie Arnoult was a member of this mission. At the time of preparing this paper, we anxiously await the report and its recommendations. A preliminary report from M. Arnoult makes for sober reading:

- "The area of the archives [in the National Library building] was probably looted before being totally destroyed by fire."
- "A number of plastic bags (about 40-50) are stored in a mosque in Revolution City (formerly Saddam City) with books of the National Library....The content was mostly archival documents from the mandate period up to 1958."
- "Conditions are very bad (high temperature and humidity, dust, insects and rodents)."
- "The structure of the building [National Library] is destroyed: it cannot be restored and must be pulled down."
- The restoration unit of the Centre for Manuscripts has been completely looted."
- "The [Basra central Public Library] has been totally looted and burnt. Nothing remaining except walls weakened by fire. It is not possible to restore the building."

Clearly a huge effort is required, not only to retrieve, restore, protect and re-house the historic materials, but also to build a modern archives, library and information infrastructure as part of the process of rebuilding the state of Iraq.

Until now, that is as much as we have been able to do: urge, exhort governments and agencies, issue statements, gain publicity, and encourage greater awareness via the media among the public of the irreversible damage being done to our cultural heritage.

We also encourage the establishment of national Blue Shield committees. So far, committees have been established in: Belgium, Benin, the Czech Republic, France, Italy, Macedonia, The Netherlands, Norway, Poland and the United Kingdom & Ireland. National Committees are also being established in Australia, Canada and Peru.

These committees can sometimes carry out positive action, for example, by sending experts and equipment to other countries, in response to emergencies. In some cases, they can raise funds to support local response teams. Typically, national Blue Shield committees bring together representatives of the four professional disciplines, the military authorities and the emergency services. Apart from responses to emergencies, they can encourage institutions to prepare disaster plans and train military and emergency services personnel in the steps to be taken to protect cultural institutions and collections. They can also work with customs and police to identify cultural property that is illegally imported or exported.

Very soon, we hope that ICBS will be able to undertake positive action in response to emergencies. Up to now we have had no resources of our own, and no direct access to any external funds. Very shortly, we hope to be able to announce that an emergency rescue fund will be set up in partnership with a respected foundation in The Netherlands (see note 1). The intention is that, with the minimum of red tape, we will be able to mount a rescue mission, send some equipment or essential materials to make a real difference "on the ground." Success in modest actions like this, we hope, will enable us to draw down funds from other foundations, so that we can intervene in a larger number of situations.

When the Second Protocol comes into force, ICBS will gain official recognition. We will act as advisors when an application is made to designate a cultural institution or collection as needing enhanced protection. My hope is that this recognition will, of itself, enable us to attract greater financial resources. Meanwhile, in cooperation with ICOM and ICOMOS, we hope to establish a small office in Paris.

What can you do to help make the Blue Shield to be more effective?

- You could urge your government to ratify the Second Protocol of The Hague Convention, if it has not already done so. A full list of the countries that have ratified the Protocol is available on the Blue Shield pages of IFLANET. The sooner twenty countries ratify, the sooner it will come into effect (see note 2).
- You could contact your national Blue Shield committee. They almost certainly will welcome your support. A full list of the national committees and those in the process of being established, together with contact details, is on the Blue Shield pages on IFLANET.
- If your country does not have a committee, you could take steps to set one up. The criteria for a national committee to be recognised by ICBS are listed on the Blue Shield pages on IFLANET.
- You could publicize the activities of ICBS and the national committees, and the need to protect cultural heritage by writing to the professional and national press.

The protection, rescue and restoration of our cultural heritage are vital tasks. To do the job properly, we need the same energy, commitment and resources – and recognition – available to the Red Cross.

My hope is that, one day the term "Blue Shield" will have the same resonance as the "Red Cross," and that we shall have the resources to establish the cultural equivalent of *Médecins Sans Frontières*.

Notes

Since the preparation of this article:

1 The Cultural Emergency Response, a joint initiative of the International Committee of the Blue Shield and the Prince Claus Fund of The Netherlands was announced. Launched in Delft on September 26, 2003, in the presence of Prince Johan Friso and Prince Constantijn of The Netherlands, this initiative provides emergency assistance in the event of destruction or damage of contemporary and traditional cultural heritage, either by war or natural causes. The first action was to support the restoration of the reading room of the central university library in Baghdad.

2 The Second Protocol to the to the 1954 Hague Convention on the Protection of Cultural Property in the Event of Armed Conflict came into force on March 9, 2004. With the accession of Costa Rica, the twentieth state to have acceded on December 9, 2003, the necessary number of states for its coming into force was achieved.

References

Arnoult, Jean-Marie. 2003. *Iraqi libraries: a general outline.* A report presented during the World Library and Information Congress, Berlin, August, 2003. http://www.ifla.org/IV/ifla69/papers/180e-Arnoult.pdf

Boylan, Patrick. 2003. The 1954 Hague Convention on the Protection of Cultural Property in the Event of Armed Conflict and its 1954 and 1999 Protocols. In Koch, Corine (ed.), *A Blue Shield for the protection of our endangered cultural heritage: proceedings*

of the open session co-organized by PAC core activity and the Section on National Libraries. International Preservation Issues 4:4-15.
http://www.ifla.org/VI/4/news/ipi4-e.pdf

MacKenzie, George. 2003. The Blue Shield: symbol of cultural heritage protection. In Koch, Corine (ed.), *A Blue Shield for the protection of our endangered cultural heritage: proceedings of the open session co-organized by PAC core activity and the Section on National Libraries.* International Preservation Issues 4:16-18.
http://www.ifla.org/VI/4/news/ipi4-e.pdf

IFLANET International Committee of the Blue Shield (includes a link to The Hague Convention)
http://www.ifla.org/blueshield.htm

Shimmon, Ross. 2003. *Letter to President George W. Bush,* March 7, 2003. IFLA Ref. R2/rs.

The Author

Ross Shimmon was Secretary General of IFLA from 1999-2004 and President of the International Committee of the Blue Shield from 2003-2004. He was previously Chief Executive of the (British) Library Association. He has worked in library education in Papua New Guinea and Wales, UK; in academic and public libraries in the UK; and with the government department responsible for libraries in England and Wales. He received an OBE (officer of the Order of the British Empire), and an Honorary Fellowship of the (British) Library Association in 1999.

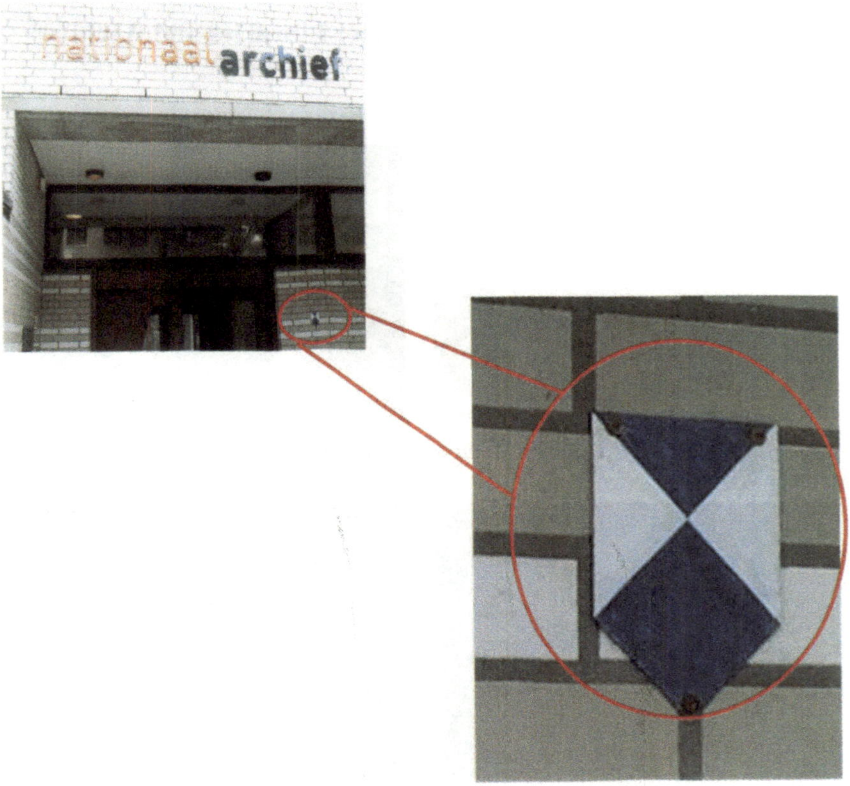

The building housing the National Archief, The Hague, showing the use of the Blue Shield – the symbol specified in the 1954 Hague Convention for marking cultural sites to give them protection from attack in the event of armed conflict. It is also the name of an international committee set up in 1996 to work to protect the world's cultural heritage threatened by wars and natural disasters.

Photo courtesy Josche Neven.

Assessment of Iraqi Cultural Heritage: Libraries and Archives June 27-July 6, 2003.

All photos courtesy Jean-Marie Arnoult.

Bags filled with archival documents in a mosque in Iraq

National Archives in Iraq, part of the stores.

Entrance of National Archives, Iraq.

Basra University Central Library: books destroyed by fire.

Basra University Central Library: Sciences reading room (looted).

Basra Central Public Library: public rooms opening on a patio.

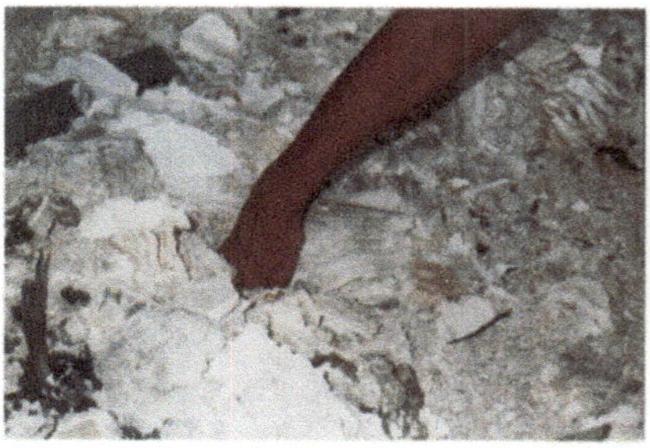

Basra Central Public Library: books burnt to dust.

Facade of the National Library and National Archives in Baghdad.

Facade of the National Library and National Archives in Baghdad.

Books of the National Library stored in a mosque.

SESSION 3: INSTITUTIONAL PLANNING

This session focused on disaster planning at the institutional level. The emphasis was on the theoretical, but also what has been shown to work based on practical experience in libraries and other sectors, and reported in the literature. What are the human resource and response issues? What are the training requirements? How is training best implemented? What are the trends, challenges, pitfalls and success factors?

EARTHQUAKE PREPAREDNESS AT THE ISTANBUL MUSEUMS

Nevra Erturk

Research Assistant, Faculty of Art and Design, Museum Studies Graduate Program, Art Management Program, Yildiz Technical University, Istanbul, Turkey

Abstract

Earthquake poses the highest risk among all natural disasters in Turkey. According to seismologists, in the near future there will be a major and devastating earthquake in the Marmara Region, which includes Istanbul.

The damage resulting from the 1999 Izmit and Duzce Earthquakes in Turkey is proof of the power and devastating force of earthquakes. These two major earthquakes provided the impetus to review and reformulate Turkey's planning against earthquake hazard.

This paper provides a general evaluation of earthquake preparedness before and after the 1999 earthquakes in Turkish museums and presents new earthquake preparedness programs that have been put forward at national and institutional levels. The discussion concludes with a description of earthquake preparedness programs to protect museum visitors, museum buildings and collections, with a focus on the Istanbul museums, which daily host thousands of visitors and house the irreplaceable cultural heritage of world civilizations.

Introduction

Natural disasters can cause loss of human life and economic crisis, as well as loss of cultural properties that are irreplaceable. Earthquake poses the highest risk among all natural disasters in Turkey. According to seismologists, 96 percent of Turkey is in an earthquake zone.

Earthquakes have the capacity to destroy instantaneously, without warning, causing extensive and often irreparable damage to cultural heritage. The damage resulting from the 1999 Izmit and Duzce Earthquakes in Turkey is proof of the power and devastating force of earthquakes. However, a positive outcome came as a result of these events. The 1999 earthquakes provided the impetus to review and reformulate Turkey's planning against earthquake hazard.

These two major earthquakes marked a turning point for the museum sector. After the 1999 earthquakes, authorities and museum professionals recognized that an earthquake could severely damage or even destroy the irreplaceable heritage materials that are exhibited and stored in the museums of Turkey. In Istanbul, there are about 60 museums, which house historical and cultural heritage and host thousands of visitors in a day. According to the scientists, there will be an earthquake in Istanbul in the near future; therefore, museum staff must learn to improve earthquake preparedness to protect their visitors, buildings and collections.

Earthquakes in Istanbul

Istanbul experienced 588 earthquakes between 400 B.C. and 1894. The most important ones were on: August 24, 358; September 25, 438; September 25, 477; August 15, 554; December 14, 557; October 26, 740; January 9, 860; October 26, 989; November 2, 1037; 1343; September 10, 1509; May 25, 1719; May 22, 1766; and July 10, 1894. (Sakin 2002, 19-37)

The major faults near Istanbul are likely late in their earthquake cycle with no major shocks since 1894, and thus, the earthquakes that damaged Istanbul in the previous 2400 years attest to a significant hazard. According to scientists, the probability of an Istanbul earthquake climbs to 62±15 percent during the next 30 years and 32±12 percent during the next decade. (Parsons at al., 295)

The Izmit (Golcuk-East Marmara) and Duzce Earthquakes

The August 17, 1999, Izmit Earthquake and November 12, 1999, Duzce Earthquake are the largest natural disasters of the 20th century in Turkey, after the 1939 Erzincan Earthquake. These two major earthquakes, both exceeding magnitude 7, occurred within three months of one another and ruptured a 200-km (124-mile) segment of the Northern Anatolian Fault. Two consecutive earthquakes with magnitudes over 7 in the same region are rare in world seismic history. (Sucuoglu 1999)

The Izmit Earthquake occurred at the north branch of the Northern Anatolian Fault Zone, and, for the first time in Turkey, about ten cities and many other locations were affected directly, just as in the Duzce Earthquake. Istanbul lies just northwest of this region. During these earthquakes, the death toll exceeded 18,000, over 100,000 buildings were destroyed and financial losses reached an estimated $10-25 billion (US). Building structures and precast concrete facilities that did not possess sufficient seismic resistance played the most important role in the large losses of life and property. (Parsons et al. 2000, 296; Petal and Turkmen 2002, 39-40; Sucuoglu 1999)

Earthquake Preparedness in Museums

Earthquake preparedness involves a variety of activities, including preparing the museum building and its collection against earthquake, preparing and equipping staff to implement an emergency plan, training staff in evacuation procedures, compiling and maintaining up-to-date contact information, stockpiling supplies and, additionally, training staff and volunteers how to use them. (Dorge and Jones 1999, 4)

Museum Visitors

Museum staff must be trained periodically against a possible earthquake. Museum visitors mostly do not know or care about how to act when an earthquake happens – they only focus on visiting the museum. However, they need to be aware of how to act during an earthquake in the museum and from where to evacuate. Trained museum staff, in concert with simple booklets for museum visitors about earthquake hazards and evacuation procedures, will be helpful to ensure the safety of visitors.

The Museum Building

A seismic survey of the museum building should be done with the help of structural and seismic engineers. These engineers should check the building structure, advise on its stability, and estimate the degree of damage the museum building might suffer during an earthquake. The structural engineer must check the structural integrity of the building, as well as other elements, such as added gallery dividers, decorative elements, and furniture and fixtures. (Podany 2001a, 1-2)

Collections on Exhibition

Collections on exhibition can be protected against earthquake by a variety of mitigation methods. The types of objects, specific needs of the objects, and their primary and secondary threats must be identified through a survey. This work should also include categorizing the exhibition furniture and fixtures, as well as the exhibition galleries in which the collections are housed. An evaluation of the fixtures and furniture should take into consideration their condition, stability, resistance to earthquake motion and potential to become a threat to the collections on exhibition during an earthquake. (Podany 2001a, 1-5)

Collections in Storage

Collections in storage are just as much a concern as those on exhibition. They are, in fact, most probably tomorrow's exhibition materials. Objects that are shut away in storage are not necessarily safe. In many ways, they are at greater risk, and in many museums the majority of the collections are in storage. Unfortunately, storage areas are often less protected and pose the greatest number of secondary threats. They are often crowded, badly located, difficult to access, badly organized and lack mitigation features. (Podany 2001a, 5-6 and 2001b, 1-5)

Earthquake Preparedness at the National Level in Turkey

There are about 200 museums in Turkey, most of them archaeological and ethnographical. Istanbul, with the highest population in Turkey, also has the greatest number of museums. Since Istanbul leads the nation in most respects, one could expect that the two projects mentioned below will be emulated by other Turkish museums and will provide a basis for earthquake preparedness for all.

After the 1999 Izmit and Duzce Earthquakes, a "Museum Disaster Preparedness Program" was conducted by the Bogazici University, the Kandilli Observatory and the Earthquake Research Institute, Disaster Preparedness Education Program. The aim of the program, which started in September 2000, is to provide education and support for the Istanbul museums, thus enabling them to begin disaster preparedness and protection of their collections.

Another project, which started in July 2003, is entitled "Seismic Conservation of Historical and Cultural Treasures of a World City: Sizing the Need and Formulating An Action Plan for the Museums of Istanbul, Turkey". It is a six-month project supported by the World Bank's Hazard Management Unit on behalf of the ProVention Consortium. The project will determine the need for non-structural risk mitigation at Istanbul museums, accompanied by the production of educational reference and hands-on guidance materials to help initiate systematic preservation efforts. However, project findings will have universal applicability to many other countries in the developing world, as well as in all Turkish museums.

The project consists of:

- compilation and classification of examples of non-structural risk mitigation measures taken by museums worldwide;
- preparation of an educational multimedia presentation explaining non-structural hazards and mitigation methods for museum collections on exhibit and in storage;
- development of survey instruments for museums that will help the project team to collect information on seismic preservation needs, as well as information on technical,

financial, physical, staffing and other resources of the museum affecting the local economy;

- organization of an educational seminar for authorities, representatives of the Istanbul museums and other stakeholders;
- visits to 15 museums selected according to their type, management, collection content and number of visitors; and
- a summary report of findings to inform authorities on the scope of non-structural mitigation work that is needed at the Istanbul museums, accompanied by suggestions on how to organize such work.

Earthquake Preparedness at the Institutional Level in Turkey

The Kandilli Observatory and Earthquake Research Institute of Bogazici University, Museum Disaster Preparedness Education Program, organized a series of seminars, meetings and workshops. The "Emergency Planning and Earthquake Preparedness" seminar was held at the Topkapi Palace Museum in October 2000. Mr. Wilbur J. Faulk from the J. Paul Getty Museum gave a lecture to the Topkapi Palace Museum's staff, along with other museum directors and professionals of museums in Istanbul, working under the Turkish Ministry of Culture and Tourism.

Another seminar, "Emergency Planning for Earthquakes," was organized in cooperation with Yildiz Technical University, Museum Studies Graduate Program and held at the Topkapi Palace Museum in December 2000. The target audience was museum directors, museum professionals of the Istanbul museums and directors of libraries.

Dr. Jerry Podany from the J. Paul Getty Museum gave a four-day workshop in cooperation with Turkish Ministry of Culture and Tourism from May 8-11, 2001. The workshop, "Measures Against Earthquakes in Museums," focused on hazard assessment and seismic protection of collections both on exhibit and in storage. It also provided hands-on exercises with the Topkapi Palace Museum and the Istanbul Archaeological Museums.

Community-based Disaster Mitigation Best Practices Day, directed by the Bosphorus University Kandilli Observatory and Earthquake Research Institute, was held in June 2003. The program included sessions on: Basic Disaster Awareness, Community Disaster Response, School Disaster Preparedness, Health Sector Disaster Preparedness, Museums and Cultural Preservation, Structural Mitigation, Non-Structural Mitigation, Media and Education, and Neighbourhood Disaster Preparedness.

Participants evaluated the sessions as being extremely helpful. Several museums followed up by having "Basic Disaster Awareness" training for their staff. Two museums have started to implement preparedness and mitigation measures against earthquake hazard in their exhibition galleries and storage areas. These are the Topkapi Palace Museum and the Sadberk Hanim Museum.

Topkapi Palace Museum Earthquake Preparedness Program

Topkapi Palace Museum is one of the world's largest museums. Located on the promontory of the historical peninsula in Istanbul, it overlooks both the Marmara Sea and the Bosphorus.

In 1453, Fatih Sultan Mehmed conquered Istanbul, building his first palace in Beyazit. Later the eye-catching beauty of Sarayburnu persuaded him to have another palace, the "New Palace," built from 1475-1478. The New Palace is a complex of separate houses and gardens covering an area of 82,000 m^2 (882,670 ft^2). Because of the gates, it was called Topkapi and the palace came to be known as Topkapi Palace. Topkapi Palace was not only the residence of the Sultans, but the administrative centre of the Ottoman Empire between 1478 and 1839. Meetings and ceremonies were held here. It was converted into a museum and opened in 1924 by the order of Ataturk. (Onder 1983, 82-83) Parts of the palace such as the Harem, the Baghdat Pavilion, the Revan Pavilion, the Sofa Pavilion, and the Audience Chamber are renowned for their architecture, while in the other sections of the palace, objects that reflect the palace life are exhibited. The Palace operates under the Turkish Ministry of Culture and Tourism.

Topkapi Palace Museum has fourteen permanent and temporary exhibition galleries and is the most highly-visited museum within the Istanbul museums. The museum sections are: Palace Attire and Garments, Imperial Treasury, Books, Maps and Calligraphic Documents, Miniatures, Portraits of the Sultans, Clocks, Chambers of the Sacred Relics, Porcelains, Guns, and Armory.

After the August 17, 1999, Izmit Earthquake, structural and seismic engineers conducted a seismic survey at Topkapi Palace Museum and an earthquake preparedness program was initiated on October 1, 1999. Because of the limited budget, the museum has given priority to its exhibition galleries and storage areas housing the unique and more fragile objects.

In the exhibition galleries, some objects were removed and measures taken against objects falling onto each other. Staff used sand bags and covered some of the showcases with security film. In some of the storage areas, objects were removed from shelves and put into boxes, and steel cabinets were affixed to the walls. In the last three-and-a-half years, steel nails have been used during tile restoration as an earthquake mitigation measure.

In addition, the Imperial Treasury Exhibition Gallery was completely renovated to reduce earthquake hazard. New showcases, part of the museum building, were put into niches, the lighting systems were taken out of showcases, and the overall number of exhibited objects was reduced. Objects on exhibition were all put into plexiglas cavities and fastened with monofilament line. The Imperial Treasury Exhibition Gallery was reopened to the public on July 3, 2001.

Earthquake hazard identification forms and information cards on basic disaster awareness were distributed to all museum staff. By 2000, disaster preparedness training and meetings started at the museum, such as "ABCD Basic Disaster Awareness Education", "Community Disaster Volunteers" training, "Community-Based Disaster Mitigation Best Practices Day" conducted on behalf of the Disaster Preparedness Education Program, and "Basic Principles of Disaster Management" conducted by the Istanbul Technical University, Disaster Management Center.

Dr. Jerry Podany gave a seminar, "Measures Against Earthquake in Museums", based on practice at Topkapi Palace Museum in May 2001. As part of the seminar, some sections of the museum were visited and discussions took place on how to secure objects.

One of the museum specialists at Topkapi Palace Museum, who had researched earthquake measures in Japan, gave a seminar entitled "Measures Taken Against Earthquakes in Japan Museums" in March 2002. The seminar focused on earthquake measures in exhibition galleries and storage areas, with emphasis on new materials and techniques.

Sadberk Hanim Museum Earthquake Preparedness Program

The Sadberk Hanim Museum opened to the public in 1980. The first private museum in Turkey, it occupies two separate buildings. The original building is a three-story wooden mansion, occupying 400 m^2 (4,305 ft^2) of space set in grounds measuring a total of 4,280 m^2 (46,071 ft^2). New acquisitions mandated the purchase and restoration of a semi-dilapidated building adjacent to the first museum building. The new museum building opened in 1988 with a total exhibition space of 625 m^2 (6,728 ft^2). (Anlagan et el. 1995, 9) All the exhibition galleries were sealed off from daylight and the showcases are illuminated in keeping with modern exhibition techniques.

The Sadberk Hanim Museum has a collection of about 17,000 objects. Its sections are: Anatolian Civilizations, Ion and Hellenic Civilizations, Roman Civilization, Byzantine Art, Lamps, Jewellery, Sculptures and Stellae, Glass Objects, Beads, Coins, Islamic Art, The Ottoman Period, Women's Costumes and Traditions. The museum's project, "Measures against Earthquake Hazard," was initiated in both the exhibition galleries and the storage areas after the 1999 earthquakes. A private museum, it has a relatively extensive budget for earthquake preparedness, in comparison with Topkapi Palace Museum, although its area and collection size are smaller. Therefore, Sadberk Hanim Museum can implement an earthquake preparedness project with greater ease than can the Topkapi Palace Museum.

Museum staff participated in events organized by the Kandilli Observatory and Earthquake Research Institute, Museum Disaster Preparedness Education Program, including "Emergency Planning and Earthquake Preparedness," "ABCD Basic Disaster Awareness Education," "Measures Against Earthquake in Museums" and "Community-Based Disaster Mitigation Best Practices Day."

Earthquake hazard identification and information cards on basic disaster awareness were distributed to all museum staff. Glass objects were affixed to their bases with museum wax in the archaeological section. Most of the objects were secured by putting them plexiglas cavities, and some were affixed with monofilament line in the Iznik Tiles and Ceramics Exhibition Galleries. Before 1999, shelves in the storage areas were affixed to the wall. Locks were installed on cabinets, contour cavities were cut into soft ethafoam blocks to hold and protect fragile objects, objects were boxed, and netting was used on shelves for both the Archaeological and Turkish and Islamic Art Object storage areas.

Conclusion

The 1999 earthquakes could have destroyed the irreplaceable historical and cultural heritage of world civilizations that are exhibited and stored at the Istanbul museums. Fortunately, while very little damage occurred during the 1999 earthquakes, there was both structural and non-structural damage at the museums located in the earthquake region.

According to seismologists, the occurrence of an Istanbul earthquake in future is a scientific fact. Fortunately, the custodians of the rich heritage of the region are now well aware of and very much involved with the active development and implementation of earthquake preparedness programs.

There are many measures that can be taken to mitigate the effects of an earthquake. Some involve expensive technologies, but many practical and inexpensive measures can be taken. Topkapi Palace Museum and Sadberk Hanim Museum are the first of the Istanbul Museums to rigorously implement earthquake preparedness measures. The Hagia Sophia Museum, the Istanbul Archaeological Museums, the Turkish and Islamic Art Museum, the Dolmabahce Palace Museum and the Rahmi Koc Industry Museum have also started to work on mitigating earthquake hazards.

Even though Topkapi Palace Museum's and Sadberk Hanim Museum's management, museum facility area, collection content and size are different, the measures that these two museums have implemented have many commonalities. They have both been taking practical, easy and less expensive precautions against earthquake hazard, such as reducing the number of the same type of objects on display or safely boxing objects in storage. The aim now, is to make this knowledge more widely available and to further develop more practical seismic mitigation action plans, both structural and non-structural.

References

Anlagan, Cetin, Tanju Anlagan, Yesim Gunsenin, Hulya Yilmaz and Sebnem Akalin. 1995. *Sadberk Hanim Muzesi.* Istanbul, Turkey: Vehbi Koc Vakfi.

Dorge, Valerie and Sharon L. Jones, comps. 1999. *Building an Emergency Plan: A Guide for Museums and Other Cultural Institutions.* Los Angeles, California: The Getty Conservation Institute.

Onder, Mehmet. 1983. *The Museums of Turkey.* Ankara, Turkey: Turkiye Is Bankasi Cultural Publications.

Parsons, T., Aykut Barka, Shinji Toda, Ross S. Stein and James H. Dieterich. 2000. Influence of the 17 August 1999 Izmit Earthquake on Seismic Hazards in Istanbul. In Barka, Aykut, O. Kozaci, S. Akyuz and E. Altunel, eds. *The 1999 Izmit and Duzce Earthquakes: Preliminary Results.* 295-310.

Petal, Marla and Zeynep Turkmen. 2002. *ABCD Temel Afet Bilinci El Kitabi.* Istanbul, Turkey: Beyaz Gemi Yayinlari.

Podany, Jerry. 2001ba. *Seismic Susceptibility Survey.* Istanbul: Bogazici Universitesi Kandilli Rasathanesi ve Deprem Arastirma Enstitusu, Istanbul Afete Hazirlik Egitim Projesi.

Podany, Jerry. 2001b. *Disaster Preparedness for Museum Collections.* Istanbul: Bogazici Universitesi Kandilli Rasathanesi ve Deprem Arastirma Enstitusu, Istanbul Afete Hazirlik Egitim Projesi.

Sakin, Orhan. 2002. *Tarihsel Kaynaklara Gore Istanbul Depremleri.* Istanbul, Turkey: Kitabevi.

Sucuoglu, Haluk. 1999. The 1999 Kocaeli and Duzce-Turkey Earthquakes. http://www.metu.edu.tr/home/wwweerc/guncel/koca-dzc.pdf (1 July 2004).

The Author

Nevra Erturk completed her BA in Classical Archaeology and her MA in Museum Studies. She is a PhD candidate in the field of Architectural History and Theory and works as a research assistant in the Museum Studies Graduate Program, Art Management Program at Yildiz Technical University. She has participated in several excavations and has been involved in disaster management training programs. She is one of the research grants for Disaster Risk Reduction Program of the World Bank's Hazard Management Unit. She has written various articles, reports and a book about museology, earthquake preparedness and archaeological heritage management. She will be starting work as a graduate intern in the J. Paul Getty Museum, Department of Antiquities in September 2004.

DISASTER MANAGEMENT AND LIBRARIES; PLANNING INTO ACTION: THE INSTITUTIONAL PERSPECTIVE

Graham Matthews

Professor of Information and Library Management, School of Business Information, Faculty of Business and Law, Liverpool John Moores University, Liverpool, UK

Abstract

This paper, based on research and literature review, considers key institutional factors that contribute to effective disaster management in libraries. The written disaster control plan is the crucial framework around which action should be planned. Devising and implementing a plan needs more than words on paper. It will determine, outline and prompt a range of activities across the phases of disaster management. It will indicate who has responsibility and who is to lead and be involved and will offer a schedule for monitoring compliance, review and updating. Clear institutional strategy and support at the top level are essential. Individual institutions must plan according to their own circumstances, but it is important to think within and without the institution – very few will be able to cope on their own in the face of a major disaster. Libraries must ask what resources are available in-house and within the parent organization, and what other expertise or assistance, might be available locally, regionally, or elsewhere, and from other sectors. Cost implications must be addressed and phased programs for implementation developed. Awareness-raising and training, including practical exercises, for all levels of staff, are vital – people are at the heart of effective disaster management. Training can contribute to organized yet flexible approaches to different incidents and build confidence to think and act quickly and decisively in difficult situations. This paper concludes with a view of current strengths and weaknesses in the field.

Introduction

My main research interest over the last 15-20 years has been preservation management in libraries, in particular, disaster management. I have, fortunately, never been personally involved in a major library disaster but through research and professional contacts have been able to share the experiences of those who have, both in the United Kingdom (UK) and elsewhere in the world. Through their willingness to talk about and reflect upon what they were faced with and how they dealt with it, I have been able to gain a privileged insight. In the mid-1990s, with colleague Paul Eden, I led a major research project, funded by the (then) British Library Research and Development Department, which achieved an overview of disaster management practice in British libraries and provided guidelines based on good practice (Matthews and Eden 1996a). This involved consulting and interviewing, not only librarians, but archivists, fire officers, museums officers, an architect and representatives from disaster salvage and recovery companies, heritage organizations, an insurance company and loss adjusters. Recently, with Professor John Feather, I edited a book on disaster management for libraries and archives published by Ashgate (Matthews and Feather, editors, 2003). Contributions by academics and practitioners from around the world include a review of disaster control planning, risk assessment and management, dealing with fire and flood, co-operation and networking, the impact on staff and users, and the role of counseling, war and its effect, and short- and long-term service continuity.

This is not a paper on 'how to do' disaster management – there is plenty of advice on that in the literature. For example: Alire, ed. 2000; Anderson and McIntyre 1985; Ashman

1995; Batchelor 1999; Coult 2001; Doig 1997; Dorge and Jones, comps. 1999; East Midlands Museums Service 2001; Kahn, 1998; and Wellheiser and Scott 2002, who themselves refer to many other sources. On the World Wide Web (WWW) – the Conservation OnLine (CoOL) website brings together useful links, and other institutional and association websites such as those of the European Commission on Preservation and Access (ECPA), the International Federation of Library Associations and Institutions (IFLA) Core Activity for Preservation and Conservation (PAC), the International Committee of the Blue Shield (ICBS), the M25 Consortium of Academic Libraries, the Library of Congress Preservation Directorate, and the National Library of Australia, do likewise. The focus of this paper is to consider the institution – what can or should an institution do, or be required to do, to facilitate effective disaster management in libraries? It begins by considering strategy and the key role of the written disaster control plan, then moves on to look at people and resources. It ends with a personal view of strengths and weaknesses in this area and a summary of key current issues.

Strategy

Libraries are usually part of a larger institution or organization to which they are responsible. Public libraries may be governed by a local authority or national body, academic libraries by a college or university administration, and commercial libraries, their parent company. It is important that any individual library strategy relating to disaster management is in line with institutional strategy and mission. It is also important to note that in a major disaster, responsibility for action is likely to rest with the parent body and decisions will be made at that level by managers or executives who are not 'library' people. It is therefore vital that senior library management make senior institutional management aware of library disaster preparedness and recovery requirements and help them understand the real impact on the institution and its mission as a whole of an incident affecting the library. Experience indicates that it is not easy to do this in the throes of dealing with an emergency situation. It is preferable to achieve this in advance as part of disaster control planning, to find out who the key people are at the institutional level and to engage in dialogue with them about disaster management and the library. Explain library matters (and jargon!) to them and make them understand both the rationale for intended actions and the cases for associated funding and other requirements, as well as the consequences for both the library and the institution of taking no or insufficient action. Involve other departments at this stage. The need for this has recently been underlined by Muir and Shenton (2002, 122):

> As for disaster plans, a key constraint appears to be the necessary reliance on other departments of the parent organization. Although they may provide expertise, they may not respond effectively when asked for assistance during a disaster. Because of the difficulties, a number of respondents suggested a credo of self-help. This is a difficult problem to overcome, and would require commitment of disaster management at the very highest level and clear communications between departments in the parent [organization].

While it will be necessary to involve other departments, it is likely that this pursuit of support and funding will be 'in competition' with other departments in the institution, each with their own agenda. It is thus vital to put forward a strong case to ensure the top-level support and relationships necessary at the institutional level for effective disaster management for the library. Awareness of institutional strategy and procedures will also facilitate their integration and/or compatibility with those of the library.

The key activity around which such a case may be built is disaster control planning. The activities involved in devising and implementing an effective written disaster control plan such as risk assessment, consulting external agencies and training will identify requirements and potential solutions and their consequences, strategic, financial or otherwise.

Disaster Control Plan

The disaster control plan traditionally comprises four stages: prevention, preparedness, reaction and recovery. While templates and examples of disaster control plans are increasingly available (as evidenced by sources in "References and Select Bibliography and Websites" at the end of this article), it is important that disaster control plans are tailored to individual library circumstances:

> Individual organizations must decide for themselves their own disaster management needs, based on a consideration of their own resources and other priorities ... . Each [disaster control] plan needs to be building-specific and to work within a unique organizational context. (Matthews and Eden 1996a, 3)

The disaster control plan is not just something that should sit on a shelf until an incident occurs. It should be a document determining and prompting actions. It is more than words; it is a framework for a range of activities. Components must be practiced, tested, reviewed, and updated. It needs to be worked on constantly; it is never 'finished'. All involved need to be aware of the plan and their roles. It must therefore be straightforward and flexible. As Roze (2002, 11) states, "un plan d'urgence doit être écrit clairement de façon à être immédiatement compris de tous. Il est mis à jour très régulièrement et diffuse aussitôt à l'intérieur et à l'extérieur de l'établissement."

No one can predict exactly what kind of incident might occur, what the level of impact might be, and when it might happen, but preplanning may help prevent it, reduce its effect or assist reaction, service continuity and recovery. If an incident does occur, the plan will provide a starting point for a course of action, and it will provide details of contacts, options and procedures. In its own right, the plan will not resolve the issue but it will help to manage it. This is underlined by accounts of recent major flooding incidents in two university libraries, one in the US, and the other in the UK:

> In a disaster of this magnitude, you are not in control. Whilst it is essential to have a disaster plan, you may find that your plan simply doesn't work for a variety of reasons. You will be at the mercy of your central administration, the insurance companies, and outside contractors for the help you need in saving your collection and restoring your building. Make sure in advance that your administrators are well-educated in the special problems faced by libraries when disaster strikes. (Enssle and Tweedie 2000, 96)

> Above all, I am convinced disaster planning is absolutely essential – and not much use when something as bad as this happens ... In the end you just cope. (Shorley 2003, 47)

A colleague qualifies this:

> The second lesson is the value of having a written disaster plan. Although the plan had no direct effect on the outcome of the disaster, the reading and discussions that accompanied it were invaluable in helping us react to the flood. We already knew where to begin. (Howes 2003, 186)

Resources

Within the Institution

It is important that all potential existing resources within the library and within the parent institution are identified and their suitability and availability checked. As indicated in the Strategy section above, this will involve identifying key institutional personnel and establishing relationships with them.

> The disaster manager must be able to build a rapport with staff in other departments within the parent organization ... [as] it may often prove difficult for the library to obtain the information it requires from them. (Matthews and Eden 1996a, 12)

One librarian consulted in the mid-1990s illustrated this by commenting how difficult it had been to find out if an institutional plan was in existence, and who was responsible for its development and implementation. There will be a need to liaise with colleagues in other institutional departments such as estates, finance and security. Identify the key people and what they can and can't do, explain the library, its role and services and try to establish a working relationship. Is the value of collections known? If library staff do not know this, why should finance officers in the parent organization be expected to know it? Find out who has responsibility for insurance coverage within the institution. Identify what insurance exists and check that institutional coverage is adequate (covering, for example, buildings, collections, computer hardware and software, fixtures and fittings, legal liability with respect to employees and the public and consequential losses). A paper published recently based on the experience of a major flood at the University of Sussex's Library repository at Lewes offers advice on insuring collections and making claims. (Howes 2003)

It is also important that institutions are not only aware of legal requirements relating to disaster management but also of those of any registration scheme membership to which they aspire. (In the UK, the recently published *Registration scheme for museums and galleries: registration. Draft for consultation* (Resource, March 2003), includes among requirements, an emergency (or disaster) plan, which must include "a risk assessment of threats such as fire, water, theft and vandalism or other disasters," "procedures to be followed by staff on discovery of an emergency," and it " ... must cover arrangements for staff and visitors as well as collections and buildings." (Resource 2003a, 14) Further non-mandatory elements are also suggested in an appendix. (Resource 2003a, 42) A checklist for benchmarks in collection care published recently by Resource: the Council for Museums, Archives and Libraries (UK) provides concise benchmarks for emergency preparedness at the level of basic, good and best practice (Resource 2002a, 65-68).

Outside the Institution

It is unlikely, especially in the event of a major disaster, that any library will be able to cope on its own. In the prevention and preparedness stages of a disaster control plan, there will be a need to involve external agencies. For example, the fire service will be required to check compliance with fire regulations, specialist consultants for advice on detection and suppression systems, commercial salvage and recovery companies, local archivists, and conservators, to name but a few.

It is worth looking for fellow professionals locally who have prepared and/or implemented disaster plans to seek their advice. Consider how to learn from experience elsewhere. There may be local or regional networks you can tap into for help and support. Look at websites and organizational newsletters for potential contacts and training events where you may strike up useful relationships. Co-operative networks may enable cost sharing, such as providing central storage and access to equipment and supplies needed in an emergency. It may be cost-effective to arrange training on a collaborative basis. If such arrangements are to be effective they really need to be formalized. They could, for instance, cover agreements on temporary access to member libraries for users of a participating library whose services have been stopped or interrupted by disaster, off-site storage and back-up of data files, the number of days that staff may be loaned to other member libraries to help with recovery. Advice and support nationally should also be identified – contact your national library. Check to see if there are any national initiatives in which you may become involved. Ask if there are any sources of funding support. Staff there will also be able to advise of any international agencies, such as the ICBS, IFLA, and UNESCO (United Nations Educational, Scientific and Cultural Organization) whose assistance you may be able to draw upon.

People

In addition to the need for top-level support mentioned above, it is also imperative for the institution to ensure that the "right" people are in the "right" jobs with regard to disaster management. For example, the "boss" might be the best person to manage and run an efficient library service in normal circumstances, but may not be the most appropriate person to lead disaster reaction in an extraordinary situation. There may be other individuals who work well under pressure in adverse conditions, leaving their manager to focus on service continuity, whilst they lead reaction and initial recovery. It is worth thinking about this in advance, and determining which senior managers might be best suited to different roles. Effective disaster management, in fact, will depend on the involvement and cooperation of *all* staff at *all* levels. It is vital that all staff are vigilant and aware of disaster plans, and know what is expected of them, whether they are team leaders or members. The person in charge must have authority within the institution to act as they deem necessary, albeit with specialist advice. They will need, for example, to authorize expenditures and will be under pressure to make such decisions quickly!

Training

Training at all levels is thus crucial; without it the disaster control plan will remain words on paper. Training itself can help ensure that this is not the case. It should not all be one way; those taking part should be encouraged to ask questions and raise issues that concern them. Their local knowledge or 'shop floor' experience may contribute to effective planning and review. Training will range from general awareness-raising to targeted advice and instruction for individuals with specific roles. For example, all staff, including cleaners and caretakers, needs to know how to raise the alarm. Those charged with writing the disaster control plan need training to support this, and others may need an insight into salvage and recovery options or how to deal with health and safety or insurance issues or dealing with the media. There must also be refresher courses; existing staff need reminding of procedures and new or recently employed staff must not be overlooked. The author has expanded on training elsewhere. (Matthews and Eden 1996b) [See also a report of a research project on preservation management training (Thebridge and Matthews 2000) and proceedings of a National Preservation Office seminar on this topic. (Thebridge, ed. 2000)]

The aims and objectives of training must be clearly determined in line with institutional strategy and individual requirements. Training should thus be focused and targeted in line with this, and with regard to the experience, expertise and physical capability of individuals. Issues relating to security may determine that some training is restricted to those with a "need to know." All aspects of disaster management (prevention, preparedness, reaction and recovery) need to be addressed. Methods of training can be varied, and may include 'brainstorming' sessions with personnel from the library and the parent body, as well as tours of the building pointing out evacuation routes, assembly points, etc. Practical exercises or simulations are essential – practice runs of the full disaster control plan, or its elements can show what does and doesn't work, but they can be difficult and time-consuming to organize. Practical workshops can offer experience, for example, in sorting and salvaging various fire- or water-damaged materials. Demonstrations and use of different types of equipment such as fire extinguishers or emergency supplies are also valuable in familiarizing staff with procedures and building their confidence. In all training, feedback and discussion should be encouraged. Training should also be evaluated. Outcomes of these should be incorporated into future sessions or discussed elsewhere as appropriate. (Matthews and Eden 1996b)

It is also appropriate to think about the training aids and support materials to be used. Disaster control plans and floor plans will be the basis for many exercises dealing with different scenarios. Videos and photographs are often used to illustrate points, and to try to bring to life what it is really like when dealing with a disaster. Many images are now available over the Internet, as are examples of training packs and programs. It is important to consider who will lead or take the training; they must have appropriate knowledge and skills. There is an up-front financial element to consider here too, if, for example, it is necessary to bring in outside trainers or consultants or to pay to send staff for external training. Collaborative training, locally or regionally, and cross-domain (for example, involving archivists and librarians) is one way that organizations have addressed this issue. (Matthews and Eden 1996b)

Training is vital to the effective deployment of the disaster control plan:

> Disaster control plans may be executed in response to a variety of incidents, from the minor and seemingly straightforward to the major, where staff will have to operate in strange and trying circumstances. They are much more likely to be successful if staff are fully aware of what to expect and what to do, and if they have been given the opportunity to practice their roles beforehand. (Matthews and Eden 1996b, 37)

But, as Davis underlines (Davis and Kern 2003, 121), in talking about sending staff to assist at a disaster in another library, there is nothing like the real thing: "It may sound callous, but helping at someone else's library disaster is one of the best training techniques for staff in disaster response – far better than any planned workshop."

Strengths and Weaknesses

Matthews and Eden (1996a), in their recommendations following research into disaster management in the UK in the mid-1990s, suggested that further attention should be given to risk assessment, installation of modern fire detection and suppression systems, increased availability of reliable information via the World Wide Web, more cross-domain cooperation (viz. with archives, museums and 'heritage' organizations), establishment of a register of 'approved' sources, and local and regional resource-sharing. In terms of future research, they suggested more was needed on health and safety issues and different salvage and conservation methods. Topics that needed to be addressed by training included conservation treatments; dealing with the media; recognizing risks to buildings, collections, contents, and facilities; salvaging damaged materials; and valuing and insuring collections.

In a more recent overview of disaster planning worldwide, Wellheiser and Scott (2002, 4) comment that the "current"

> ... reality is that many organizations, despite their good intentions, have yet to realize these intentions in the form of a disaster plan or integrated planning.
>
> On a more positive note, recognition of the necessity and value of disaster planning has increased overall. This is demonstrated by the great strides that have been made in certain areas such as the growing body of disaster planning literature, improved technical expertise in the recovery of various media, increased training opportunities, the formation of local support networks and, in some instances, the development of national disaster management initiatives.

This positive view is echoed by Mansell (2003, 38), reflecting on the situation in Australia, who says that "It is interesting to note that while there is a multiplicity of approaches to counter-disaster management, there is also a high level of consistency across organizations as to how disasters are prepared for and actually dealt with."

Strengths

Depending how you look at them, many factors that are strengths can also be viewed as weaknesses, so you will see some aspects of disaster management under both headings below.

Looking on the bright side:

- a tradition within the sector of cooperation and networking; reinforced by national and international initiatives;
- growing literature and sharing of experience via the Internet;

  It is pleasing to note in the UK, for instance, the ongoing development of the United Kingdom and Ireland Blue Shield Organization website, offering news and advice, and that of Resource (changed name to Museums, Libraries and Archives Council [MLA] in February 2004), with, for example, its pages covering Collections, including benchmarks for collection care, and those addressing Managing Risk, which cover security and emergency preparedness.

- experience/advice/lessons to draw on (unfortunately); sharing knowledge;

  Including recently, the impact of 9/11 and lessons learned from the business community, especially relating to electronic information/storage and access, and service/business continuity.

- training as a clearly defined concept, and in response to major disasters, national libraries, cooperative organizations, professional associations and others have organized training;
- steady, if slow, progress addressing disaster management issues in some institutions; and
- evidence of successfully dealing with disasters – coping with massive unexpected disasters, both natural and man made, and emerging positively from this on the other side – through enthusiasm, hard work, fortitude, and vision.

Weaknesses

It'll never happen to me:

- Disaster control plans – how many institutions have a well-developed written disaster control plan?

  It is not only important to have a disaster control plan, it is important that it is sufficiently developed. Polišenský (2002, 4-5), writing about the recent flooding in Czechoslovakia, underlines the significance of a plan still being under development:

  > The other important element which enabled [us] to cope with floods was the disaster plan. After discussions in 1999 and 2000, a directive was approved in 2001; this directive identifies specific categories of publications for rescue priorities, determines responsibilities, areas for the temporary deposit of publications, means of transport, etc. A crisis commission of managers and special teams ... headed by experienced employees or experts were established. Unfortunately, all proposed measures have not been taken. For example, the agreement with a freezing plant and a removal company had not been concluded, protective aid...had not been bought...Some employees did not know that they had been designated to be part of the crisis teams ... .

  This emphasizes that it takes time to produce a plan, it is better to have a plan than not have one, and that it is important to make a start. Once devised, disaster plans should not be kept on the shelf – they need to be tested. Research is needed into how testing of disaster plans might be carried out prior to a disaster and into the effectiveness of disaster control plans that have been activated (Muir and Shenton 2002, 122). And while, generic disaster control plans may be useful starting points, those who use them must be careful that they develop them in an institution-specific manner. And, no matter how well planning is undertaken, there has to be a realization that this on its own will not prevent incidents: "Disaster planning obviously cannot prevent all disasters; we have to be conscious of the need to cope with whatever happens, however well we have planned." (Shorley 2003, 46)

- Do/can we actually learn from past experience elsewhere?

  Is it, in fact, easy to find relevant information? Muir and Shenton (2002, 121), for example, assert that "Only large scale disasters tend to be reported in the professional or general press." While not necessarily in total agreement with this, it does make me reconsider how relevant or transferable information from previous incidents really is. Shorley makes an interesting point in this respect about how helpful it was to visit Norwich Central Library destroyed by a fire in 1994 (see Creber 2003) and expresses gratitude for the generous advice she was given, yet adds "... but, of course, technology had moved on a good deal in the following years which made the issues somewhat different for us." (2002, 47) So previous experience must be considered in the current institutional- and incident-specific context of a disaster.

- Information overload and reliability

  Linked to the previous point is the fact that while professionals in this sector are generally good at sharing information and advice, there may be a danger of overload, thanks in particular to the Internet, which in recent years has offered a vehicle for greater dissemination. As a recent report to *Resource* notes, "The web is an excellent place to look for resources to support stewardship at all levels." (M Squared Consulting 2003, 61) There is now, apparently, a lot of information available relating to disaster management, but increasingly much of this repeats what is found elsewhere. It may not be easy to determine, especially in a hurry, what might be relevant to a particular situation or indeed which information might be reliable or authoritative, or which choice from conflicting advice might be "right" in a particular set of circumstances. M Squared Consulting (2003) has recently evaluated stewardship resources on the web using a simple rating scale it has developed. Perhaps something more sophisticated could be developed for disaster management-specific sites or pages on sites with broader preservation coverage.

This situation also suggests the need for an authoritative information/advisory/referral service. It is interesting to note that *Resource* has just (June 2003) published a brief for consultants to bid for a project " ... to examine six options for the delivery of advice and information on technical and professional issues associated with the management of collections to practitioners." (*Resource* 2003b) This will cover, *inter alia*, conservation and collection care, security and preservation in the archive, library, and museum domains. There is here probably an element of recognizing that it may be necessary to approach commercial services and consultants, i.e., to bite the bullet and pay for advice and services! It is not always clear when this point has been reached, especially if finances are tight.

- Unprecedented scale and range of threats – terrorism, war, natural disasters

What Stephens (2003, 34) says with regard to business may also be applied to cultural heritage organizations – "The terrorist attacks changed the face of disaster preparedness. In their wake, traditional disaster recovery practices have been shown to be inadequate. Businesses must now prepare for the kinds of threats on a scale of potential damage never before imagined." This is underlined by Cox et al (2001, 6), who say that "We must be able to understand how disaster preparedness and recovery concepts and practices have been altered by the new threats of terrorism."

It is also important to bear in mind, especially if the impact of a disaster is region-wide, what the position of libraries will be in terms of overall reaction and recovery priorities. Other vital services and institutions will have priority (e.g., hospitals, local government, water, food supplies and distribution, security, and transport infrastructure). There may be a need to "go it alone" for a period of time while emergency services are stretched. Conversely, it is vital to convince civil emergency planners of the key role that libraries can play in times of civil emergency, for instance, as "neutral" and reliable providers of official information to local communities.

- Don't rely on cooperative tradition

There may be a feeling in some institutions that it will never happen here, and if it does, we'll get help from elsewhere. Institutions shouldn't rely on this. Likewise where there are formal collaborative arrangements, it is worth reviewing how sound these are. Some such ventures may rely too much on enthusiastic, dedicated individuals. What level of institutional support do they receive? And what if such individuals move elsewhere or retire? Kenney and Stam (2002, VI, Site visit results: summaries) found in a recent survey in the United States that "The record on cooperative ventures is mixed...Some people are frankly skeptical about cooperative activities...There is at least tempered interest in sharing skills and experience."

The importance of shared responsibility, "a network is a collaboration of equals," is stressed by Davis and Kern (2003, 139), who acknowledge, however, that "To ensure continued productive activity, each network needs a core of members who are committed to the missions and goals of the network (and are supported by their home organization)."

- Integration versus disappearance

  Integration of disaster management into overall institution management is justifiably recommended as good practice, but there is a need to be careful: this should not mean it gets buried, i.e., it becomes too discreet or pervasive as to be invisible – a case of "out of sight, out of mind"? Maintaining a high profile stresses its ongoing significance and the need for constant vigilance.

- Institutional scale

  Many of the above issues have been identified, albeit relating more broadly to preservation management, in the report of a recent survey of preservation in American college and research libraries, whose third recommendation includes:

  > Organizational context and timing are as important as content is. The delivery of information should respect differences among and be tailored for various institutions. What works in a large institution may not be effective in a smaller one; the missions and operating procedures of public institutions are different from those of private institutions ... . Services and guidance designed to aid preservation work in local institutions must take into account circumstances, size, mission, and other factors characteristic of these institutions. (Kenney and Stam 2002, III Action recommendations, Recommendation 3)

  It is imperative that those responsible for strategies, standards and benchmarking relating to disaster management acknowledge what can be done by different kinds of libraries. There has to be a realistic, overall approach which acknowledges different circumstances and levels of resources (for example, between national and one-person libraries). Training requirements and delivery should also be looked at in this context. That said, all institutions should strive to ensure that good and often inexpensive basic housekeeping and other preventative measures are employed.

Conclusion

In conclusion, I should like to focus on several aspects of disaster management that I feel institutions need to address now in their own right, and that also have training implications for institutional support, in particular, for those managers charged with managing disaster management.

Digital Environment

We are now very much in a digital age with electronic resources and networks playing a key role in the provision of information and library services. These bring with them their own disaster management requirements. The impact of loss of or interruption to electronic services must be considered with regard to overall service continuity. Institutions must determine appropriate levels of security and who is responsible for this. It is important that institutions talk to service providers and suppliers – they should be aware, for example, of any changes in procedures that may have an impact on security and archiving of data files. Brennan and O'Hara (2002, 72) outline these kinds of issues on the basis of a very real and unfortunate experience in an American college library. They urge that

> Regular *ongoing* communication must take place. The communication must involve all three points of the triangle: the library staff, the college systems staff, *and* the vendor. Had the vendor been in touch with the IT department more often, there

> might have been fewer questions on how to back up the data properly. Had we been in touch with the IT department more often, such discussions might have raised questions about how our data was being backed up. Had we communicated with the vendor more often we would have known who our new customer service representative was, and we would have had an advocate during the emergency. Communication is particularly important during periods of staff changeover.

On the positive side, institutions should consider as part of their disaster planning how they might use electronic services to provide temporary service in the aftermath of a disaster and to advertise that service and inform users of alternative arrangements and make progress reports on return to normal provision.

There is much activity relating to digital materials and libraries at present, some of it relating to their preservation including security and disaster management. It is important that institutions are well informed of such developments and of advice available from organizations such as the Digital Preservation Coalition and the Arts and Humanities Data Service in the United Kingdom, and the Research Libraries Group (RLG) with the Online Computer Library Center (OCLC) Digital Attributes Working Group in the United States, which has international membership. There also needs to be consultation and collaboration between those organizations dealing with preservation of digital materials and those with 'traditional' materials so that each is aware of the other's activities and plans, can learn from them, and check that nothing falls through any gaps. A recent paper underlines the significance of learning from past experience:

> To understand how preservation will be addressed in the 21st century, we need to look at how librarians have responded to preservation needs in the past and ask what can we learn from the experience to enable our culture save in usable form its proliferation of electronic information. (Marcum and Friedlander 2003, 1)

Such activity can be made difficult by the number of initiatives and projects underway. What Robin Dale (RLG) says of digital preservation could apply more broadly here:

> A lot of initiatives begin because people need a quick fix to a "local" problem – this can be at an individual institution or within a small, informal consortium. Unfortunately these local imperatives are common to a great many institutions and multiple – often duplicative – efforts arise. Information about these projects often comes too late to prevent duplication of effort, though fortunately, this is not always the case. Sometimes these similar efforts can be woven together to form a common, community-based result. Sometimes the focal points are just different enough for the efforts to remain separate, though complementary. (Dale 2002)

Dale (2002, 6) also makes an interesting point with regard to institutions and change:

> Our cultural heritage institutions usually lack the organizational infrastructure necessary to support digital preservation. People who have never been involved with cultural heritage institutions have had to come in and help restructure institutions, at least virtually. We're working with computer scientists more than ever before and perhaps to a greater extent than many could have imagined. It has been a big learning curve and organizational change is difficult to bring about.

Risk Assessment

In recent years, there has been a movement to develop and establish preservation needs assessment surveys as a basic tool in effective preservation management (see Matthews 2002). Institutions need to put the same emphasis on risk assessment relating to disaster management, and librarians should seize all opportunities to make sure that libraries are included in institutional risk assessments. This does seem to be happening but with varying take-up institutionally and from country to country.

Not doing this, if not a case of burying one's head in the sand, suggests perhaps an element of unease – of not really wanting actual proof of what one already suspects – that there is much to do, and with what budget? And, formally identifying this opens it up institutionally, with potentially awkward questions and much work ensuing. Take a positive approach to this. Through risk assessment, a clearer picture of what needs to be done can be achieved, action can be planned and prioritized – and surely prevention is better than cure?

Deal with Common, Recurring Issues

Over the years, accounts of disasters seem to throw up many of the same, recurring issues, for example,

- communication and dealing with the media
- insurance, loss adjusters and valuing collections

and these, and the more general literature on disaster management, also often mention

- training
- impact on staff and users.

Has enough, or appropriate, attention been given to these professionally?

Funding

Effective disaster management will cost. It may be difficult to persuade institutional budget holders to spend money on something that may never happen, especially when there are many other pressing cases for the funds. In this sense, disaster management reflects the situation with regard to preservation management in general:

> ... In some cases, preservation is looked on favorably but is deferred when it involves additional staff, time, and money. All too often, the consequences of deferred preservation or inadequate preparation (e.g., disaster planning) are insufficiently understood or fail to be compelling in comparison with more immediate concerns, such as maintaining library hours, supplying Internet connections, or staffing the reference desk. (Kenney and Stam 2002, III Action recommendations, Recommendation 6)

Managers also need to be aware of potential internal and external sources of funding; they will need institutional support and training to assist them to write effective proposals.

Networking and Collaboration

While there will be factors, such as security, that institutions will want to keep in-house, institutions should look outwards too, within the cultural heritage sector *and* beyond to develop more effective disaster management. Collaborative ventures should be reviewed. In the current digital environment and with increasing cooperation within the broader cultural heritage sector, are all aspects addressed? Are new partners with new or different expertise and experience needed? This may lead to cost sharing (for example, with regard to emergency supplies or training events), as well as sharing ideas and expertise.

Government and Links with Civil Disaster Organizations

In response to recent events worldwide – war, terrorism, large-scale natural disasters – governments and international agencies have stepped up their efforts. This has resulted in the creation of new, or further development of existing, national and regional emergency agencies and networks. Libraries need to improve links with civil disaster organizations. They need to get all the external help they can, but they can also promote the positive role they can play in times of national or local disaster. Joint training events might be a way of facilitating such interrelationships.

It is pleasing to note international collaborative efforts responding to the needs of cultural heritage in times of war and natural disaster. Libraries, through their professional associations, need to continue to lobby and bring pressure on governments to act in ways that do not jeopardize the world's cultural heritage, but safeguard it. International strategy is thus important and conferences like this can play a big part in discussing and promoting issues that can be taken up by individuals and institutions at national and international fora.

The Disaster Control Plan

Finally, and to return to where I started, the significance of disaster control plans must be stressed and institutions encouraged to devise, test and update them. A report on the impact of September 11 on the cultural heritage noted that:

> Although the events of September 11 were caused by an unprecedented act of terror, we found that standard, proven emergency management plans and responses turned out to be the most effective way of dealing with the disaster. (Heritage Preservation 2002, 20)

No plan can cover all contingencies, but, as Mansell (2003, 38) has commented:

> We need to be aware that dealing with disaster is a creative process, that there is no "right" way. By creating a framework (a DCP [disaster control plan]) we become familiar with the concepts and principles which enable us to deal with the unexpected.

Mansell also notes (2003, 14) constructively of the situation in Australia:

> A number of organizations report that DCPs [disaster control plans] form part of a bigger, corporate emergency plan which also covers risk management, staff, business resumption, information technology (IT), security and the media ... . Increasingly the responsibility for counter-disaster management is being spread through organizations and being funded at corporate level. The onus is no longer on conservation and preservation specialists, although they still need to play an active role in the process. Support at corporate level has added authority to the whole process.

There is no room for complacency; indeed the situation in all countries and institutions may not be this advanced, but it is a positive note on which to end. It shows that there can be progress institutionally, that the institution is a key factor in effective disaster management in libraries and, it illustrates the significance and the success of personal and professional relationships and interaction at all levels in the institution in tackling disaster management.

References and Select Bibliography

Alire, C., ed. 2000. *Library disaster planning and recovery handbook.* New York: Neal-Schuman.

Anderson, H. and J. E. McIntyre. 1985. *Planning manual for disaster control in Scottish libraries and record offices*. Edinburgh: National Library of Scotland.

Ashman, J. 1995. *Disaster planning for library and information services*, Aslib Know How Series. London: Aslib.

Batchelor, K. 1999. *Records management: a guide to disaster prevention and recovery*, DISCPD0013:1999. London: British Standards Institution.

Boss, R. W. 2002. *Disaster planning for computers and networks*. Chicago: American Library Association, Public Library Association, Tech Notes.
http://www.ala.org/ala/pla/plapubs/technotes/disasterplanning.htm

Brennan and O'Hara. 2002. Murphy was a librarian: a case study in how not to handle a systems crash. *Computers in Libraries* 22(3):10-12, 72.

Coult, G. 2001. Disaster recovery. *Managing information* 8(8):36-39.

Cox, R. J., et al. 2001. The day the world changed: implications for archival, library, and information science education. *First Monday* 6(12).
http://www.firstmonday.dk/issues/issue6_12/cox/

Creber, J. 2003. Aftermath – service continuity and recovery. In Matthews, G. and J. Feather (eds.), *Disaster management for libraries and archives*. Aldershot: Ashgate. 191-211.

Dale, R. 2002. Digital preservation. where we are, where we're going, where we need to be. *CIMI* [Consortium Museum Intelligence] *Awareness* March:1-5.
http://www.cimi.org/wg/awareness/awareness_rd_012002.pdf

Davis, S. and K. Kern. 2003. Cooperative activity in the U.S., or misery loves company. In Matthews, G. and J.P. Feather (eds.). *Disaster management for libraries and archives*. Aldershot: Ashgate. 117-141.

Doig, J. 1997. *Disaster recovery for archives, libraries and records management systems uhin Australia and New Zealand*, Topics in Australasian Library and Information Studies No.12. Centre for Information Studies, Riverine Wagga Wagga, New South Wales, Charles Stuart University.

Dorge, V. and S. Jones, comps. 1999. *Building an emergency plan;. a guide for museums and other cultural institutions*. Los Angeles, Calif.: Getty Conservation Institute. .

East Midlands Museums Service. 2001. *The EMMS emergency manual for historic buildings and collections*. Nottingham: East Midlands Museums Service.

Available as interactive CD ROM; for further details, see http://www.emms.org.uk

Enssle, H. and C. Tweedie. 2000. Why can't facilities fix this? In Alire, C. (ed), *Library disaster planning and recovery handbook*. New York: Neal-Schuman. 91-122.

Heritage Preservation. 2002. *Cataclysm and challenge. Impact of September 11, 2001 on our nation's cultural heritage*. A report from Heritage Preservation on behalf of the Heritage Emergency National Task Force, Project Director Ruth Hargeaves. Washington, D.C.: Heritage Preservation. http://www.heritagepreservation.org/NEWS/Cataclysm.htm

Howe, C. 2002. Business risk management: an emerging market? *Library+Information Update* 1(9): 32-34.

Howes, R. 2003. After the disaster: drawing up the insurance claim. *Aslib Proceedings* 5(3):181-187.

Kahn, M. 1998. *Disaster response and planning for libraries*, Chicago: American Library Association.

Kenney, A. R. and D. C. Stam. 2002. *The state of preservation programs in American college and research libraries: building a common understanding and action agenda. A joint study by Council on Library and Information Resources, Association of Research Libraries, University Libraries Group Regional Alliance for Preservation.* Washington, D.C.: Council on Library and Information Resources.
http://www.clir.org/pubs/abstract/pub111abst.html

M Squared Consulting. 2003. *Stewardship resources on the Web: raising awareness of the role stewardship plays in ensuring the preservation of cultural material.* London: Resource.
http://www.mla.gov.uk/documents/id693rep.pdf

Mansell, H. 2003. The disaster control plan, In Matthews, G. and J.P. Feather, (eds.), *Disaster management for libraries and archives.* Aldershot: Ashgate. 13-40.

Marcum, D. and A. Friedlander. 2003. Keepers of the crumbling culture. What digital preservation can learn from library history. *D-Lib Magazine* 9(5).
http://www.dlib.org/dlib/may03/friedlander/05friedlander.html

Matthews, G. 2002. Preservation needs assessment in libraries. In *Encyclopedia of Library and Information Science*, v. 71, supp. 34. New York: Marcel Dekker. 258-284.

Matthews, G. and P. Eden. 1996a. *Disaster management in British libraries. Project report with guidelines for library managers, Library and Information Research Report 109.* London: The British Library.

Matthews, G. and P. Eden. 1996b. Disaster management training in libraries. *Library Review* 45(1): 30-38.

Matthews, G. and J. Feather, eds. 2003. *Disaster management for libraries and archives.* Aldershot: Ashgate.

Muir, A. and S. Shenton. 2002. If the worst happens: the use and effectiveness of disaster plans in libraries and archives. *Library Management* 23(3):115-123.

Polišenský, J. 2002. Floods in the Czech Republic and their impact on libraries. *International Preservation News* (28):4-8.

Resource. 2002a. *Benchmarks in collection care for museums, archives and libraries: a self-assessment checklist.* London: Resource.
http://www.mla.gov.uk/documents/benchmarks.pdf

Resource. 2002b. *Overview of collections information and advice in the library domain.* London: Resource. http://www.mla.gov.uk/documents/id526rep.pdf

Resource. 2003a. Registration scheme for museums and galleries: registration. Draft for consultation. London: Resource. (see http://www.mla.gov.uk)

Resource. 2003b. Appraisal for the delivery of collections management advice to museums, archives and libraries. Project brief and invitation to tender. London: Resource. (see http://www.mla.gov.uk)

Resource. 2003c. *Security in museums, archives and libraries: a practical guide.* London: Resource. http://www.mla.gov.uk/documents/security_manual.pdf

Roze, J-P. 2002. Sinistres: un plan d'urgence pour le sauvetage des collections [Disaster planning]. *International Preservation News* (27):11-16.

Shorley, D. 2003. Disaster planning: "in the end you just cope." *Library + Information Update* 2 (3):46-47.

Sikich, G.W. 1996. "All hazards" crisis management planning. http://palimpsest.stanford.edu/byauth/sikich/allhz.html

Stephens, D. O. 2003. Protecting records in the face of chaos, calamity and cataclysm. *Information Management* 37(1):33-40.

Thebridge, S., ed. 2000. *Training for preservation management: the next step. Proceedings of the National Preservation Office Seminar held on 26th October at the British Library,* and Thebridge, S. and Matthews, G., *Review of preservation management training in the UK and abroad. The main findings from the Library and Information Commission Research Report 48*. London: National Preservation Office.

Thebridge, S. and G. Matthews. 2000. *Review of current preservation management training in the UK and abroad. Library and Information Commission Report 48*. London: Library and Information Commission.

Trotta, C.J. and M. Trotta. 2001. *The librarian's facility management handbook*. New York: Neal–Schuman.. (Chapter 7, Preparing emergency and disaster plans, 139-173.)

Wellheiser, J. and J. Scott. 2002. *An ounce of prevention: integrated disaster planning for archives, libraries and archive centres*. 2nd ed. Lanham, Md. and Ottawa, Canada: Scarecrow Press, Inc. and Canadian Archives Foundation.

Websites

Arts and Humanities Data Service
http://ahds.ac.uk/

Conservation OnLine (CoOL)
http://palimpsest.stanford.edu/

Digital Preservation Coalition
http://www.dpconline.org/

European Commission on Preservation and Access (ECPA)
http://www.knaw.nl/ecpa/

International Committee of the Blue Shield (ICBS)
http://www.ifla.org/VI/4/admin/protect.htm

International Federation of Library Associations and Institutions (IFLA) Core Activity for Preservation and Conservation (PAC)
http://www.ifla.org/VI/4/pac.htm

Library of Congress. Preservation Directorate
http://lcweb.loc.gov/preserv/

M25 Consortium of Academic Libraries
http://www.m25lib.ac.uk/M25dcp/

National Library of Australia.
http://www.nla.gov.au/preserve

National Preservation Office (UK)
http://www.bl.uk/services/preservation/national.html

Research Libraries Group (RLG). RLG and Preservation. Digital Archive Attributes Working Group. A joint effort with Online Computer Library Center (OCLC). http://www.rlg.org/longterm/attribswg.html

Resource (Museums, Libraries and Archives Council [MLA] from February 2004) http://www.mla.gov.uk/index.asp

United Kingdom and Ireland Blue Shield Organization http://www.bl.uk/services/npo/blueshield/overview.html

The Author

Graham Matthews is Professor of Information and Library Management, and Head of Research, School of Business Information, Faculty of Business and Law, Liverpool John Moores University. He was previously (and at the time of writing this paper) Professor of Information and Library Management and Director of Research, Faculty of Computing, Information and English at the University of Central England in Birmingham. He has a PhD in preservation management in libraries. He has led or been involved in several major externally funded research projects on different aspects of preservation management and has written widely on the subject. He was Project Head of a (then) British Library Research and Development Department funded project which reviewed disaster management practice and co-author of its report (Matthews, G. and P. Eden. 1996. *Disaster management in British libraries. Project report with guidelines for library managers, Library and Information Research Report 109*. London: The British Library. More recently, he is joint-editor, with Professor John Feather of *Disaster management for libraries and archives* (Ashgate, 2003). He is a member of the Chartered Institute of Library and Information Professionals Preservation and Conservation Panel and has served on other national preservation committees.

PSYCHOLOGICAL STRESS AND RECOVERY

Maj Klasson

Professor, Swedish School of Library and Information Studies
University College of Borås, Linköping, Sweden

Abstract

Every epoch has its share of disasters and catastrophes. Even in a small, quiet country like Sweden, accidents and crises – fires, traffic accidents, bank robberies occur, and people get hurt, physically or mentally (e.g., post-traumatic stress). Articles written about disasters often focus on material damage in such catastrophes. Human beings are an important asset in all organizations. Organizations and workplaces, therefore, have to be prepared for such incidents and make disaster management plans. This paper[1] discusses disaster management from a psychological point of view, based on contemporary research literature and results from a recent research project on a library fire and its consequences

Introduction

In the last decade, several major disasters opened our eyes as to how innocent citizens, war victims, people exposed to bank robberies, fire victims and others suffer from shock and stress disorders and need treatment of some kind. Methods for treating these victims have developed into several programs for traumatic stress management. My own interest started when the public library in my hometown was the target of an arson attack, which had devastating effects. I had the opportunity to collect information during the first 24 hours after the fire and for several years after, up to one year after the rebuilt library had been in use. The main foci of this were users, staff, politicians and other people involved in library management or development and their experiences and stories from the night of the fire and the following months. It resulted in a research project and the production of articles (for instance, Klasson 1999a, 1999b, 2000b, 2002 and 2003, Klasson and Persson 2000), a monograph (Klasson 2000a), and some conference papers. Students also produced their master's theses using this material at the National School of Librarianship.

The Linköping Library Fire

On September 20, 1996, a fire was intentionally started by a pyromaniac at "Stadsbiblioteket i Linköping" (the Central Town Library, Linköping). On that day the building was crowded. Linköping University celebrated its annual event, "Humanistdygnet," (Humanist around-the-clock event) of popular presentations and lectures, based on research at the university and disseminated to the citizens as a form of communication between

---

1 This paper is a short version of the chapter "Psychological aspects of disaster management" in Graham Matthews and John Feather (eds.), 2003, *Disaster management for libraries and archives*. Aldershot: Ashgate. 143-168. That book chapter in its turn is a revised and updated version of a paper presented at a conference sponsored by The International Group of the Library Association September 4-6, 1998, in Bristol and subsequently published in P. Sturges and D. Rosenberg (eds.), 1999, *Disaster and after: The practicalities of information service in times of war and other catastrophes*. London: University of Bristol; Los Angeles: Taylor Graham. 51-70.

researchers and the surrounding community. Four hundred people were strolling around and listening to poets and story tellers, researchers and writers when someone cried "fire!" Ten minutes after the fire was discovered, the whole building was a flaming inferno.

The firemen directed their actions towards preventing the fire from spreading to neighbouring buildings, among others, a home for the elderly. It was a Friday night and the staff at the home were mostly inexperienced young women, who had a terrible time trying to call relatives of the elderly people by phone when the service was disrupted by the fire.

A reason for not pouring water on the library was the risk of water damage to the collections, especially in the cellar where the literature from more than half a millennium of collecting was stored. Small fires gave off smoke for several days. Outside the library the citizens gathered. The shock was great and triggered a lot of feelings. People from all over Sweden sent letters and offers of help: authors, cultural workers, politicians, other libraries and a large number of ordinary people wanted to give their support for the rebuilding of the library. Newspaper articles, television and radio programs reported from the fire site.

The Days after the Fire

In the days after the fire, several things happened:

- The local health organizations, "Kommunhälsan" and Previa, started planning and performing psychological debriefing of staff.
- Different work groups were formed, comprising politicians and staff and other relevant municipal officials (security, police, etc.), who took care of the immediate work.
- The valuable material in the fireproof cellar was evacuated and the material brought to safer places such as cold storage. This involved crawling and crouching, in strong heat (up to 80°C [176°F]), while packing and removing smoke or water damaged material. The stench was pervasive. The ceiling hung down and was full of cracks.
- People had to find temporary work places.
- Insurance companies needed information.
- Evaluation of the lost material had to start as soon as possible.
- The extent of the damage to the computer system and local databases had to be established.
- The police called library staff and some participants at different programs that night for questioning.
- A temporary main library had to be opened soon and a new library had to be planned.
- An architect's competition was arranged.
- A project leader for the first year of work was appointed.
- A big demonstration against violence and racism was organized on Saturday, the day after the fire, with help from the local paper, "Östgöta Correspondenten" (The Ostgota Correspondent). Several hundred people gathered by the Castle and beside the library ruin. Some cried, and others were in a state of shock. Library staff huddled together, faces white, in the middle of the square. Well-known individuals from the local community stood on a platform outside the Castle. Among them were the Mayor, the Bishop, the County Governor, the Head of the University Library and the Town Li-

brary, the University Vice Chancellor, professors in local history, the Town Chancellor, spokespersons for the students, and researchers who had used the centuries-old collections.

- A billboard was put up on the initiative of young students (16-19 years of age) from the high schools in the central area a few days after the fire. It was used especially by children and young people, and in some cases, adults. High school students were allowed to demonstrate outside the library ruin and hundreds of notes filled the billboard.
- A local support group was created. Every Friday outside the library, and later in the winter, inside the temporary library, authors, researchers, and politicians gave speeches or presentations on the theme of libraries, freedom of speech and free access to books. These activities were kept alive until the opening ceremony of the new library in the spring of 2000.

Research into the Human Impact of the Fire

Initial research dealt with the psychological effects of the fire in the first year it happened. This covered the debriefing of staff, changes in work tasks and their subsequent effects, reactions from users, such as demonstrations for democracy, calls for solidarity and a non-racist society, and reactions to the loss of study-places caused by the fire. The next few years' research concentrated on the architect competition, rebuilding, user reactions and staff reflections on the various processes. During the last phase of the study, I and others carried out a study on the impact of the new library, its introduction and management.

The research data consisted of interviews, questionnaires, written notes on the billboard "The Billboard for the Freedom of Speech," newspaper articles and letters-to-the-editor in the daily newspaper, audio tapes, video tapes, pictures etc., produced in the restoration and rebuilding processes. As mentioned earlier, this paper concentrates on disaster management and thus, excludes some of the other aspects of the fire. Most empirical examples, usually in the form of quotations, come from the analyses of qualitative interviews revealing individuals' real experiences.

In the period after the fire, I started to conduct interviews with librarians, both management and front line staff. I also interviewed politicians, municipal officials, health unit personnel, fire-fighters, and users from all social classes and ages. All in all, about 40 tapes (60-80 hours of recordings) were made in order to collect stories from the days of the fire and the period that followed. A doctoral student and former head of a public library, Christina Persson, took part in several of the interviews and analyses. The interviews were taped and analysed by qualitative methods. Usually the analysis started immediately after the recording with our reflections on the interviews. Below are presented some examples from a part of the study concerning experiences during the fire and in the following six months. All interviewees have been very generous and allowed us to share their experiences and feelings. When we met them the debriefing had been carried out and finished. Most of them were in a phase where they had had time to elaborate and reflect. They could reflect upon the situation and choose what to tell us. We did not want to intrude into their lives in the first few weeks, when so many things were in a mess. From that period we have a lot of informal conversations, but nothing we will present as quotations. Although some time had passed since the fire, the interviewees give a very intense picture of what it was like when the fire started, and afterwards. Their names are excluded for reasons of research ethics.

Reading the texts, it is possible to see the different stages of the recovery process after a shock. Several interviewees express *a sense of unreality* and speak of their *feelings being locked up*. The shock makes *time stand still* but after a while things feel normal again:

> When the information was given by the politicians I felt numbed. I did not care. But then, afterwards, I went with my friends and close colleagues to a café to have a coffee. And suddenly I felt OK. Colleagues were the best medicine. To talk and talk with people who knew ... .

People *repressed* the strange situation by keeping themselves occupied in lots of detailed routine tasks, and in a state of *not being vulnerable*:

> When the alarm went off we were occupied with closing the circulation desk. So we continued to put away the material, we çounted the cash and locked it in the safe, closed the curtains, rearranged some papers and did all the routines we were used to do. There seemed to be no hurry. It was not real. We went out through the main door. When we turned around we saw the flames jump from shelf to shelf and suddenly it was all ablaze.

Sometimes, it is as if the situation never occurred:

> When I cycled towards the library site two days after the fire I suddenly *knew* the library was there like before. When I turn around the corner I will see it. It is there. Then I saw the ruin and the ashes.

Then came feelings of *deep sorrow*. "Han fattas mig" ("He's left me bereaved") Astrid Lindgren, the recently departed, famous Swedish author of children's books makes one of her characters say when he expresses his deep sorrow on a relative's deathbed. The same kind of remarks came from several interviewees talking about what the loss meant to them. Not only the building, the interior, their personal things in the offices, but also traces of years of library work:

> Suddenly all traces of my work over twenty-five years as a librarian have vanished. (Librarian)

To lose the workplace is like losing the "home at work." The pictures on the walls, colours, the welcoming of the "guests," the comfort, the feeling of having a place where you are safe and secure is a vital part of your self-esteem:

> Nothing was left. I felt lost. Yesterday I had a job and a place to go to. Today I have a job but no workplace. (Librarian)

Many interviewees expressed *anger and rage* and quite a bit of *frustration*. They felt a need to put the blame somewhere (the police, the firemen, and the management). Many interviewees gave the same impression: *The feeling of time standing still or being prolonged*:

> Afterwards I see myself strolling around in the library, up and down the stairs, talking to friends, my eyes catching every detail of the collections, exhibitions, people and scenes for hours. But according to my watch it all happened in a few minutes! (Librarian)

> We tried not to create panic so we moved slowly and talked in calm voices and we felt as if we had all the time in the world. But in reality it was a case of minutes! (Student Evening Library Guard).

The fact that it was an arson attack made some interviewees *feel queasy and frightened*:

> Every time I heard sounds like the sound of a fire engine I was frightened. And I did not want to go down in the cellar. I turned around and looked over my shoulder if I heard an unknown noise.

And, the feeling of *being an outsider*:

> I am trained as a voluntary fireman, but I did not have the authority to do anything! It was terribly frustrating! Why did they do this and not that! My feelings were inside the library and I was standing there as an outsider! (User)

Being tired, burned-out. Managers were aware that staff was tired. Someone said, with black humour, "We are fierce spirits who are burned-out"! Demand for activity at work was very low the first few weeks after the fire. Those who wished could stay home occasionally, but very soon reality knocked at the door. Lots of work waited to be done and problems needed to be solved. The first heavy work had already been performed: the evacuation of the material from the fireproof cellar. The temperature was 80°C (176°F) at the hottest point and the ceiling had to be strengthened so it did not fall down:

> I cannot forgive myself for taking part in the evacuation. I have two children at home! What would have happened to them if the ceiling had come down on me?

Those who were "homeless" had to get a temporary workplace at branch libraries, something that was not always a success. The dichotomy of *generalist – specialist* became obvious. Some main library staff expressed the view that the branch libraries worked less efficiently than they themselves did, and some branch library staff said that the main library staff was less flexible and less able to do several things at the same time. Some interviewees pointed out how interesting it had been to learn new things from each other.

Drop in morale. Sometimes interviewees felt down and indifferent. So many things had to be performed at the same time, and for staff with an average age of fifty-seven years, it could only be moderately rewarding to work towards a solution that might be put into practice by the time of their retirement.

Support group and rhetoric. Many people as well as the local support group provided moral support, but also expressed their expectations for the rebuilding of the library: traditional values on the one hand, and Sweden's most excellent, up-to-date IT library on the other. It became impossible for the politicians, as well as the library managers, to ask for a longer period of reflection on how the new library could take advantage of the situation and create something less traditional, maybe a system with equally important units in a network?

Shift in hierarchies. The new situation required competence of a kind that had not been the case before. It demanded people with ability to handle unexpected situations and great stress.

A lot of *expanded learning* took place and staff could either break out of the stress phase and use the new situation as a learning opportunity, or break down, leave the organization, or stand still and refuse to engage in the development work. Some shifts in hierarchies took place at the end of the first year.

One of the innovations managers were interested in trying was a higher degree of *teamwork.* They also wanted to engage staff in the planning of the new library, with everybody being a member of at least one team. Two years after the fire, there was one team still working: the team for the acquisition of literature. In time for the opening of the library, a little more than three years after the fire, management had set up a more team-oriented organization, applying quality management and delegated power.

Psychological Disaster Management

The day after the fire, planning for disaster management started. When dealing with psychological aspects of behaviour it is important to recognise that:

- What influences people are not the objective facts about the situation, but how *they* experience it.
- Human information management has its limits. A person's mind is not able to manage more than five to ten information units simultaneously.
- Too much information creates stress.
- New experiences means new knowledge processes (thinking, learning, memory processing and reflection).
- Negative or malfunctioning thinking patterns must be replaced by constructive and functional ways of thinking.
- Debriefing is a mild form of cognitive therapy.

What is Debriefing?

Debriefing is:

- a systematic strategy to help people through periods of extreme psychological stress in relation to catastrophes of different kinds;
- a method to learn how to cope with extreme stress in crises and to handle normal, although very strong, feelings in those situations; and
- a means to lessen the effect of the critical incident and speed up recovery. (Weisaeth 1996)

In a state of shock or deep stress individuals pass through different stages:

- *shock* that lasts minutes or days;
- *reaction* that lasts four to six week;
- *reparation* that lasts six months to one year; and
- *re-orientation.*

Atle Dyregrov, a Norwegian psychiatrist, has conducted several studies on debriefing. He has also written manuals and scholarly books on the subject (Dyregrov 1988, 1989, 1992 and 1997). Debriefing is used not only on people who have experienced disasters and traumas, but also to help personnel working with victims of disasters (rescue-teams, health care workers, police, firemen, etc.) to cope with their feelings. He and other researchers have found that debriefing shortens the period of severe shock and helps people recover more quickly. In some cases, reactions after disasters can remain for several years. More about the research literature on debriefing and examples of library fires (Kennedy 1995, MacKinnon and Morgan 1989, Simpson 1994, Thorburn 1993, Mäntykangas 2000, and others) is presented in my full paper in Matthews and Feather (2003). Articles from this literature search mainly describe the restoration process in relation to materials, acquisition and preservation. In only a few articles are the psychological effects mentioned.

Debriefing and Emotional Stress Management

The debriefing material that was used at Linköping comes partly from the SOSCON (Social Science Conference) on organization and leadership in crises held in 1996, and a presentation by the psychiatrist Lars Weisaeth. He describes the debriefing method as a process with several stages (author's translation):

Introduction Phase

The leader describes the goals and the rules. The rules are as follows:

- Once you are a member of a ring, a defined group, you have to be present every time. You are not allowed to be absent. If you are absent, you will be asked to come back. It is important that no one stays behind.
- Within the group you speak freely but you do not tell anyone outside the group what has been said.
- You are expected to share your experiences and feelings with the others, but you are allowed to choose to be silent.
- You speak about your own experiences, not of others. You use rounds, you answer the questions one after another, nothing is too small or dull, and all reactions are all right.
- No documentation is allowed. (The examples of reactions we give in this paper come from later interviews.)
- No criticism or actions are taken against anybody. No reaction is "Wrong." No accusations are directed to persons by name.

Fact phase

During this phase, you talk about "What happened" and "What did you do when it happened?" Everybody describes his/her exact memories.

Thinking phase

During this phase, members talk about what they thought when the disaster happened and afterwards.

Reaction phase

During this phase, members talk about what they thought was their worst experience and what things they would rather have missed. They also add their thoughts on how they can handle the present situation.

Symptom phase

In this phase, the conversation turns to how they felt physically, mentally and emotionally when it happened, afterwards and at the moment.

Phase of learning

During this phase, the theme is how you define what a normal reaction to an abnormal situation is from a physical, mental and cognitive point of view.

Reorientation phase

In order to be prepared for the future, you must discuss how you feel right now, if some things went wrong, was there anything that was OK? And what did you learn for the future?

In the debriefing process at Linköping public library, a psychiatrist, Dr. Thomas Eriksson, who had had experience of debriefing soldiers in Bosnia, took responsibility for the more severe cases, including acting as a counsellor for managers and assistant managers. Before the debriefing took place, a tradition was established. It consisted of daily, informal, morning meetings with coffee and information and "sympathy" open to everybody. Staff from different parts of the library system could meet and talk and exchange information about the fire and subsequent actions. Experts from the police, municipal security service (for example, firemen), politicians from the town council, and others were invited to answer questions or to give information. For many of our interviewees, this was the best therapy for overcoming problems in the period after the fire. The first two days of the treatment mainly involved the presence of health organization staff available to talk at any time.

The debriefing opened with the creation of a number of groups, selected in "rings." Some groups had full debriefings, but some had only a kind of structured conversation. The first ring of about eight persons consisted of people who were present and working the night of the fire. The next group were those who evacuated the material from the cellar in terrible heat. (The fire was still burning in other parts of the building. In the narrow cellar compartment the ceiling was temporarily strengthened so as not to fall down. It was a very tough job.) Then several more rings were created, with people with similar experiences. Those who did not have any formal debriefing were staff from the branch libraries whose workplace was located elsewhere. Some of them did afterwards regret that they did not get any debriefing. Their recovery from shock might have been easier.

Evaluation of the Debriefing

Six months after the library fire, Dr. Thomas Eriksson was asked by the authorities to produce an evaluation of the actions related to the psychosocial treatment. (Eriksson 1997) He carried out interviews with library staff and staff at the information bureau. He also was in contact with doctors, health organization personnel, personnel administrators, the police, and security (firemen). Library and information bureau staffs were able to express their opinions about the support and actions that took place after the fire. They also answered two questionnaires, a General Health Questionnaire (GHQ 28) and the Impact of Event Scale (IES 15), which are used to provide an assessment of psychological health conditions. Thomas Eriksson´s results are summarized as follows:

- Staff was positive about the debriefing.
- Some individuals were criticized on how they managed their responsibilities during and after the fire.
- Physical and mental problems still remained to some degree.
- A plan was suggested for action in extreme situations.

Comments on the Debriefing

All interviewees were positive towards the debriefing they had received, or thought that it did not do any harm. Those who had no debriefing, such as branch library staff, wished they could have had some. The first year showed some problems, e.g., the enforced work, the disappointment that according to the personnel "the wrong architect" won the competition, conflicts between external organizations' experts and local library senior managers. The interviews and the informal conversations reflect a period of dissatisfaction. You could call it the difference between:

- pure system thinking and more organic thinking;
- rationality against relations and feelings;
- trespassing into territories and questioning the knowledge of authorities against defending local know how; and
- the indulgence and demand for quick results against patience and acceptance of the fact that the psychological processes take time.

But, as time goes by and the work is stabilized, the remarks become more positive. In the interviews with staff several years after the incident, very few say they have any symptoms in their own opinion; they usually say: "We do not talk of the fire any longer. Now we concentrate on the work in our new library, which is, we understand, very well liked." The very skilful and pedagogic architect succeeded in creating a dialogue with staff. This seems to have reduced the dissatisfaction from the first phases of the planning of the new library. In press articles and the municipal information newsletter, the voices express more and more satisfaction with the way they feel.

Critical Views of Debriefing

All are not in favour of the debriefing method or suggest there are difficulties in interpreting results (Robinson and Mitchell 1993; British Psychological Society Working Party 1990). Martin Deahl (2000) argues that many of those psychological debriefing studies have "methodological shortcomings." Some of the problems with these studies are:

- some debriefing is of bad quality;
- lack of baseline data;
- variable timing;
- low response rate and sampling bias; and
- results from questionnaires are sometimes compared with results from interviews.

The critics come mainly from medicine and the concept of evidence-based medicine or evidence-based nursing holds a strong position within the medical and nursing professions and their research. Ranking orders for more or less accepted research methods based on the degree of significant results are in use. Randomized, controlled experiments are valued as best and case studies and qualitative studies are at the bottom.

There are, however, many researchers within social sciences, including the present author, who undertake qualitative research, and hold a different opinion. We feel that when one deals with emotions, very personal feelings and problems, qualitative interviews under conditions of full trust between interviewer and interviewee make it possible to achieve more meaningful and deeper knowledge. The interviewee's voice, his/her own words, facial expression and body movements together give a better insight into the phenomenon Post-Traumatic Stress Disorder, (PTSD). Interviewees may give the best evidence on how different target groups experience and describe the effects of disasters and inform the process of overcoming the problem PTSD causes. Interviewees may also be the best evaluators of what they have learned from their experiences.

One of the results that researchers agree upon in the studies on psychological debriefing is that debriefing that lasts longer, and is repeated after a month, will have a better effect than a single event. David Richards has arrived at the same results in a study comparing critical incident stress debriefing (CISD) with critical incident stress management (CISM). (Richards 2001) The latter method includes other actions like pre-incident training, counselling and advice, follow-ups of more severe cases by psychotherapy, recurrent meetings, team training and so on. Better results come from integrated programmes where debriefing is but one part of a battery of activities. (Mitchell and Everly 1997) In the Linköping case, we have found that several other activities accompanied the psychological debriefing, and maybe we should talk of critical incident stress management instead.

Critical Incident Stress Management in Linköping

Besides the debriefing, other activities might have had an impact on the psychological processes in the aftermath of the fire. Such activities were:

Informal communication among colleagues. Moving staff around the remaining library branches, working together on immediate evacuation, reparation and restoration tasks knitted staff closer together. The sharing of experiences of the fire and the very strong emotions it evoked made the peer-group a resource for healing and reflection.

Teambuilding.

Pre-training of staff in case of disasters. There had been some evacuation training in case of a fire. Staff had also received instructions on how to carry out surveillance of the library premises regularly and act on suspicious situations as several serious threats had been delivered in the months before the fire.

Individual treatment of the most vulnerable cases by debriefing experts.

Informal information meetings every morning where coffee was served and time was set aside for informal conversation. Experts from the police, the fire brigade and municipal security service were invited to give information and answer all the questions asked.

Support groups. It is important to draw attention to the co-operation and communication between library staff and support groups. Several arrangements were made this way.

A channel created by the local media for users to express their love of and sympathy for the library and its staff. This channel also made it possible for citizens to express their rage against the arsonist, to organize demonstrations for the rebuilding of the library and to keep the informed citizens interest alive until the opening hour of the new library.

Users' support and sympathy as shown orally, in writing, by flowers, by demonstrations for a new library, in positive comments in questionnaires and interviews, in articles and in the notes on "The Billboard for the Freedom of Speech."

User Reactions

As pointed out earlier, users did not take part in any debriefing as it was given exclusively to those staff present the night of the fire and those who took part in the dangerous rescue of literature from the cellar. The users created other channels to express their feelings and to alleviate the absence of the main library. One example was the Borggården demonstration, another the notes put on "The Billboard for the Freedom of Speech." The ongoing programs in the temporary library and mass media participation also played a vital role. We also have a lot of material in the project from questionnaires and interviews. A more complete description is found in the full paper and in other articles (see reference list).

The texts have been analysed by a qualitative method and documented (Klasson, 2000; 2002). We found the same feelings and categories as we found in the early interviews. The billboard writers express strong feelings of confusion, insecurity and shock. They feel sorrow, rage, hate against the arsonist who is disloyal towards other users. They express demands for law, justice, confessions, and punishments. A few billboard writers express a wish to understand the offender and the psychology of his mental health and actions. Some writers use irony as a means of coping with the strange situation. The library is looked upon as a mirror of time, a symbol of free speech, the defender of democracy. It also stands firm against racism. The library stands for good books and culture. It is a "public home", a social milieu and a meeting place. It is a link to history and the homeland for immigrants. It is like a living creature: it lives, burns, suffers, gets murdered, dies and resurrects. It gives and it receives positive feelings. It offers a positive study environment. The library stands for established values and ideologies in society. It mirrors a societal discourse. The library becomes a discursively loaded artefact whose mission is to disseminate societal thinking patterns.

Some new knowledge relating to how to provide channels for users to express and process their feelings was gained:

- Help people feel they are there and taking part in the case together with library staff, politicians and other groups.
- Encourage people to participate in the rebuilding work by: commenting on the architects' plans, helping to find items for the library, lobbying political parties for funding, answering questionnaires on how they want the service to be in the new premises.
- Organize channels in the press and on billboards for expression of feelings and opinions.
- Keep interest alive by events such as a series of lectures by experts, author presentations, demonstrations, and information meetings on the rebuilding process open to the public.
- Arrange a temporary library as soon as possible even if it is small, so regular, daily visitors do not forget where to go.
- Users are not only interested in their own affairs and the library as a means for delivering books and information! The library has a very strong symbolic value as a free and open space, and as the defender of a democratic society. This must be observed and taken into account in the planning of activities during the period of restoration.

Some Recommendations on Psychological Aspects of Disaster Management

Finally, here are a few recommendations based on the research for library managers:

- Is there a national library or other body with national responsibility to give advice on disaster matters and to offer courses on library materials, as well as the psychological side of disaster management? If not, create a network with that aim. The International Federation of Library Associations and Institutions (IFLA) and the International Committee of the Blue Shield (ICBS) have a lot of usable knowledge to offer.

- Check your disaster control plan regularly. If you do not have one, create one!

  The plan should give advice on escape routes, and provide: contact details of individuals with specific responsibilities; telephone lists with numbers of crisis management teams; doctors; psychologists; security personnel; fire service; book, painting and other library material salvage and conservation experts; and details of regular practice for different disaster scenarios. This should be displayed in visible places close to lifts, main doors, etc. A site on the library homepage with this kind of information is useful.
- Prepare a training and education plan for middle-management in strategies and activities for unexpected crises.
- Devise a ready-made plan addressing how to take care of staff in extraordinary stressful situations.
- Prepare a plan for involving users' expertise in restoration work and lobbying for extra finances for rebuilding the library, and collection development.
- Devise a strategy for making the users' situation easier. Can they be involved in the restoration process in any way? How can services they require continue to be delivered with as little disruption as possible?
- Welcome support groups, but do not let them take over the show. In Linköping, a support group was founded. It organized regular information programmes with lectures by celebrities and ordinary people who had something to pass on to the participants, architect, authors, firemen, police, head of the library, the governor, and others. In this way, interest could be kept alive and sparkling, and the threat of closing down part of the service was made almost impossible
- Put up a billboard or space in/near the premises and/or on the Internet where anyone can express their feelings or views about the library. This works as a means of releasing some stress. The "Billboard for the Freedom of Speech" in the library park in Linköping was used by children, young people and some grown-ups to express their feelings after the fire and acted as a kind of common man's crisis therapy. Many a feeling was aired and brought into the open.
- Evaluate the process regularly to get good ideas from different groups of players. In Linköping, users were also asked to take part in questionnaire surveys and interviews by researchers and newspapers to reveal their reactions and comments on different issues, and take part in the dialogue for the whole three and a half years of the rebuilding process.
- Be prepared to take care of people's feelings as soon as possible after the disaster, and undertake some checking and evaluation during the following year. This seems to have a positive effect on staff and saves a lot of money for managers. A manager with knowledge of psychological disaster management will be a winner, avoiding more severe illness and absence from work, and will earn trust and support from his/her staff.

References

Deahl, Martin. 2000. Psychological debriefing: controversy and challenge. *Australian and New Zealand Journal of Psychiatry* 34:929-939.

Dyregrov, A. and J.T. Mitchell. 1988. Psykologisk debriefing. *Tidsskrift for Norsk Psykologforening* 25:217-224.

Dyregrov, Atle. 1989. Caring for helpers in disaster situations: psychological debriefing. *Disaster Management* 2:25-30.

Dyregrov, Atle. 1992. Manual för genomförande av debriefing (Manual for performing debriefing). In: Dyregrov, Atle *Katastrofpsykologi*. Lund: Studentlitteratur.

Dyregrov, Atle. 1997. The process in critical incident stress debriefings. *Journal of Traumatic Stress* 10:589-605.

Eriksson, Thomas. 1997. *Evaluering av branden vid Linköpings stadsbibliotek*. (Evaluation of the fire at Linköping Public Library). Linköping: Kommunhälsan (Draft).

Kennedy, Jean. 1995. Norfolk Record Office fire: an initial report, *Journal of the Society of Archivists* 16(1):3-6.

Klasson, Maj. 1999a. *Linköpingsbor om sina biblioteksvanor före och efter branden 1996. En enkätstudie*. (Linköping citizens on their library habits before and after the fire. A questionnaire study). Borås:University College of Borås, Library and Information Science.

Klasson, Maj. 1999b. Debriefing as a means to overcome the reactions after a devastating fire catastrophe. In Sturgess, Paul and Diana Rosenberg, eds. 1999. *Disasters and after: The practicalities of information service in times of war and other catastrophes*. London: Taylor & Graham. 51-70.

Klasson, Maj, ed. 2000a. *Röster. Branden vid Linköpings stadsbibliotek* (Voices. The Linköping library fire). Borås: Valfrid.

Klasson, Maj. 2000b. Röster från klotterplanket. (Voices from the Bill Board) In: *Röster. Branden vid Linköpings stadsbibliotek* (Voices. The Linköping library fire). Borås: Valfrid. Ss. 45-73.

Klasson, Maj. 2002. Rhetoric and realism: Young user reactions on the Linköping fire and its consequences for education and democracy. *Library Review* 51(3-4):171-180.

Klasson, Maj. 2003. Psychological aspects of disaster management. In Matthews, Graham and John Feather (eds.), *Disaster management for libraries and archives*. Aldershot: Ashgate. 143-168.

Klasson, Maj and Christina Persson. 2000. Röster från branddygnet. (Voices from the day of the fire) In: *Röster. Branden vid Linköpings stadsbibliotek* (Voices. The Linköping library fire). Borås: Valfrid. Ss.13-44.

Mackinnon, Alison and V.E. Morgan. 1989. Fire and Flood, Disaster Contingency Planning and Management for Libraries. *HKLA Journal* 13:93-98.

Mäntykangas, Arja . 2000. Biblioteksbranden i Boxholm (The Library fire in Boxholm). In: Klasson, Maj, (red.), 2000. *Röster. Biblioteksbranden i Linkpåing*. (Voices. The Library fire in Linköping). Borås: Valfrid. 147-158.

Mitchell, J.T. and G.S. Everly. 1997. Scientific evidence for CISM. *Journal of Emergency Medical Services* 22:87-93.

Richards, David. 2001. A field study of critical incident stress debriefing versus critical incident stress management. *Journal of Mental British Health* 10 (3):351-362.

Robinson, R.C. and J.T. Mitchell. 1993. Evaluation of psychological debriefings. *Journal of Traumatic Stress* 6:367-382.

Simpson, Edward. 1994. The Norwich Central Library fire. *Paper Conservation News* (72):10.

Stoker, David. 1994. Only burning people is worse than burning books. *Journal of Librarianship and Information Studies* 26(4):177-179.

Thorburn, Georgine. 1993. Library fire and flood – successful salvage, but beware of the cowboy. *Aslib Information*, 21(2):76-78.

Weisaeth, Lars. 1996. Organization och ledning i kris. Emotionellt ledarskap. *SOSCON, Arlandastad 28-29 mars*, 1996.

The Author

Dr. Maj Klasson is Professor, Library and Information Studies, University College of Borås, Linköping, Sweden. In addition to her recent research on the effects of a library fire on users, staff and society, other research interests include the development of library and information studies, as well as that of adult education in Sweden, the Nordic countries and Europe, university libraries and change, educational aspects of user education, and information strategies among emigrants and female members of popular movements. She has published widely in Sweden and abroad.

SESSION 4: DISASTER PLANS IN ACTION

This session presented stimulating case studies of institutions that have experienced disasters. Speakers described their experiences, what the consequences were, and how they coped with what actually happened. If the institution had a disaster plan, what happened when disaster hit? Did it work? If the institution didn't have a plan, what happened? Would a disaster plan have helped? How were resources mobilized? What lessons were learned?

THE DEVELOPMENT AND USE OF DISASTER PLANS: THE BERLIN EXPERIENCE

Annette Gerlach

Head of Historical Collections, Zentral- und Landesbibliothek Berlin, Berlin, Germany

Abstract

Disaster plans are not only necessary for large natural catastrophes, but also for response to smaller emergencies, e.g., burst pipes. The Zentral- und Landesbibliothek Berlin (the "Central and Regional Library of Berlin") has some experience in this area because of the age of its buildings. In the last two years a disaster plan has been developed by the library. Since co-ordinated planning is recognized to be very useful, model plans were developed together with other institutions in Berlin. These model plans can now be used by any of the libraries and archives in the city for developing their own disaster plans. This paper emphasizes the experience of cooperation, as well as the practical aspects of implementing disaster plans.

Introduction

There are a substantial number of references to disaster control and disaster control planning. An inquiry, using the Internet search machine Google and entering the subject "disaster control plan," produces approximately 200,000 results. There are numerous sample plans, a much respected and practice-oriented brochure by the former German Libraries' Institute (Ehemaliges Deutsches Bibliotheksinstitut), and training courses organized by the Federal Government (Civil Defence) on issues of disaster control. Yet, there are still archives and libraries that have no local disaster control plan in place. We have known the importance of disaster control planning for many years, at least since the large floods in 1997 in the region of the river Oder on the border between Germany and Poland, and especially since the great floods in Saxony last year. But we don't only know major disasters. A library accommodated in a building that has never been renovated may experience small disasters on a daily basis, such as burst heating pipes, rusty water pipes causing slow but constant leaking, the penetration of rain through defective discharge pipes, etc. This paper describes the practical criteria used by the Zentral- und Landesbibliothek Berlin (The Central and Regional Library Berlin) over the last three years to develop and repeatedly test a disaster control plan, as a basis for initiating open discussion and offering practical advice to other cultural institutions.

Zentral- und Landesbibliothek Berlin / The Central and Regional Library Berlin

Established in 1995, the Central and Regional Library Berlin is the result of an amalgamation of the Berlin City Library (founded in 1901) and the America-Memorial-Library (opened in 1954 in the former West Berlin). Today, the Central and Regional Library Berlin is, as the name implies, the central library for the Berlin region, hence, for the capital of Germany. It has a legal deposit privilege, currently offers more than 2.5 million items for loan and reference, has nearly 100,000 users and between 5,000 and 7,000 visitors daily, and over 3 million loans every year (excludes onsite, reference-only media).

Traditionally, the library and its predecessors have had a keen interest in contemporary media. As a consequence, you will find not only books, newspapers and periodicals, but also music records, CDs, DVDs, video tapes, slides, and CD-ROMs, as well as an art lending library with paintings, graphics, and sculptures. In addition, there is an EDP system throughout the library for the purposes of acquisition, indexing, the circulation of media, etc., as well as a network of nearly 200 PCs, an extensive CD-ROM network, and computer work stations for library users with and without Internet access. Understandably, apart from a highly developed network structure, sophisticated server architecture is essential. For the safety and security of these systems, specific concepts have been in place for a long time, practice sessions on how to deal with various emergency situations take place on a regular basis, and safety checks are carried out daily. Specific members of staff to be contacted in case of emergency have been designated and emergency "do's and don'ts" have been established.

Today, the Central and Regional Library Berlin is located at two sites, one in central Berlin (Berlin-Mitte) and the other in Berlin-Kreuzberg, about half an hour's distance from each other. The Berlin City Library is accommodated in what used to be the royal stables of the former imperial castle built in the 19th century. In 1966, rooms accessible to all library users were added to the building complex. The offices and the closed stacks are located where previously the coachmen lived, and where the horses and carriages were kept. The building was badly damaged during World War II; after its reconstruction only the facade retained its original shape. Inside the building, however, nothing reminds us of its former history.

The America-Memorial Library building, a donation from the United States, was constructed in the early 1950s. At the time, it was the most modern public library building in Germany, much influenced by concepts of American public libraries. At the end of the 1980s, there were plans for an extension to the building which could not be realized due to the political situation in 1989-1990 and the amalgamation with the Berlin City Library in 1995.

For some years now, the Central and Regional Library Berlin has intended to create a modern building at *one* common site, centrally located at the site of the former Imperial Castle in Berlin. Considering the city's desperate financial situation, however, it remains to be seen whether and to what extent these plans can be realized. For many years, there have been offsite closed stacks in what used to be a factory, and for about a year, a second offsite storage building has been rented. A part of the Protestant central archives, it was built two years ago according to required standards for storage and preservation. The closed stacks are fully air-conditioned; therefore, in terms of preservation all is well for the stock in this building. However, despite its overall positive situation, a desiderata remains for the new building as to disaster control planning, certain issues of which still need to be clarified between the main user of the building and its owner, the Protestant Regional Church of Berlin and Brandenburg.

Risk Analysis of the Library Buildings

In 2002, the staff responsible for issues of preservation carried out an analysis of the damage to the buildings in relation to any obvious threats to the entire stock. The age of the buildings and the fact that necessary renovations, particularly of the pipe and heating system, had not been carried out are potential risk factors. Therefore the following items were identified:

- water pipes were unsecured, partly defective;
- water-deflectors were partly missing;

- connection/rain flaps/drainage pipes needed a check-up and some repair work to be carried out (signs of corrosion, traces of humidity);
- the old heating system was never dismantled, no or poor isolation of heating pipes;
- heating: few thermostats, hence, no adjustments possible, few or defective return valves;
- no air purification was provided, hence, no controlled supply of fresh air;
- there were no possibilities for an air conditioning system;
- in certain areas of the building the removal of mold from the walls was urgently required;
- fluorescent tubes used at present were completely unsuitable for lighting purposes in the closed stacks; and
- no blinds in the windows of the closed stacks on both sides of the building.

Problems at the America-Memorial Library buildings:

- the existing air conditioning system did not allow for the regulation of humidity (occasionally, critical peak values equated with mold infestation may be reached);
- mold formation in some areas, due to persisting problems caused by damage to the flat roof.

Meanwhile, some past problems that have repeatedly led to damage caused by penetrating water have gradually been solved:

- renewal of most defective or too small discharge pipes (causing strong back pressure during rainfall); and
- redevelopment of the roof of the America-Memorial Library building in 2002-2003.

In September 2000, a massive inrush of water into the closed stacks at both sites following heavy rainfall led to intensified efforts regarding the repair of damage to the buildings. Much, however, remains to be done. At the same time, the development of a comprehensive disaster control plan was speeded up. The incident stimulated further detailed investigations. Mold infestations were discovered during various investigations. Fortunately, the results pose no health hazard to staff working normal hours in the closed stacks. The recommendations included a thorough cleaning of the books and a renovation of the buildings. These investigations and the written report initiated a major preservation project, which has been carried out for some months now. The project, which was financed by the Lottery Foundation Berlin, included the removal of mold as well as a process of mass deacidification. While the project may not succeed in saving all the books, it certainly is an excellent step in the right direction.

Development of the Disaster Control Plan

The disaster control plan incorporates the experiences of other libraries and archives. The Anhaltische Landesbücherei Dessau, for instance, offered their own disaster control plan as a sample plan. An extensive body of literature was consulted and frequently discussed with staff from the regional archive of Berlin, who were very concerned when their archive moved to a new building nearly two years ago. And we have drawn on the experience of various other Berlin archives, such as the Federal Archive, which have been cooperating with each other on disaster control planning for many years.

As a first step, a short telephone list of management staff and heads of departments within the Central and Regional Library Berlin was compiled, including contact persons within the departments of administration and preservation (the head of bookbinding, etc.). It took some time and sorting out, as some members of staff want to take it upon themselves to judge the extent of the damage and to effect any repairs by themselves. It is essential for expert bookbinding staff to be informed in every single case, so that any hidden damage or excess humidity in the closed stacks may be discovered as early as possible. At the same time, guidelines were drawn up containing general instructions on how to deal with media at different levels of damage. It proved necessary to provide an action plan including essential instructions, as well as an edited shorter version, including a continually updated telephone list of the persons to be contacted in an emergency. During another inrush of water, however, the action plan turned out to be too general and too abstract.

Last year, during the renovation of the flat roof of the America-Memorial-Library and due to the incompetent construction work carried out, there were frequent opportunities for putting the theoretical paper into practice. Both the full and the detailed versions of the plans were adapted specifically with a view to the condition of both buildings and presented in a third version. Interestingly, in this case, it was the head of the reader services department who took the initiative rather than the staff responsible for issues of preservation. Thoroughly familiar with the specific practical aspects within his department, the presence of staff and the organization of tasks within the closed stacks, he was able to modify the different scenarios appropriately.

It was equally important to set up immediately the "disaster boxes", i.e., a kind of cupboard in each of the two closed stack areas containing emergency supplies according to standard recommendations. It was not easy to find the right location for the boxes, which must be easily accessible in case of emergency and at the same time not block any passageways in the closed stacks. Staff not familiar with the large closed stack areas were shown the exact location of the boxes to avoid any misunderstanding of the terminology used in the plans. However, the intention remains to set up a disaster box in the offsite stacks as well. The head of bookbinding, who is very much involved with all issues of disaster control planning in our library, carries out the ongoing task of replacing any supplies as well as updating the plans; including checking alarm plans and telephone lists for accuracy and completeness (staff turnover occurs faster than previously assumed). Disaster control plans are placed in suitable locations, and the head of bookbinding personally ensures that only the most up-to-date version is distributed.

Additional Organization

In recent years, the Central and Regional Library Berlin has compiled general disaster control plans, addressed issues of security and dealt with outbreaks of fire, bomb alerts, etc. The fire alarm plans have already been put to the test at the America-Memorial-Library, and an exercise is pending at the Berlin City Library. A few weeks ago, a fire alarm system was installed enabling staff to be alerted immediately of an emergency within the large intricate building. The development of plans was further motivated by events following September 11, 2001, when a false bomb threat to a neighbouring library posed a potential threat to the America-Memorial-Library and necessitated additional police protection. Older staff members of the America-Memorial-Library have experienced similar situations in the past, such as demonstrations and smaller bomb threats due to anti-American sentiment; hence, there is a generally heightened awareness among security staff. The experiences in the aftermath of the September 11 terrorist attacks in the United States caused all staff to be sensitive to, as well as supportive of, issues of security.

The responsibility for the development of disaster control plans lies with the administration department of the Central and Regional Library Berlin. And it soon became clear that the disaster control planning for buildings and the emergency planning for the safeguarding of the stock are closely related. Responsibilities and contact persons must be clearly identified. Upon the initiative of the Berlin Senate for Science, Research and Cultural Affairs, all relevant institutions were requested to nominate contact persons for disaster control. The Central and Regional Library Berlin decided to nominate the head of administration as being responsible for issues of disaster control, and the head of bookbinding as his deputy. Close cooperation and ongoing coordination are thereby guaranteed.

A disaster control group was set up, with its members selected from the nearly 300 staff of the Central and Regional Library Berlin to be the first to be contacted to provide assistance and to prevent further damage in an emergency. Their selection was based on two criteria. First of all, their competency in handling books in terms of preservation and conservation. Secondly, the frequency and extent to which an area, such as the closed stacks, might be hit by emergencies would be greater than in the acquisition department. Therefore, the bookbinding staff, as well as some staff in the closed stacks, was trained in handling damaged books in an emergency. The focus remains on what is seen as the worst case scenario for books: damage caused by water. Practical testing, onsite training in the closed stacks and regular refreshers turned out to be indispensable. There will be annual refreshers for the members of the disaster control group. Issues related to leadership and responsibility in emergency situations had to be clarified, too. In principle, each member of staff within the public sector is obliged to provide assistance according to general regulations of industrial law. In a real emergency, the term 'assistance' needs to be further specified to cover emergencies after working hours, during weekends, or on late shifts when only few staff are present. Mock scenarios were set up, and decision-making within the scenarios was specified. Primarily, this concerns management staff, but also, depending on the time of day, late shift group leaders who are responsible, among others, for potential conflicts with users of the library. This may involve the delegation of responsibilities to subject librarians who, also need to be trained and made aware of relevant issues.

Let me give you an example to illustrate the sources of potential problems. On Saturdays, there is only a minimum of staff required for providing direct services to library users. In an emergency (e.g., caused by a burst water pipe), it has to be decided whether the loan of books from the closed stacks is stopped to enable closed stack staff to help prevent any damage caused by water, or whether librarians are to be withdrawn from the information desks in order to provide assistance, etc. This is the kind of problem that cannot be solved *once and for all,* but discussions of potential scenarios and possible solutions will further both knowledge and awareness of the issues involved.

The responsibility for authorizing orders and making other financial decisions during a real emergency (e.g., the freezing of books) had to be identified beforehand. It was determined that the final decision rests with the director general. The non-existence of a disaster control and emergency budget is due to the fact that no disaster or emergency can be foreseen, especially in its financial dimensions. In addition, there are more financial means available for unforeseen expenditures at the beginning of the financial year than towards the end, although this does not imply that essential measures would necessarily fail because of a lack of financial means.

The experiences reported on during the time of the flood in Saxony revealed sources of potential conflicts. The preservation specialists in many places had made safeguarding of the books a priority. Problems arose when companies demanded payment for services rendered (e.g., the freezing of books), before any donation funds became available. Therefore, the regional administration department for preservation in Saxony (founded some years ago at the Regional Library Dresden) strongly recommended that a thorough advance assessment of the costs of relevant measures, as well as a comparison of the prices of various service providers be included as part of the disaster control planning. The detailed evaluation of this empirical report about a major disaster faced by various cultural institutions clearly demonstrates the divide between theory and practice. In most cases, it proved difficult to reach the responsible disaster control staff when no librarian or archivist was involved. At times, there was only scarce knowledge about the preservation or handling of salvaged but damaged books. At times, the existing structures of preservation and conservation, and specialized providers of the services required (e.g., for freeze-drying processes) were simply not known. On occasion, librarians and archivists were prevented by disaster control staff of administration departments or members of the military forces from accessing any damaged buildings or stock. Readiness to help was abundant, yet at times it led to over-eagerness. The regional administration for preservation in Saxony sees its job in the future not only in terms of cooperating with librarians and archivists, but also in providing qualified training and information to special disaster control staff of government and military services.

Moving back into previously flooded buildings turned out to be a great challenge. The report emphasizes warnings not to rush things, but to make sure to wait until the buildings have completely and verifiably dried out. The problems that emerged in many private households, even one year after the flood, proved this point. While the flood might have withdrawn after a few days or weeks, a rash renovation and reuse of the buildings has caused penetrating humidity. The reports on the flood, specifically on the experiences of archives, sparked much discussion about the best viable methods of drying processes for large quantities of books. Vacuum freeze-drying appears to be the most effective despite the costs involved. Many questions still remain unanswered. The case of Saxony demonstrates that a disaster of any magnitude is too much for *individual* institutions to cope with on their own. Instead, cooperation is required far in advance of the actual disaster, in the form of disaster control planning. This remains a major task to be tackled by the Central and Regional Library Berlin, as well as by all other cultural institutions.

Co-operation in Berlin

In terms of planning, The Central and Regional Library Berlin did not limit itself to its own organization. We encouraged the Berlin Senate to gather all the staff responsible for preservation and conservation in cultural institutions, such as libraries and archives in Berlin, in order to establish a working group for mutual information exchange. A Round Table for Preservation Issues in Berlin was established two years ago – I am the head of the working group for disaster control planning.

Meanwhile, various relevant topics have been cooperatively discussed and worked on by individual working groups. In the beginning, we drew on the results of a similar working group dealing with archives in Berlin. And we used the disaster control plans of our library and the regional archive in Berlin to develop sample plans for other cultural institutions. We designed a sample plan for the disaster boxes and outlined all the issues to be addressed during mock disaster scenarios, as well as numerous suggestions for solving potential problems. These were distributed in autumn last year on the condition that they be adapted to the various specific requirements of the various different institutions. However, difficulties remain due to different staff situations and building conditions.

Disaster control planning is easier to carry out in an archive located in a newly renovated building, such as the regional archive, than it is in a university library, such as the Free University of Berlin located in a central building or smaller departmental libraries in other institutions. They do not have their own restoration, preservation, or bookbinding department, and perhaps only one staff member with many responsibilities, of which preservation is only one. Therefore, where disaster control plans meet with hesitation, it may be due to the struggle with very real problems rather than ill will. At the last meeting of the Round Table for Preservation Issues in Berlin; however, we noticed that twelve months had passed and none of the cultural institutions had started an internal discussion on disaster control planning, or adapted any of the sample plans – which is quite unfortunate. The importance of disaster control planning and general issues of preservation and conservation for our institutions is intimately related to our responsibility to ensure the safety and security of our stock. Sadly, this attitude cannot always be taken for granted even in the case of people involved with issues of preservation.

The working group for disaster control issues suggested development of a list of contact persons and experts on preservation within each institution, including telephone numbers and addresses, so that they might be called for assistance in an emergency situation. To guarantee help in advance of every emergency situation is not really feasible. Rather, there are decisions to be made in every specific situation. One of the positive outcomes of this development has been not only, a list of contact persons and expert staff available for general communication, but also fruitful exchange of information and experiences about disaster control issues in various cultural institutions. The lack of contacts with the Technisches Hilfswerk Berlin (a German technical relief organization) and, particularly, with the disaster control staff of the Senate for Internal Affairs remains unsatisfactory. In order to be effective, these contacts must occur within a cooperative framework involving all institutions concerned. The potential availability of closed stacks to be used in cases of major emergencies, for instance, is a matter of regional as well as national cooperation. Current delays are due to the internal restructuring of the Senate and an associated office transfer to staff not yet completely familiar with the issues at hand. A discussion and an information exchange are planned for September which should mark the beginnings of improved cooperation in the future.

Another problem that remains to be solved is that of carrying out exercises, including those on a larger scale. Due to the previously described structural problems of the buildings of the Central and Regional Library Berlin, we have already had several opportunities (on average three to four times a year over the last few years) to put the disaster control plans into practice, if only on a minor scale. The exercises confirmed that the action plans established in theory can essentially be applied in practice. At the same time, the experiences gained have been translated into some detailed improvements. For example, it was determined that the terminology used for the content of the disaster boxes must be clear and comprehensible to staff who are not concerned with issues of preservation on a daily basis. During one particular emergency situation in our library, the list of contents of the disaster cupboard caused some confusion and showed the need for subsequent revision. This instance goes to show that practical exercises best highlight any divide between theory and practice.

Conclusion

What results of this work and the experiences gained by our institution might be relevant for other institutions? A clear and detailed delineation of responsibilities including general guidelines for handling damaged media are crucial in any emergency situation. Each disaster control plan must consider the whole range of different media rather than limit itself to books alone. In an emergency (most frequently involving water damage), staff must know right from the start how to handle wet disks, videotapes, or other media. It is essential to provide ongoing training for a sufficiently large group of staff that will be called upon first to provide assistance. Such staff must also be competent to train auxiliary staff. Disaster control plans including telephone lists must be up-to-date at all times. An ongoing revision of relevant details must be a firmly embodied task that follows clear regulations. No aspect of disaster control planning should be left to the memory of individual staff. Guidelines contained in the plans must be detailed, yet concise, to allow instant action in a case of emergency. An extremely difficult problem to solve concerns the financial aspects of a potential disaster, which cannot be planned and prepared for in advance, as is the case for other forms of budgeting. Many other aspects of handling a disaster are, however, grounded in meticulous planning and based on ongoing training in order to minimize any potential consequences.

The Author

Dr. Annette Gerlach is the Head of Historical Collections of the Zentral- und Landesbibliothek Berlin, where she is also responsible for preservation and digitization. Prior to this position, she was deputy director of the Anhaltische Landesbücherei Dessau. Her academic training is in history, German literature, and theology.

THE PRAGUE FLOOD DIARY

Jiří Vnouček

Head of Conservation Department, National Library of the Czech Republic, Prague, Czech Republic

Abstract

In August 2003 floods struck the Czech Republic. Water surged from South Bohemia through Prague to the north of the country. Although the water level in several rivers was very high during the flood, the major role was played by the Vltava and the Labe. In most cases, the water level of the rivers was at least about four to five meters (13 to 16 feet) higher than normal. The amount of water, its power and speed overcame all predictions. In the first days, a so-called "20 year flood" was projected. In fact, after the flood, it was calculated that we had experienced a "500 year flood". The flood caused enormous damage. Several people died, and considerable property and infrastructure were destroyed. There was no electric power, public transport, etc.

The flood affected many libraries, archives and museums, including their storage repositories where different types of paper documents were held. Books, paper documents and other museum artifacts were submerged in water that contained mud and other types of pollution from upstream. Thanks to prompt action, most of the wet documents were successfully frozen – an estimated total of 4,000 m^2 (43,060 ft^2) of material. No one was able at the time to estimate how long the drying process and conservation of damaged material would take.

Fortunately, the impact on the National Library of the Czech Republic collections was minimal, thanks to an effective disaster preparedness plan. However, the damage to other libraries and institutions, such as the Municipal Library of Prague, was substantial. The National Library coordinated the overall recovery efforts for many other institutions. A vacuum-pack drying method, invented in the United Kingdom by Dr. Nicholas Hadgraft and Stuart Welch, was used for the first time for the large-scale recovery of wet collections. The National Library vacuum-packing equipment, acquired from the British Council, was used for this purpose and the process was considered to be a successful, albeit slow, method for the drying of special collections where process control is important. Other collections were dried in timber-drying rooms, 10,000-13,000 volumes at a time.

This paper, presented almost exactly one year after the flood, described the drying and conservation processes. The development of the flood and its results were presented in the form of diary – following the flood minute by minute, then day by day, and later month by month. The early moments of flooding and the rescue operations were described in detail. Attention was paid to comparing expectations and preparedness plans with the reality when disaster struck. The situations and reactions of several institutions were described, as well as the development of drying methods and equipment used.

On behalf of the National Library of the Czech Republic and other institutions, the Library would like to express its gratitude to all governments, institutions and individuals for their assistance. This assistance is detailed in the article by Dr. Polišenský.

Notes

1. The text of this paper is unavailable: however, a selection of photographs with extended captions is provided.
2. Since the presentation of this paper, the National Library continued the drying of collections, and then shifted its focus to the actual conservation of book collections damaged by the flood. A newly equipped studio has been created, and the Library will soon to able to accept students and conservation volunteers who are interested in this kind of conservation work.

The Prague Flood Diary, 2003

All photos courtesy National Library of the Czech Republic.

General view of the historic district in central Prague during the flood.

Measurement of the water level at the outset of the flood. In the stone wall (lower left), the head of a bearded man can be seen. Throughout history, if his head was under water, the flood threat to the city was considered serious. A water level at the top of the vertical white stick indicates a water level of 5 meters (16.4 feet) higher than normal.

A flood barrier was built to prevent the water from entering the streets of Prague.

View of the River Vltava during the flood taken from the Astronomical tower of the Clementium, the historical building housing the National Library of the Czech Republic.

The Charles Bridge during the peak of the flood at lunchtime on August 14, 2003. The water flow was 5,000-6,000 cubic meters/second (~176,600-212,000 cubic feet/second), the highest ever recorded. Normal flow is about 300 cubic meters/second (~10,600 cubic feet/second).

View of an underground storage area at the National Library of the Czech Republic, where water has penetrated through the walls and drainage system.

Damaged rare book collections from the Prague Municipal Library after flood water was pumped from a storage room.

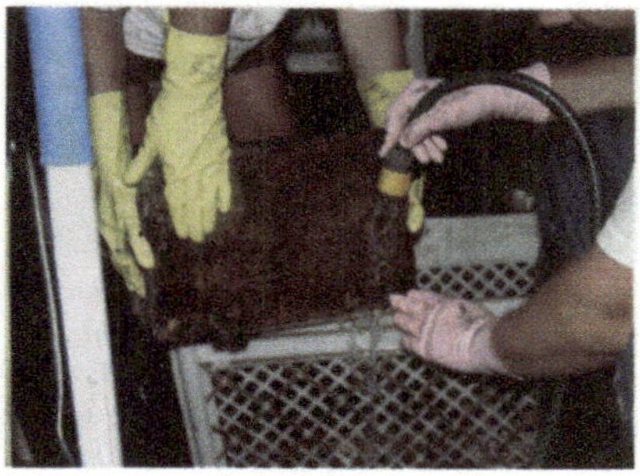

Careful removal of mud from books using streams of fresh water.

Preparing wet books for transport to the cold storage/freezer facilities at Kladno.

Removal of wet architecture plans from storage.

Example of collapsed shelving in a collection storage area.

Architecture plans packed into plastic foil in preparation for freezing at Kladno.

View of the salvaged collections in cold storage at Kladno. A total of approximately 5,000 cubic (~176,000 cubic feet) meters of wet material was frozen to stabilize the collections, prevent mold and allow for a staged recovery.

Preparing stacks of collection items in advance of a vacuum-pack drying process, one of the drying techniques used to recover the wet collections. In this process, items were interleaved with filter paper and packed with newspaper before the actual vacuum-packing. Newspapers were used instead of blotters because of cost--the flood waters were contaminated with various pollutants, and packing materials could not be re-used.

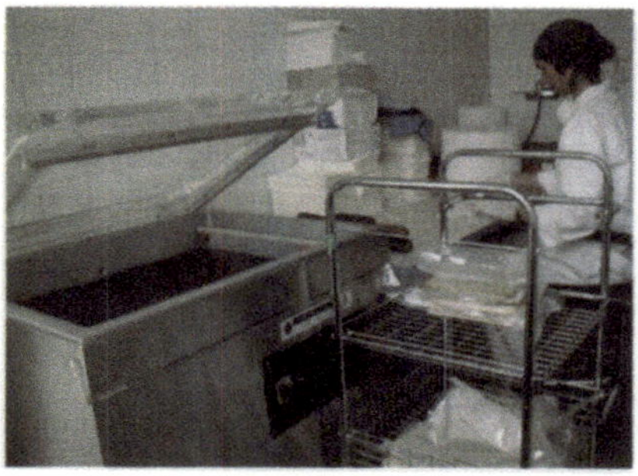

View of the National Library vacuum-packing equipment.

A stack of collection materials being vacuum-packed in plastic. The pages separate slightly during the initial pull of the vacuum, and then, as the vacuum increases, water is evacuated from the edges of the collection materials and is absorbed by the inserted newspaper. The aim is to create as airless an environment in the bag as possible, to aid in moisture removal and suppression of mold growth.

Vacuum-packed books awaiting drying in controlled environmental conditions.

Drying the collections using controlled environmental conditions – relative humidity and temperature. Note the ceramic block weights used to keep the books and other materials flat during the drying process. While the vacuum-pack drying process is labor-intensive, it offers a number of advantages. Pages dry with no or minimal blocking. Also, an item can be removed from its vacuum-pack, checked, and if not dry, can be readily vacuum-repacked for further drying.

A book being checked for dryness after removal from its vacuum pack. The drying time varied from one to three weeks. It was found that a thick book needed to be re-packed approx. fifteen times, while a thin book only needed to be repacked several times. There were no problems observed with the migration or running of inks and dyes. No mold growth was observed in the vacuum packs during this treatment.

References

Balik, Vojtěch and Jiří Polišenský. 2004. The National Library of the Czech Republic and the floods of 2002. *Alexandria, The Journal of National and International Library and Information Issues* 16(1):17-24.

Bradford, Owen. 1999. *Vacuum drying books using an Archipress 1000.* University of Newcastle on Tyne website. August 26, 1999
http://www.staff.ncl.ac.uk/owen.bradford/technique.html

Hadgraft, Nicholas and Stuart Welch. 1999. *Vacuum packing and its implications for conservation and preservation of library, archive and related materials.* Conservation by Design website. January 1999.
http://www.conservation by design.co.uk/flood.html

[Information on Flooded Municipal Library of Prague]
http://www.mlp.cz/eng/flood.htm

Polišenský, Jiří. 2002. Floods in the Czech Republic and their impact on libraries. *Newsletter of the IFLA Core Activity on Preservation and Conservation* 28:4-8.

Welch, Stuart M. 1999. *Drying and humidification using vacuum packing & anoxic enclosures.* Conservation by Design website. January 1999.
http://www.conservation by design.co.uk/oxyfree/oxyfree29.html

The Author

After book and paper conservation studies in the Czech Republic, Jiří Vnouček interned with Christopher Clarkson at West Dean College, England in 1992-93. In 1993, he became head of the Conservation Department at the National Library of the Czech Republic. He has taught book conservation at the Institute of Restoration and Conservation Techniques in Litomyšl (IRKT) and the Academy of Fine Art at Brno (FAVU). And since 2000, he has participated on several research projects covering topics such as the conservation of medieval illuminated manuscripts, conservation surveys for collections, and parchment research – Improved Damage Assessment of Parchment (see http://www.idap-parchment.dk/portal/DesktopDefault.aspx). During the 2002 Prague flood, he was a consultant for document recovery operations for several institutions and recently, he has been organizing a new studio dedicated to the conservation of flooded documents at the National Library in Prague.

VIETNAMESE LIBRARIES: THE COLLECTIONS, THEIR VALUE, AND THE PROTECTION OF THE DOCUMENTARY HERITAGE FROM DISASTER

Chu Tuyet Lan

Director, Department of Documentation and Information, The Institute of Han-Nom Studies, Hanoi, Vietnam

Abstract

Vietnam is a tropical country in Southeast Asia with a long cultural tradition. Our Vietnamese ancestors bequeathed to us a large number of written documents, of which the most important are printed and manuscript books written in Han (classical Chinese) and Nom (Vietnamese demotic script). The collections of Han-Nom documents found in Vietnamese libraries are large in size and richly diversified in content; the majority are history and literary works. Because of the hot and humid climate, the country's political history that includes numerous wars and full or partial occupations of the country, and the resulting economic difficulties, it has been difficult to ensure the survival of the cultural heritage, despite the best efforts of the Vietnamese people and government to keep the collections alive. This paper briefly introduces the system of libraries and archives in Vietnam, gives a rough evaluation of the collections (especially the unique Han-Nom collection), and shares our experiences in protecting the documents during continuous wars and armed conflicts.

Introduction

According to the latest statistics, there are a large number of libraries in Vietnam (about 20,000 units of all kinds), as well as a small number of museums (under 100 units) at the national and provincial levels. The libraries in Vietnam are being established within the framework of a national governmental program and act as educational institutions and information agencies to serve the development of the country.

Generally speaking, libraries in Vietnam are grouped in two major systems: scientific and public. The scientific library system includes the National Library of Vietnam (NLV), the Central Library of Science and Technology (now National Center for Scientific and Technological Information and Documentation-NACESTID), the Library for Social Sciences (now Institute of Social Sciences Information–ISSI), libraries belonging to various ministries and state committees, and special libraries. The public library system also includes NLV, provincial libraries, district libraries, and rural libraries.

Most libraries of the scientific library system also have the status of "information centers." The libraries and information centers in Vietnam are integrated in a network called the National System of Scientific and Technological Information (NSSTI). In addition, there are archival documents kept at the State Archives Department of Vietnam (SADV).

Vietnam has an old cultural and literary tradition. The literary heritage includes materials written in Han (classical Chinese) and in Nom (demotic Vietnamese script), as well as in modern Vietnamese using Latin script. These collections are said to be the most important in the world for the study of early Vietnamese history and classical Vietnamese literature. It goes without saying that the collections housed at the Institute of Han-Nom Studies (IHNS), the State Archives Department of Vietnam and the National Library are the most valuable and significant collections in Vietnam. The entire fabric of Vietnamese intellectual and scientific activities, including research programs, studies, and publications, is often based on the availability of these collections. What follows is a description of the most precious collections that were carefully protected in stone caves far away from Hanoi during the Vietnam War and other armed conflicts, but are now preserved at these three locations.

Institute of Han-Nom Studies

The Institute of Han-Nom Studies is the largest center in Vietnam devoted to collecting, preserving and researching the Han-Nom heritage that originated in the collection of the Ècole Française d'Extrême-Orient (EFEO), established in 1900. The EFEO was the focus of most of the early scholarship on Southeast Asia and remained active in Vietnam until 1958. The EFEO library became the center for all documentation resulting from archaeological explorations, research projects, and acquisitions, which included a vast range of epigraphic, printed and manuscript materials from East and Southeast Asia. After the closure of the EFEO in 1979, according to the decree of the State of Vietnam, the Social Sciences Information Institute of the State Committee for Social Sciences (now the Vietnamese National Center for Social Sciences and Humanities) transferred all of the collections devoted to *Han* and *Nom* to the Institute of Han-Nom Studies.

At present, the collection of the Institute contains about 20,000 Han-Nom books, including genealogical registers, folk religious legends, Imperial decrees, land registers, etc. The collection also contains books of minority nationalities, such as Dao, Tay and others written in Han and Nom, and more than 40,000 paper rubbings from stone steles, bronze bells, stone gongs and wood plaques (including stele inscriptions left by the Cham minority group), dating from the Ly dynasty (1010-1225) to the Nguyen dynasty (1802-1945). In addition, the Institute holds more than 15,000 units of wood block printing and around 14,000 copies of specialized reference books and serials written in modern Vietnamese, Chinese and other languages. Most are the original works that reflect the tradition, custom, history and culture of Vietnamese in the past.

State Archives Department

The State Archives Department of Vietnam consists of three national archives centers, which together have 30 kilometers of nationally significant records. The records preserved in the centers have high political, economical, cultural, scientific and historical value and have been produced since the fifteenth century in Vietnam by agencies and organizations, as well as by prominent individuals and families.

The National Archive Center No. 1 preserves the records formed during the activities of agencies and organizations under the Vietnam feudal regime and the French colonial and Japanese fascist regimes prior to 1945. Predominant among these are the records of the last reigning dynasty, the Nguyen dynasty in Hue City, which ruled from 1802 to 1945. One of the most important categories among the Nguyen court records is the *Chau ban*, or the so-called "vermilion" records. Most of them are documents written in Han and Nom that were submitted to the Emperor for comment (*chau ban* is derived from the vermilion ink used by the Emperor). These records cover all reigns of the Nguyen dynasty and include seventeen volumes in Romanized scripts from the reign of the last Nguyen Emperor *Bao Dai.* They are divided into various categories, including correspondence, memorials from various offices of court, memorials from the provinces, and even materials relating to medicinal practices of court doctors. Currently there are 786 volumes of *Chau ban* preserved in Center No. 1. However, the major part of the Center's collections are documents in French produced by the French colonial agencies and organizations in Indochina from 1858 to 1954, such as the Indochina Governor's Residence, the Tonkin Governor's Office, and their subordinate services.

The National Archive Center No. 2 currently contains ten kilometers of records, which were produced during the activities of the Governor's Annam and Cochinechina offices and pro-American Saigon administrations in the south of Vietnam before 1975, as well as those records of revolutionary agencies located from Quang Tri to the south of Vietnam. There are also 55,000 units of *Moc ban* (wooden blocks), which were used for book printing during the Nguyen dynasty.

The National Archive Center No. 3 acquires and preserves the records of national significance created after 1945.

National Library of Vietnam

The National Library of Vietnam (NLV) was founded in 1917 and has a collection of about 1,000,000 books, 8,000 periodicals, 9,000 doctoral dissertations and 2,000 volumes of Han-Nom books, as well as large collections of pictures, microfilms, CD-ROMs, maps, atlases, music disks, etc. Because the NLV receives materials according to deposit laws, it has the most comprehensive collection of books, newspapers and periodicals published in Indochina from 1922 to 1945 and in Vietnam from 1945 forward.

The three repositories described above hold the collections that are considered the most precious documentary heritage in Vietnam. They ensure a vital link between the past, present and future. They constitute a major part of the country's intellectual and cultural property and reflect the diversity of Vietnamese language, culture, and history, which is why these collections were carefully protected during wars and armed conflicts in the long history of Vietnam.

Protection from Disasters

Floods, fires, hurricanes, storms, and earthquakes are the most common major disasters, yet for the Vietnamese people, wars and armed conflicts have been the most terrible ones. During the country's long history, the Vietnamese people faced many aggressors and invasions and had to undergo decades of conflict. They had to make every effort to overcome difficulties caused by war and conflict in order to protect the documentary heritage. Nevertheless, losses have been sustained. The earliest devastating loss resulted from the Chinese Ming Dynasty invasion of 1407-1427, when the Yongle Emperor ordered that all original Vietnamese books be sent to Nanking, China. It seems that the books were deliberately destroyed or were subsequently lost. Another example occurred during the four decades of the French war from 1858 to 1898. In general, documentary heritage was in the hands of the private libraries and Imperial families, and the records moved with them to safe places far away from the smoke of war. Normally, those in charge of safeguarding the records placed them in bamboo or wooden baskets and hung them under roofs of houses near doors or windows to take advantage of the natural circulation of wind and air. This was effective for Han-Nom materials, so that most of the books are still in good condition and can be used by readers today.

Between the beginning of the twentieth century and 1958, the Ècole Française d'Extrême-Orient tried to collect almost all Han-Nom materials throughout the north of Vietnam. The EFEO library in Hanoi gathered many of these materials, some 800 titles in both Han and Nom, and transferred the negatives to Paris. After the departure of EFEO in 1958, its library became the Central Library of the Vietnamese State Committee for Social Sciences, later the Institute of Social Sciences Information. In 1979, almost all valuable Han-Nom materials were transferred to the Institute of Han-Nom Studies. In many cases, the preservation of the Han-Nom heritage required considerable effort. For example, after the success of the 1945 August revolution, a large part of the collection of the Bao Dai library (the library of the last Emperor in Vietnam) was moved to Hien Si, where staff carefully packed and buried the collection under the earth in large ceramic jars to avoid important losses and serious damage by acts of war, bombardment, and fire.

The saying "an ounce of prevention is worth a pound of cure" sounds even better when applied to book preservation, if we say that preparing for a disaster is the best prevention. Because of the climatic condition and geographical position of the country, the Vietnamese people coped very well with disasters – both natural and human-made.

The Case of Armed Conflict

Acts of war, bombardment and fire, whether deliberate or accidental, expose archives to severe risks and inevitable damage. In the thickest of armed struggle, cultural heritage collections are threatened with destruction. Archival records may even become the target of the conflict and are willfully annihilated. In the case of the anti-colonial movement, for example, aggrieved citizens swooped on the records offices, since they were colonial government property and thus represented the enemy. In other cases, archives can be a good source of useful intelligence information for the opponent and thus are liable to be destroyed if they cannot be evacuated. They are also often accidentally damaged by either side in an attempt to hit other targets. As in other aspects of life, prevention is the best medicine for books and documents. To help keep damage and loss to a minimum, after 1954 the libraries and archives in Vietnam had to be relocated many times to safe places.

Never before in the history of Vietnam has there been a century in which there have been as many wars as in the twentieth. They include the French war (1945-1954); the American war (1954-1975, known in the West as the Vietnam War; and the Chinese invasion (1979). To avoid the damage and destruction of war, almost all the unique and rare collections had to be evacuated to places of safety.

During the American war, the archives that were to be housed in the Imperial Pavilion of Hue were moved and stored in Da Lat for the whole duration of the fighting. Most of the Nguyen archives were subsequently moved to Ho Chi Minh city following the liberation of the South in 1975; they remained there until 1992, after which many items went to Hanoi for preservation activities. In Hanoi, some of the rare and precious collections were moved to stone caves in Son Duong district, Tuyen Quang province, more than 166 kilometers from Hanoi. Many others were taken to the Lap Thach district, Vinh Phu province, nearly 50 kilometers from Hanoi, to be preserved in houses on stilts. Never will we forget the hard time of the American war; under the smoke of war, the first class of Han-Nom studies was taught in the shelters and trenches. Whenever materials were needed as textbooks for the class, we had to send someone to the caves to borrow the documents, carry them on bicycles for the class to study, and then return them to the cave the next day. No air-conditioners, no vacuum cleaners, no equipment ... but those who had responsibility for the collection tried their best to protect the country's cultural property so it could be available for use in the future. This calls to mind these beautiful sentences: "Today, modern research libraries and archives have a dual responsibility to their users. First, they must provide scholars with the materials necessary for ongoing research. And second, they have to preserve valuable library materials for the future, as part of the intellectual heritage of the past." (Cunha 1988)

Damage can be limited even in the face of large-scale disaster, so during the fighting our staff members took good care of the records, although it was hard to avoid damage and loss due to natural deterioration and transfers from place to place. During wartime, there was no time or energy to write disaster plans, but those responsible had preparedness in mind and trained staff members to be prepared to react quickly in case it was needed. About such circumstances, one can say that "difficulties create smarts."

In late 1978 and early 1979, the Chinese army threatened to invade Vietnam, so once again staff moved almost all of the rare and precious collections to Da Lat, nearly 2,000 kilometers from Hanoi, to avoid the kind of total destruction that had occurred when the Ming invaded Vietnam in the 15th century. All of the books and rubbings of stone inscriptions were carefully packed and placed in the steel cabinets to be moved by truck to Da Lat. The staff members were sent there to protect these collections for nearly two years, with no weekends and vacations at all. Recently, on a business trip to the South in mid-June, my colleagues and I went to Da Lat to pay a visit and recollect the hard time we had to endure.

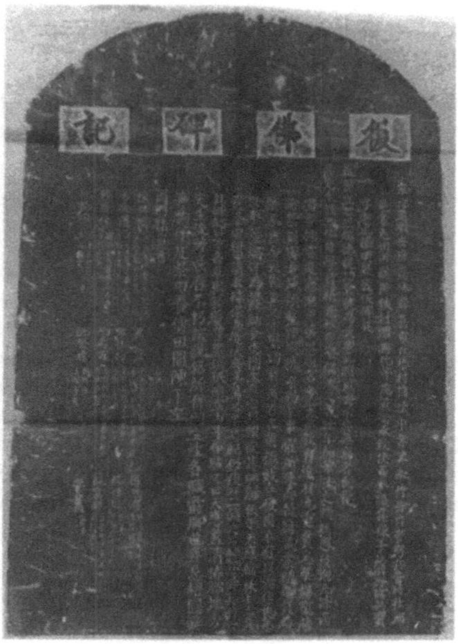

Rubbing of stone inscriptions.

Courtesy Chu Tuyet Lan.

The hard experience of safeguarding the documentary heritage during the continuous wars and armed conflicts in Vietnam is a sad story, but it must be shared with others so that they may avoid unnecessary damage and destruction to cultural materials caused by war. Living in the third year of the 21st century, Vietnamese librarians who lived and worked during the hard time of war wish to forget the past and think toward the future of living in a world without war. We also take pride in saying that we successfully fulfilled our task of preserving our documentary heritage, which has been of vital importance in maintaining the cultural identify of the Vietnamese people, in linking the past with the present and in shaping the future of the country.

References

The ancient works and the new task. 1978. Hanoi, Vietnam: Social Sciences Publishing House.

Cunha, George M. 1988. *Methods of evaluation to determine the preservation needs in libraries and archives: a RAMP study with guidelines.* Paris: UNESCO.

Documentary on vermilion records (Chau ban) of the Nguyen dynasty. 1992. Archives Review, no. 3.

The Institute of Han-Nom Studies; 30 years of construction and development. 2000. Hanoi, Vietnam: Social Sciences Publishing House.

Looking back to the Han-Nom studies in Vietnam in the twentieth century. 2003. Hanoi, Vietnam: Social Sciences Publishing House.

The Muong in the Hung King's ancestral land. 2001. Hanoi, Vietnam: Culture Information Publishing

The National Library of Vietnam; 85 years of construction and development. 2002. Hanoi, Vietnam: National Library of Vietnam.

Nguyen Thi Tam. 2002. *Some activities on preservation and providing access to the National Archives of Vietnam.* Workshop on Preservation and Access to Southeast Asian Documentary. Hanoi, Vietnam, February 4-8, 2002.

Workshop Manual. 1989. The Milton S. Eisenhower Library, Johns Hopkins University.

The Author

Chu Tuyet Lan has worked for the Institute of Han-Nom Studies in Hanoi, Vietnam, since 1979, becoming Director of the Department of Documentation and Information in 2001. Ms. Chu has a BA in philology from the National University of Vietnam and an MLS from Simmons College. She has made presentations and written papers on several topics, including international cooperation among libraries, traditional medicine and pharmaceutics in Vietnam, and preservation in Vietnam and Southeast Asia.

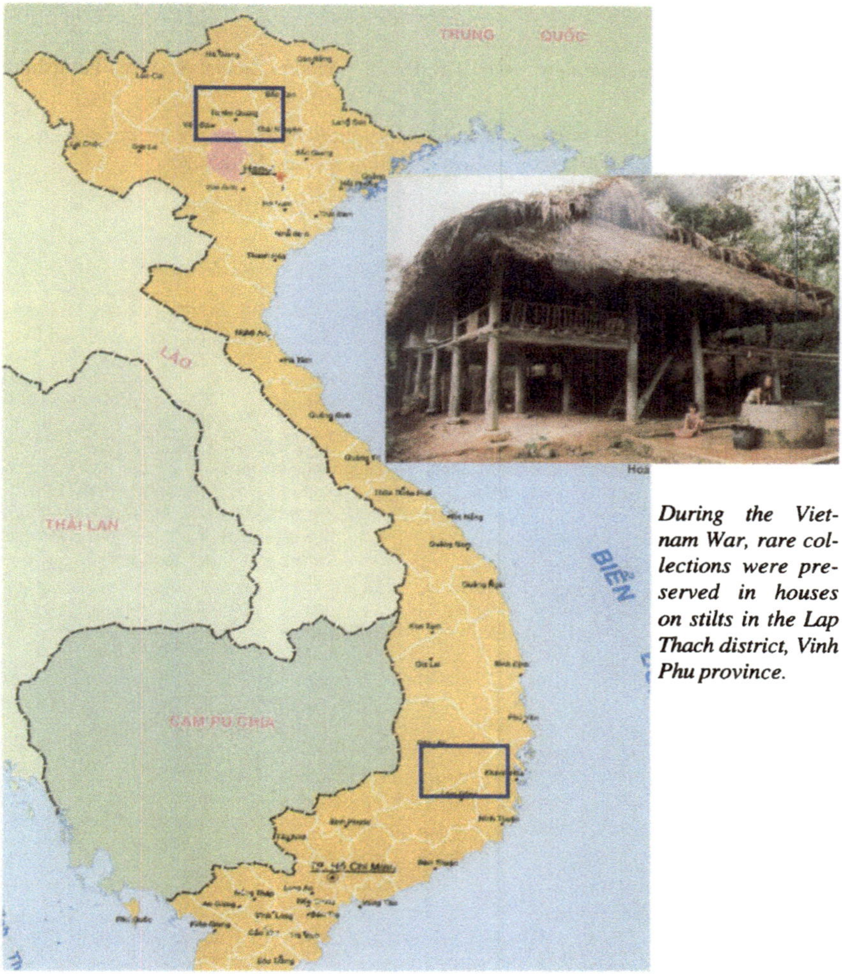

During the Vietnam War, rare collections were preserved in houses on stilts in the Lap Thach district, Vinh Phu province.

Rare manuscripts were moved to stone caves in Tuyen Quang province, 166 kilometres (103 miles) from Hanoi, during the Vietnam War (blue box at top). Archives of the Imperial Pavilion of Hue were stored in Da Lat (blue box at bottom).

Photos (Muong 2001) courtesy Chu Tuyet Lan.

HURRICANES AND DISASTER RESPONSE: LESSONS LEARNED IN JAMAICA FROM "GILBERT"

John A. Aarons

Government Archivist of Jamaica, Jamaica Archives and Records Department, Spanish Town, Jamaica

Abstract

Hurricanes are tropical cyclones that affect the Caribbean, Central America, states of the Gulf region and the eastern seaboard of the United States of America between June and November each year. These natural disasters, that can affect an area for several days at a time, are characterized by strong winds, heavy rain, flooding, and storm surges. Paper-based materials are easily damaged or lost in this type of occurrence. Hurricane Gilbert, one of the worst hurricanes of the 20th century, struck Jamaica in September 1988 and caused extensive damage to the country. The experiences gained by library personnel in Jamaica in salvaging books and documents that suffered water damage as a result of the disaster are described in this paper. These salvage operations were carried out in an environment in which response measures regarded as common in North America and Europe such as freezing of wet materials and vacuum drying them were not options as a result of the disruption of electricity services. Response mechanisms within the context of a small tropical island state trying to cope with a situation of national devastation are presented.

Introduction

Friday, September 9, 1988, was a normal workday in Jamaica ending an uneventful week. The weather forecast for the weekend merely stated that a tropical wave would be moving across the island causing showers and maybe thunder showers. As this was "hurricane season", this type of weather was not unusual and was no cause for alarm. Everyone went home that evening expecting to report for work as usual after the weekend. This however was not to be. At 10 a.m., on Monday, September 12, a hurricane with winds of over 111 mph (179 km/h) struck the eastern end of Jamaica, and during the next eight hours the eye or centre of the hurricane crossed the entire length of the 144 mile-long island. This was Hurricane Gilbert that became known at the time as the "storm of the century".

The country's Office of Disaster Preparedness later said that the hurricane "swept over Jamaica like a gigantic bulldozer spreading destruction, confusion and despair over the two million people living in the island". Damage was catastrophic – 26 persons killed, hundreds of thousands of people homeless, 40% of houses damaged or destroyed, roads impassable, electricity and other utility services disrupted and agricultural crops totally wiped out. It was, in the words of the then Prime Minister Edward Seaga, "the worst natural disaster Jamaica has experienced in its modern history." (Pan American Health Organization 1988, 5)

Hurricane Gilbert is significant in the history of hurricanes, not only on account of the extensive damage it caused in Jamaica and in other countries, but because it was the first of the mega hurricanes of the closing years of the 20th century. It was the precursor of later and more dangerous hurricanes such as Hugo (1989), Andrew (1992), Mitch (1998), and Lili (2002). As a result of changing climatic conditions in the world, hurricanes have become larger and more dangerous and thus, increased attention is being paid to them. Their progress from the African coast across the Atlantic Ocean is closely monitored.

Hurricanes

A hurricane can be described as an intense tropical weather cyclone with a well-defined circulation, and wind speeds of at least 74 miles per hour (118 km/h). These affect the countries of the Caribbean, Central America and the states of the Gulf Region and the eastern seaboard of the United States of America between the months of June and November. Hurricanes are like giant whirlwinds, in which air moves in a large spiral around the centre of an area of low-pressure that is called the "eye". Hurricanes are measured on a scale of 1 to 5 with Category 5 being the most severe. The first category is "minimal"; the second "moderate"; the third "extensive"; the fourth "extreme" and the fifth "catastrophic". A Category 5 hurricane has wind speeds in excess of 155 mph (249 km/h) and storm surges higher than 18 feet (5.5 meters).

Preparing for the "hurricane season" that begins in June is a regular activity in the Caribbean region. There is a traditional rhyme associated with the hurricane season that says:

June	–	too soon
July	–	stand by
August	–	come it must
September	–	remember
October	–	all over

However, this rhyme is no longer accurate, as the hurricane season – as least as far as the Western Caribbean and Gulf of Mexico are concerned – now peaks in September. Sometimes there are hurricanes in October, and in 1997, Hurricane Lenny, which was one of the worst hurricanes that year, formed in mid November. Hurricanes are therefore, unpredictable, and their number and strength vary from season to season.

Before the start of the season, the names that will be attached to hurricanes are published along with predictions of the likely intensity of the season. Previously, only female names were used to identify hurricanes, but now, in the era of gender equality, male and female names are used alternately. For the 2003 season, there has been Ana, Bill, Claudette, Danny, etc.

The National Hurricane Center in Miami monitors hurricanes from the time they develop as tropical waves off the coast of Africa. It issues advisories that are carefully monitored by the countries in the region. Based on these predictions, standard procedures are put into place when there is a hurricane threat. An area is placed on hurricane "alert" if hurricane conditions are likely within 72 hours. A hurricane "watch" is issued if hurricane conditions are likely to occur within 36 to 48 hours, while a hurricane "warning" is issued if a hurricane is likely to strike within 24 hours. Evacuation procedures are put into place for low-lying areas if flooding is likely to occur.

Hurricane Gilbert

Hurricane Gilbert originated on September 8 as the twelfth tropical depression of the 1988 season. A tropical depression is an organized system of clouds and thunderstorms with defined circulation and top winds of less than 39 mph (63 km/h). It developed rapidly and became tropical storm "Gilbert" on Saturday, September 10. A tropical storm has winds from 39 mph (63 km/h) to 74 mph (119 km/h). It was upgraded to a hurricane on Sunday morning, September 11, and by the time it hit Jamaica, it was classified as a Category 3 hurricane with winds over 111 mph (179 km/h).

Although the eye of "Gilbert" came ashore on Jamaica at 10 a.m. on the morning of September 12, the island had been experiencing hurricane conditions – rain and high wind – since the previous night. Although the most intense damage occurred during the passage of the extreme weather associated with the 'eye of the hurricane, the wind and heavy rains associated with the whole system lasted for some 36 hours. The hurricane took a whole day to cross the island and after exiting, it intensified and by the time it reached the Yucatan peninsula it was a Category 5 hurricane.

The damage caused by the hurricane was due to high winds, torrential rain and flooding caused, in part, by storm surges in low lying costal areas. The rain continued for several days following the passage of the hurricane. Jamaica was not prepared for a disaster of this magnitude despite the existence of the Office of Disaster Preparedness that, since its inception in 1979, has done much to educate the nation on potential disasters and their likely consequences. The last hurricane to have struck Jamaica occurred in 1951, so a whole generation had grown up without experiencing a hurricane.

Damage to Books and Records

Damage to books and records was widespread. Fortunately, none of the country's major libraries or the national archives suffered any major damage to their buildings, so their collections were unharmed. Preventative measures were in place in some institutions, such as the National Library of Jamaica, where every Friday of the hurricane season, the metal shutters over the windows on the exposed southern side of the building are routinely closed and the drains around the building checked and cleaned. This saved the Library from serious damage. Many libraries were saved by the action of their staff members who went to their workplaces that Sunday afternoon when the island was already coming under the influence of gusty winds.

At the Library of the University of the West Indies, some members of staff worked late into that night to secure windows, doors and other weak and vulnerable areas. Incredibly, a number returned in the morning before the hurricane struck and only stopped to return to their homes before the wind and rain became too intense. Although much improvisation had to be done, the damage would have been far more severe had it not been for the heroic actions of these people.

Most libraries were affected by the hurricane to some degree, and many suffered serious damage when the roofs of their buildings were badly damaged or were removed altogether. Even when the roofs of buildings remained intact, water damage was widespread caused chiefly by flooding and leaks. The driving force of the wind was so strong that it drove water though the louver blades of windows. Damage to the all-island public library service was widespread with three of the 13 parish library buildings sustaining major damage to workroom/storage areas and garage roofs. Many small branch libraries housed in rented premises were badly damaged.

It took time for the full extent of the disaster to be known, especially in remote areas as internal communications was disrupted. Most telephones were out of order and many roads were blocked. This affected, in particular, salvage operations at the Jamaica Library Service with its over 900 service points all over the island. Most areas of the country were also without electricity, as the hurricane had damaged power lines and poles were down all over the country. With overseas assistance, power was restored slowly on a phased basis to the essential services, and then to residential areas over a four-month period. Private generators were hard pressed to maintain emergency services and store perishable food items and medical supplies. In such a situation, salvaging books and documents was hardly a national priority.

Recovery Efforts

As a result of many factors, such as the widespread damage to homes and people's preoccupation with issues relating to their personal survival, the continuous rain and the disruption of communications, salvage operations in many institutions were slow in starting. When they did start, they were seriously hampered by the absence of electricity, as areas with controlled environmental conditions to dry materials could not be established. The humidity was high, as a result of the damp conditions, and the temperature was in the high eighties. Fans could not be used to circulate the air, so drying operations were often done in the open, and these were continually being interrupted by rain. Materials were often soaked several times, which only worsened their already serious condition.

Salvage operations were also affected by the fact that there was a general lack of knowledge among library and information personnel on how to cope with water-damaged materials. This caused delay in dealing with the situation and resulted in the unnecessary loss of material. In many institutions, when salvage operation started, they were done on an ad hoc basis. One library, for example, lost irreplaceable photographs, as the area in which they had been stored was overlooked in the anxiety to rescue printed items, which in the final analysis could have been replaced.

It was therefore, not surprising, that under the conditions which existed, materials were soon affected by mold and combating its rapid growth was one of the major problems encountered in salvage operations. Facilities and personnel with experience in coping with mold were chiefly confined to the conservation units at the University of the West Indies Library and the National Library. These institutions could not have coped with the volume of materials that required treatment or assisted all the institutions that required help. Unlike in developed countries, there are no private conservators with specialized laboratories who could have been called in to assist. Therefore, the advice given in disaster preparedness manuals to "call in the conservators" was not applicable.

Nevertheless, the library institutions noted above played a vital role in salvage operations. A team from the National Library visited a number of institutions to provide advice and assistance in recovery efforts. While genuine appreciation was shown for these visits, many did not result in the intended benefits. This was not only because some of the material had already been lost, but because many persons were not psychologically prepared to cope with the problems confronting them as they had given no prior thought to disaster preparedness measures and, in particular, to identifying their vital and important material.

The Government was aware of the damage done to their paper records in various buildings that had been destroyed or damaged, and asked the National Library, as a matter of urgency, to produce and circulate guidelines for salvaging water damaged records. These were published in the newspapers and aired over the radio. In the guidelines, emphasis was placed on dealing with mold, and the advice had to be simple enough to enable persons to deal with their particular situation, using materials that were readily available. The response received showed that the information was valuable not only to institutions but to private individuals, many of whom regretted not having the information earlier.

In spite of the problems experienced, a surprising amount of material was dried out and rehabilitated, although done under less than ideal conditions. As damage within the country was so widespread, it is difficult to provide accurate figures on the amount of material lost. The Jamaica Library Service said it lost over 150,000 books island-wide. Losses at the University Library were moderate – 500 books and periodical volumes at the main Library and 1,510 periodical items at the Science Library. There was significant loss of books and periodicals at the library of the Norman Manley Law School, as the building suffered structural damage. An account of what took place at that library will be used as case study to illustrate the problems encountered in trying to salvage materials after the hurricane.

Norman Manley Law School Library: A Case Study

Background

The Norman Manley Law School is situated on the Mona campus of the University of the West Indies in Kingston. The University campus is situated on the Liguanea plains between two mountain ranges. It was one of the areas badly affected being right in the path of the eye of the hurricane. The Library of the Law School is located on the upper floor of a modern two-storey building, named after National Hero Norman Manley. The building had been officially opened in 1975 by Queen Elizabeth II on a visit to Jamaica, and it was regarded as one of the most attractive structures on the campus. Most of the wall space of the Library consists of large panes of plate glass, each 8'-3" x 4'-3" (2.5 m x 1.3 m), which slope outwards at an angle. In the 1975 Governor General's Awards for Architecture, the building had received an Award of Merit "for clarity in planning and articulation of the functional elements...and for excellence in intellectual disposition of the Moot Court and the Library." (Jamaica Architect 1975-6, 8)

At the time of the hurricane, the Library had no written disaster preparedness plan. However, it did have metal hurricane shutters for the windows and these were hurriedly put up by the University's maintenance staff over the weekend when hurricane warnings were issued. The deputy librarian visited the Library on the Sunday afternoon to ensure that the shutters had been installed.

Hurricane Damage

During the hurricane, it is believed that the high winds with speeds of over 111 mph (179 km/h) dislodged two of the shutters and one of the panes of glass broke. Wind entered the building, causing the internal pressure to build up. This resulted in a whole wall of 15 panes of glass to blow outwards. The panes of glass in their metal frames with the shutters still attached to them fell onto the roof below. A section of the roof was also removed. The driving wind blew the rain inside and soaked a large part of the collection, scattering books and papers and damaging furniture. The carpet was also soaked. During this period 50-75% of the collection was exposed to water damage.

Recovery Efforts

When members of staff were able to reach the Library a day or two after the disaster, they were in a state of shock. As there was no disaster response and recovery plan, they were not certain how to proceed. The National Library only learned of their problems 10 days after the hurricane – telephone service took some time to be fully restored. When a team led by the author of this paper visited the Library, efforts were being made to dry some books in the sun. The humidity in the room was high, as a result of the heat and the continuous dampness, caused chiefly by the wet carpet. As the broken windows had not been repaired, and rain fell daily, books were continually being wetted. Books which had not been affected before were now wet.

As a result of advice from the National Library conservation team, blotting paper and paper toweling were obtained to interleaf wet materials and ethanol was supplied by the chemistry department to spray on the books to kill the mold spores which were threatening to destroy the materials. Damaged photographs were removed from their frames and placed on blotting paper to dry.

There was a delay in repairing the building because the University's maintenance crew was stretched in repairing the lecture rooms and the halls of residence to allow the University to reopen. As the University itself had suffered significant damage, there were few dry areas in adjacent buildings to which the affected books could be moved. To complicate the situation, it rained every day.

Nevertheless, attempts were made to dry the books by interleaving them with paper toweling and placing them outdoors in the shade. In order to kill mold growth, which by this time was heavy, the affected materials were sprayed lightly with a solution comprised of thymol crystals (see Note 1) dissolved in industrial alcohol or ethanol. The materials were then allowed to dry, after which the mold was brushed off. Two weeks after the hurricane, sheets of plastic covering were placed over the shelves to protect the books from the rain and the wet carpet was removed after much deliberation. The carpet removal helped to reduce the moisture level; however, the shelf coverings, while providing protection for the books, increased the amount of moisture in the area.

This situation continued for another week and an indication of how frustrating the matter had become can be seen from the following extract from the diary of the National Library's team leader for October 3, three weeks after the hurricane (Aarons 1988):

> *Took out books from shelves. Mold growth very heavy. Blue covering keeps in the moisture. Roof leaking badly. Apparently rain of Friday made matters worse as more books became wet ... many books which had been dried were now wet again.*

An entry for October 4 noted "more water than ever coming down on shelves. The card catalogue which had been fairly dry earlier was now wet and some cards were covered with mildew.

The diary entry for October 13, a month after the hurricane, noted the good news that the *"Roof of Law School being put back. Windows which blew out being replaced. The wet books may at last have a chance to dry out."* Fortunately, from October 3 to 13, some books had been removed to other areas of the University to be dried.

As a result of the disaster, the Law School was closed for six weeks, and even when the Library opened to students, service could only be provided on a limited scale.

The Library administration is still not certain of the exact amount of material lost as a result of the hurricane. A large amount of materials had to be discarded, and conditions were not ideal for documentation. However, a fair amount was saved, although a number of items had to be rebound before they could be returned to the shelves. Some warped and discolored tomes on the shelves of the Library today are the only reminders of the disaster which occurred some 15 years ago.

Some Lessons Learned

There are several lessons to be learned from the experience at the Law School. These are presented not as criticisms but as situations from which we should learn and benefit.

- Be prepared for the unexpected.

  Organizations should be aware of the vulnerability of their buildings to all types of damage, especially from water, and take appropriate preventative action. Total reliance should not be placed on one prevention plan such as placing hurricane shutters over windows. Other protective measures should be taken for safeguarding valuable or irreplaceable collections and fixtures from water entering through the roof, such as covering them with plastic sheeting.

- Be decisive.

  Library materials deteriorate rapidly under hot and humid conditions, and mold and mildew will develop within forty-eight hours. Quick action is therefore needed, if materials are to be salvaged. In our case, too much time was taken up in deciding whether or not to remove the carpet or to move the wet and partially dried books to other buildings.

- Know where to turn to for help and take advantage of local expertise.

  On a university campus for example, a chemistry department should be able to provide advice in dealing with outbreaks of mold and mildew.

- Ensure that members of library and archive staff know about the:
  - properties of records – paper, audiovisual and electronic;
  - susceptibility of these materials to extremes of humidity and temperature; and
  - action to take if they become wet or damaged.

- Set up an effective chain of command for decision making purposes following a disaster.

  In the case of a special library, the responsibilities of the librarian and the head of the organization need to be clearly defined, so that decisions can be taken quickly and emergency funds approved.

- Ensure that the institution has a written disaster response and recovery plan, developed and produced in advance and that staff are knowledgeable about its contents.

Decisions cannot be taken easily after a disaster, especially one that is a national calamity. People find it difficult to focus, as they are either overwhelmed by the magnitude of the disaster or preoccupied with their personal survival issues. The absence of such a plan at the library discussed above had several unfortunate consequences. These included the following:

- No member of staff had been identified as leader of the Disaster Recovery Team so there was some uncertainty in the recovery efforts.
- Staff had no guidelines to follow in salvaging materials such as the correct techniques in drying out wet books or how to deal with outbreaks of mold.
- Stabilizing the environment was not seen as a priority. It was understandably difficult to control the temperature and humidity, but the carpet could have been removed earlier.
- There was no agreed to priority in the order in which materials should be salvaged. Removing or safeguarding the card catalogue, perhaps the most important record in the room, was not done.
- The value of items did not appear to have been taken into account in salvage operations. When materials were being salvaged by the staff, there was little attempt to identify the irreplaceable and valuable items which should have received priority attention, as well as the items which were not as crucial as they could be easily replaced (e.g., unbound copies of serials).
- There were no emergency supplies on hand to deal with the treatment of wet materials.

Conclusion

A hurricane has been aptly described as "nature's weapon of mass destruction". An active season can have eight to ten hurricanes, and recent years have witnessed major hurricanes which flattened everything in their path. Because of 'global warming', the frequency of these mega hurricanes is likely to increase. This is not very comforting news to small countries in the region which are particularly vulnerable, as hurricanes can create major damage to their economies, as well as to their physical infrastructure.

Although it is over 15 years since "Gilbert" struck Jamaica, the lessons learned are still relevant to librarians and archivists of today, especially those in the developing world. The year after the hurricane, the Jamaica Library Association published a booklet outlining some of the problems caused by the hurricane and providing guidance on salvage operations (Brown 1989). This was widely circulated both locally and throughout the region. It is hoped that the experiences recorded in this publication have been taken seriously, for the hurricane demonstrated dramatically the importance of disaster preparedness, both planning and precautionary measures. This is because the speed with which the hurricane developed and approached Jamaica left little time to implement disaster plans which were already made, much less those not considered.

Response mechanisms after a hurricane have to be carefully considered. Our experience showed that, in a situation in which an entire country is affected by a disaster and people are concerned with their personal survival, it is unrealistic to expect that the treatment of wet and damaged books will be a priority. In addition, the standard disaster response in North America and Europe, in which wet materials are frozen to arrest damage, is simply not an option where electricity services are not available. The shortage of trained personnel to deal with water-damaged materials in developing countries is also a matter of concern. In Jamaica, most materials were lost not primarily because of the damage done to them by the hurricane, but by the delay, as well as the uncertainty in dealing with the materials after the hurricane had passed.

These issues pose special challenges to librarians and archivists in the region. Only by careful planning, ongoing implementation of preventative procedures, training sessions, and clearly conceived response measures can information professionals hope to secure the safety of their collections in the event of a disaster.

Notes

Fungicides, such as thymol, are now regarded as a human health hazard. Research has also identified deficiencies in the effectiveness of thymol, as well as identified risks for collection materials. In addition, there is evidence that books and papers treated with fungicides may be more susceptible to mold after treatment.

The use of chemicals in general to treat mold is no longer recommended for library, archival and museum collections. If chemicals are employed, they must only be used by trained personnel with appropriate protection.

References

Aarons, John. 1988. Author's diary of events (unpublished).

Brown, Hyacinth, ed. 1989. *Disaster planning in Jamaica: safeguarding documents and vital data.* Kingston: Jamaica Library Association.

Jamaica Architect. 1975. Governor General's Awards. *Jamaica Architect* 12:6:8.

[Jamaica] Office of Disaster Preparedness and Emergency Management. 2002. *Looking back at Hurricane Gilbert, 16 October 2002.* http://www.odpem.org.jm/articles/gilbert.html [May 2003]

Pan American Health Organization. 1988. *Hurricane Gilbert in Jamaica.* PAHO: Washington, D.C. 5.

The Author

John Aarons has been Government Archivist of Jamaica since 2002. He holds a BA (Hons.), an MA in Heritage Studies, a post-graduate diploma in Library Studies from the University of the West Indies, and a post-graduate diploma in Archives Administration from the University of London. He worked at the National Library of Jamaica from 1979 until 2002, serving as deputy director and head of the Conservation Department from 1979 to 1992, and Director (later reclassified as Executive Director) from 1992 to 2002. He has written several papers and articles on disaster preparedness and recovery.

SESSION 5: ASSESSING THE RISK

This session introduced models for assessing risk and setting priorities for salvage in libraries, archives, and museums. How does an institution arrive at decisions? Who makes the choices, and whose responsibility is it? Do politics play a role? What are the insurance considerations?

SEEKING BALANCED RISK MITIGATION: RISK ASSESSMENT AT THE CANADIAN MUSEUM OF NATURE

R. Robert Waller[1]

Chief Conservation, Canadian Museum of Nature, Ottawa, Canada

Abstract

The Canadian Museum of Nature (CMN) completed comprehensive collection risk assessments in 1993 and 1998. In between the two assessments, the CMN designed, constructed and moved into a purpose-built collection-holding building and undertook numerous collection management and conservation projects. Overall, these activities resulted in a significant net reduction in total risk to the collections.

Comparison of the results of the two risk assessments indicated differences caused by: 1) changes in perception of risks; 2) changes resulting from improved understanding of, or ability to quantify, risks; and 3) changes to magnitudes of specific risks because of specific projects. In addition to enabling us to set priorities for further collection care and conservation research activities, these repeated risk assessments have greatly increased our self-awareness of collection care issues and changes in risks to collections over time. They allow an estimation of the benefit of proposed preventive conservation measures, such as an improved emergency preparedness plan and comparison of that benefit with alternative conservation projects.

This paper outlines the CMN's risk assessment method and presents results of particular salience to emergency preparedness.

Introduction

The Canadian Museum of Nature (CMN) completed comprehensive assessments of risks to the collections in 1993 and 1998, using a method now termed the Cultural Property Risk Analysis Method (CPRAM; Waller 1994, 1995, 2003). During the five years between these assessments, the CMN designed, constructed and moved into a purpose-built collection-holding institution. In addition, numerous collection management and conservation projects were undertaken to mitigate risks to collections. These activities resulted in a significant net reduction in total risk to the collections and an improved understanding of remaining risks.

Fulfilling a fiduciary responsibility for maintaining collections requires that potential risks to collections be considered comprehensively and evaluated rationally. Comprehensiveness, clarity in purpose and scope, and rationality (minimally semi quantitative and preferably quantitative) are characteristics of any good risk assessment method (Boroush 1998, Buchanan, Porter et al. 1999).

---

1 I am grateful to my many colleagues at the CMN and elsewhere who contributed to the development of the CPRAM. I especially appreciate the consistent support of Jerry Fitzgerald who was the Director of Collection Services for much of the development time. More recently, Roger Baird, CMN Director of Collection Services has supported continuing outreach and education about risk analysis for preventive conservation including attendance at the IFLA Berlin 2003 Conference: Preparing for the Worst, Planning for the Best: Protecting our Cultural Heritage from Disaster. I thank Johanna Wellheiser, Toronto Public Library, and Laura Smyk, Canadian Museum of Nature, for assistance in preparing the manuscript.

The Canadian Museum of Nature's Natural Heritage Building, 1997. This purpose-built collection holding facility is a tangible result of collection risk analysis.

Photo by Martin Lipman, reproduced with permission Canadian Museum of Nature.

Cultural Property Risk Analysis Method

The basic steps involved in the Canadian Museum of Nature's CPRAM are:

- Define project scope including collection contents, values considered, etc.
- Divide overall institution collection holdings into units to assess.
- Identify specific risks to assess.
- Quantify risks.
- Analyze and present results.
- Plan collection care projects.
- Refine estimates of uncertain risks through research.

In the case of the CMN, collections were defined as formally accessioned objects. Excluded from the scope was material in temporary custody for research, consignment, etc., and material for consumptive use (Category 5 material within the value classification system of Price and Fitzgerald 1996). Overall collection holdings were divided into nineteen collection units according to a range of criteria including administration, nature of specimen material, primary storage hardware, and storage environment. Risks were comprehensively identified within a framework of ten agents of deterioration and three types of risk. The agents of deterioration (after Michalski 1990) are:

- Physical forces
- Fire

- Water
- Criminals
- Pests
- Contaminants
- Light and ultraviolet radiation
- Incorrect temperature
- Incorrect relative humidity
- Dissociation (custodial neglect).

Knowing that the manifestations of most agents of deterioration can range widely in frequency and severity, three types of risk are distinguished. These range from Type 1, rare and catastrophic events, to Type 3, constant but persistent processes (Figure 1). Recognizing different types of risks facilitates both identifying risks comprehensively and finding sources of authoritative information on hazards and risks.

Intensity \ Frequency	Constant	Sporadic	Rare
Catastrophic			·······Type 1·······
Severe		·······Type 2·······	
Gradual/Mild	·······Type 3·······		

Figure 1. Three types of risk range in frequency and severity.

Some examples of risks specific to the CMN included:

- Earthquake causing building collapse resulting in breakage or crushing of objects (Physical forces – Type 1)
- Earthquake causing toppling of storage units or objects resulting in breakage or crushing (Physical forces – Type 1)
- Snow loading causing roof collapse resulting in breakage or crushing of objects (Physical forces – Type 1)
- Accidental physical damage to objects during use (Physical forces – Type 2)
- Poor support causing distortion of objects (Physical forces – Type 3)
- Overcrowded storage causing abrasion, breakage, etc. (Physical forces – Type 3)

Magnitudes of risks are quantitatively estimated using the formula:

MR (Magnitude of Risk) = **FS** x **LV** x **P** x **E**

Where

FS = Fraction Susceptible

LV = Loss in Value

P = Probability

E = Extent

Each of these variables is determined for every plausible combination of specific risk and collection unit. The first step in quantification is to determine the *Fraction* (of the collection) *Susceptible* to the specific risk. The next step is, while considering objects typical of the FS, to estimate the *Loss in Value* that could result from a worst-case occurrence of the risk. The product of FSxLV can be considered the maximum "theoretical" part of the collection value subject to loss from that specific risk. The *Probability* for Type 1 risks is the chance of at least one event of a specified severity occurring over the next century. It is determined with help from appropriate national or international agencies and organizations. The *Extent* reflects the amount of the FS that will be affected, the degree to which the LV will be realized, or both. It is estimated by projecting the effect of one century exposure to the current setting and collection care and use circumstances. Simple multiplication of the four variables, which are all fractions between 0 and 1 inclusive, gives the *Magnitude of Risk*, which itself is a fraction between 0 and 1 inclusive. The *Magnitude of Risk* is the expected loss in utility value of the collection over the next century considering the current collection care situation to continue.

For most collection units, the magnitudes of risks range over many orders of magnitude, even though only those risks considered significant enough to identify and estimate were evaluated. The CMN mineral collection (Figure 2) is an example. The highest estimated risk is more than one million times greater than the lowest estimated risk, even though all of these risks are completely plausible and many would have been intuitively perceived as comparable. For this mineral collection, incorrect levels of relative humidity leading to changes in hydration, effects of pollutants within cabinets, and oxidation of sulfide specimens are the three highest risks.

The total risk to CMN's collection holdings due to each generic risk (combination of agent of deterioration and type of risk) was estimated by summing for each generic risk, across all collection units after normalizing to express risks as risk to the total (number of objects in the) CMN collections. Figure 3 shows a comparison of generic risks to total CMN holdings as assessed in 1993 and again in 1998. Although differences in perceptions, understanding, and means of assessing risks have led to some of the differences, most of the change reflects real reductions in levels of risk.

Improvements at the Museum

In 1993, CMN collections were dispersed among twelve leased warehouse spaces and significant collections were in inferior storage hardware. In 1996-1997, the time between the two assessments, the CMN designed, had built, and occupied a purpose-built collection housing building. At the same time, storage hardware was upgraded to modern museum standards. In addition, following the move, and before the 1998 risk assessment, a collection emergency preparedness plan was developed and disseminated. Training in emergency response procedures and methods was conducted.

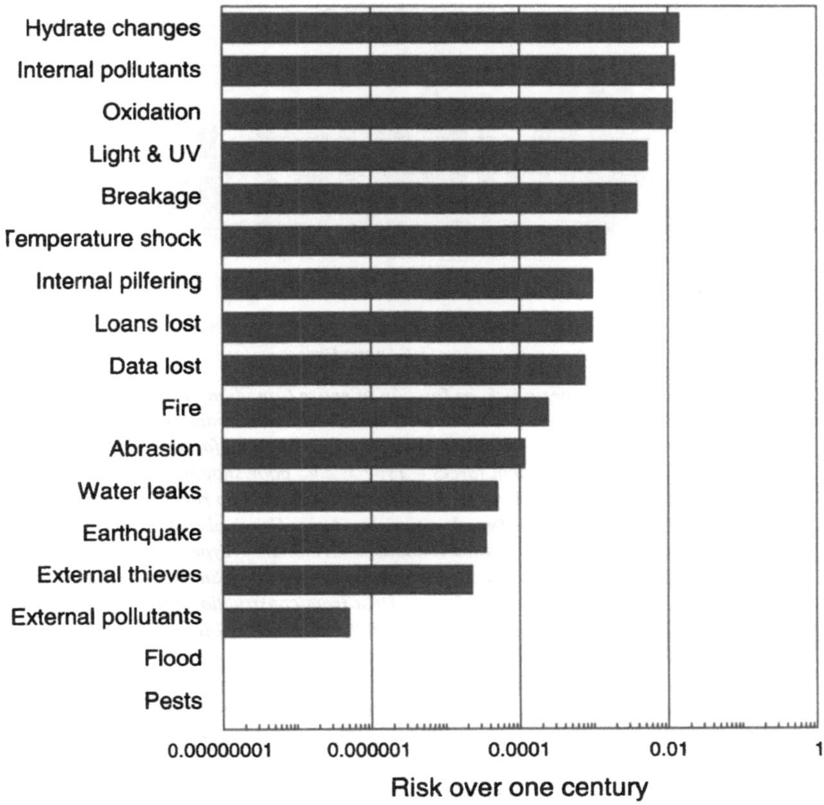

Figure 2. Magnitudes of risks to the Canadian Museum of Nature mineral collection, 1998 risk assessment data with pollutant data updated according to Waller (1999).

Of particular interest to consideration of emergency preparedness, is evaluation of the changes in Type 1 risk and the relative contribution of Type 1 risks to total risk. These comparisons are shown in Figure 4.

Over the period 1993-1998, Type 1 risks were the most reduced of the three types of risk. There are several reasons for this.

1. Much protection against the effects of Type 1 risks is afforded at the levels of location, site characteristics, and building construction and systems. These were considerably improved by the CMN National Heritage Building design and construction project.
2. Many systems that provide life safety protection also contribute to property protection from Type 1 risks. Buildings designed and built to modern building codes will afford considerable property (and collection) protection against Type 1 risks.
3. The CMN, by consolidating staff in one location and by completing, and training staff on, an emergency preparedness plan within 1993-1998 further mitigated against the effects of Type 1 risks.

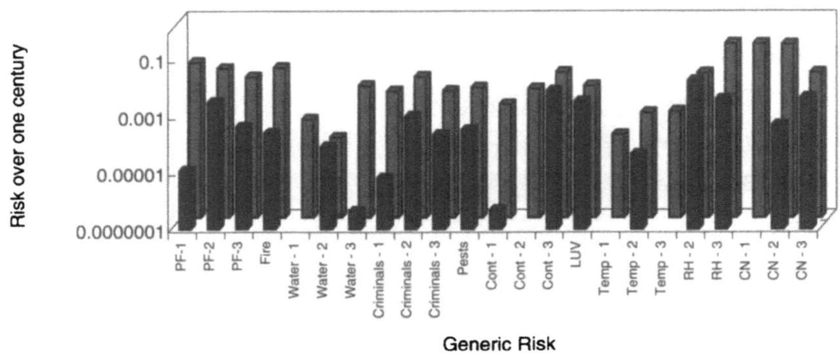

Figure 3. Comparison of generic risk, as fraction of entire Canadian Museum of Nature collection holdings, between 1993, back bars, and 1998, front bars. PF-1, Physical forces – Type 1, e.g., earthquake causing breakage; PF-2, Physical forces – Type 2, e.g., accidental breakage; PF-3, Physical forces – Type 3, e.g., poor support causing distortion; Fire – Consumption by fire; Water – Type 1, e.g., inundation by river flood; Water – Type 2, e.g., roof leaking; Water – Type 3, e.g., rising damp; Criminals – Type 1, e.g., major theft; Criminals – Type 2, e.g., isolated vandalism; Criminals – Type 3, e.g., pilfering; Pests, e.g., insects and rodents; Cont-1, Contaminants – Type 1, e.g., Smoke from a nearby disaster; Cont-2, Contaminants – Type 2, e.g., Dust from construction activity; Cont-3, Contaminants – type 3, e.g., Permanent gaseous pollutants ; LUV, Light and Radiation; Temp-1, Temperature – Type 1; Temp-2, Temperature – Type 2, e.g., Incorrect temperature causing softening or melting; Temp-3, Temperature – Type 3, e.g., Higher than ideal; RH-2, Relative Humidity – Type 2, e.g., drastic change leading to fracture; RH-3, Relative Humidity – Type 3, e.g., too high accelerating paper degradation; CN-1, Custodial Neglect – Type 1, e.g., collection abandonment; CN-2, Custodial Neglect – Type 2, e.g., misfiling a book; CN-3, Custodial Neglect – Type 3, e.g., failure to ensure title for gifts.

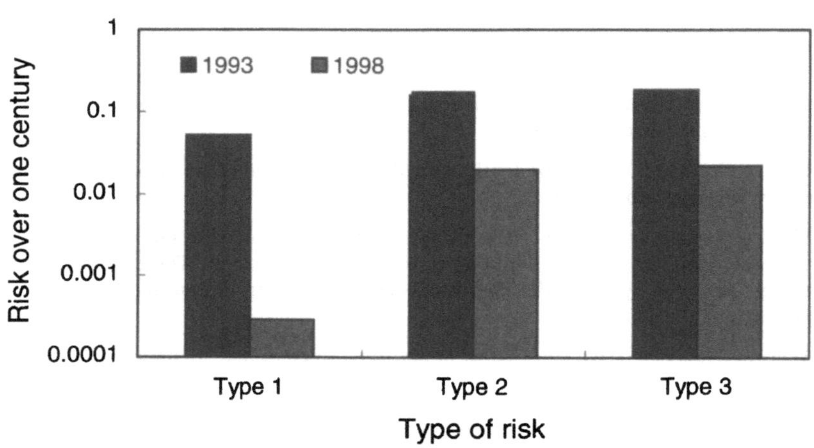

Figure 4. Comparison of risk to the Canadian Museum of Nature's collections by type of risk for both 1993 and 1998.

It is also evident in Figure 4 that the totals of both Type 2 and Type 3 risks are approximately two orders of magnitude (one hundred times) greater than the total of Type 1 risks. Consequently, current preventive conservation priorities are now focused on reducing Type 2 and 3 risks, particularly in fluid-preserved collections, as this is where our most cost-effective risk reduction is possible.

Although beyond the scope of this paper, the CPRAM defines, and sets priorities for, preventive conservation projects. In addition, conservation research needs and priorities are defined. Precise research requirements can be refined to a high degree. That is, the information required from research, whether laboratory studies, collection surveys, or other kinds of investigations can be accurately defined thereby greatly increasing the effectiveness of research investments.

Indeed, the CPRAM emphasizes the importance of focus on the rigor and quality of the preventive conservation planning process. This is essential because, due to irreducible uncertainties, preservation management can seldom obtain meaningful feedback on results of preventive conservation measures taken. As Ashley Smith (2000) has suggested, we need to become familiar and comfortable with thinking about uncertainties. Deterioration processes are inevitably too slow, damage events too sporadic, and the overall mix too confounded in cause and effect to enable significant adjustment of preventive conservation strategies (Waller and Michalski 2004). In addition, it is difficult to quantify what did not happen. Even if risk mitigation actions have prevented rare or sporadic risk events, it is often impossible, from the perspective of single institutions, to prove the effectiveness of the mitigation measures. This is not a result of mere difficulties, but a consequence of the irreducible uncertainty associated with random processes. The only escape from ignorance is through adoption of a risk analysis process such as the CPRAM.

References

Ashley-Smith, J. 2000. Developing professional uncertainty. In A. Roy and P. Smith (eds.), *Tradition and Innovation: Advances in Conservation*. London: The International Institute for Conservation of Historic and Artistic Works. 14-17.

Boroush, M. 1998. *Understanding risk analysis.* American Chemical Society (ACS) and Resources for the Future (RFF).
http://www.rff.org/rff/Publications/ReferenceMaterials.cfm

Buchanan, M., N. Porter, D. Goodwin, S. MacDiarmid and K. Knight, (eds.). 1999. *Guidelines for managing risk in the Australian and New Zealand public sector.* HB 143:1999. Srathfield, Australia: Standards Association of Australia.

Price, J. C. and G. R. Fitzgerald. 1996. Categories of specimens: a collection management tool. *Collection Forum* 12(1):8-13.

Michalski, S. 1990. An overall framework for preventive conservation and remedial conservation. In K. Grimstad (ed.), *ICOM Committee for Conservation, 9th Triennial Meeting: Preprints.* Los Angeles: ICOM Committee for Conservation. 589-591.

Waller, R.R. 1994. Conservation risk assessment: a strategy for managing resources for preventive conservation. In A. Roy and P. Smith (eds.), *Preventive conservation practice, theory and research. preprints of the contributions to the Ottawa Congress, 12-16 September 1994.* London: The International Institute for Conservation of Historic and Artistic Works. 12-16.

Waller, R. R. 1995. Risk management applied to preventive conservation. In C. L. Rose, C. A. Hawks and H. H. Genoways (eds.), *Storage of natural history collections: a preventive conservation approach.* Iowa City: Society for the Preservation of Natural History Collections. 21-28.

Waller, R.R. 1999. Internal pollutants, risk assessment and conservation priorities. In *ICOM Committee for Conservation Triennial Meeting (12th): Preprints.* London, U.K.: James & James. 113-118.

Waller, R. Robert. 2003. *Cultural Property Risk Analysis Model: Development and Application to Preventive Conservation at the Canadian Museum of Nature.* Göteborg Studies in Conservation 13. Göteborg: Göteborg Acta Universitatis Gothoburgensis.

Waller, R. and S. Michalski. 2004. Effective preservation: from reaction to prevention. *Conservation, the GCI Newsletter* 19(1):4-9.

The Author

Robert Waller is currently Chief, Conservation at the Canadian Museum of Nature. He holds a Ph.D. in Conservation from Göteborg University Institute of Conservation, and Professional Accreditation with the Canadian Association of Professional Conservators. Research interests have included: the preservation of mineral specimens; the preservation of natural materials in general; cultural property risk assessment, analysis and management, and holistic approaches to collection management and preservation. Author of more than 30 scientific and technical papers, chapters, or books on conservation, Robert Waller has taught, lectured, and served as a consultant at dozens of museums, universities, and organizations throughout North and South America, Europe and Asia. He is a fellow of the International Institute for Conservation and is a Past-Chairman of the Canadian Association of Professional Conservators.

WRITING A DISASTER PLAN: IDENTIFYING RISK

René Teygeler[1]

Consultant, The Netherlands

Abstract

The Koninklijke Bibliotheek (KB), the National Library of The Netherlands, recently developed a disaster preparedness plan for its collection. During the process, staff encountered a number of unexpected stumbling blocks and problems. For example, the creation of the new Collections Care Department forced the postponement of certain decisions. The reconstruction plans for the library's reading rooms and a new storage depot also affected the planning process. Because the solutions identified for some other problems would have been so far-reaching, management decided to defer their execution until a later phase in the process.

Risk analyses revealed that security posed one of the most significant threats to the library, in particular, minimal staff monitoring of non-library personnel who accessed the facilities. The disaster preparedness and planning process also made clear that the Collections Care Department is essential to successfully preparing for the worst. Now almost complete, the disaster preparedness plan is rich in detail that will enable the library to respond effectively in time of emergency. At the same time, the planning process made a significant step towards the implementation of a total quality management program at the KB.

Introduction

Not so long ago disasters, in particular natural disasters, were thought to occur only in tropical climates. A tornado, hurricane, earthquake, forest fire, landslide or volcanic eruption was an act of nature that hit without warning. Today we are wiser. First of all, we know that the number of natural disasters is increasing worldwide due to global climatic changes. As a consequence, nature disturbs the inhabitants of colder climate zones more frequently (Teygeler 2000). The memory of inundated villages in Central and Northern Europe is all too fresh. At the same time, we understand that many so-called natural hazards are at least partly caused by human interference. As for man-made disasters, the twentieth century with its two World Wars has been tremendously destructive to our cultural heritage, and the start of the present century does not promise any improvement. The growing consciousness of the increase in disasters, be they natural or man-made, is the very reason why this IFLA pre-conference 2003 was organized.

The Netherlands

In The Netherlands, a number of hazardous events triggered the discussion of disaster preparedness at a national level. Over the last five years, the Dutch had to cope with recurrent floods that overran existing dikes, a huge explosion in a fireworks factory that blew away a whole residential area, a blazing disco that was packed to the doors at New Year's Eve, and withal an ever-increasing number of art thefts. In reaction, a cry for more and better safety and security dominated the media – a cry that also reached the museum, library and archive world.

---

1 I would like to express my gratitude to the departments of Collections Care, Stacks Management, and Buildings and Facilities. Without their cooperation the disaster preparedness plan could definitely not have been written. In particular, I would like to thank the following persons: Theo Vermeulen, Frans Stark, Wim Smit, Rob Buying, Paulien Rings, Ko van de Watering and Ruud Ritsman.

Today, every employer in The Netherlands has to comply with the renewed Occupational Health and Safety Act (1999). Based on the 1934 Safety Act, this law helps employers prepare their own risk assessments and thus create safer and healthier working conditions. The law changes continuously and new government policies are constantly added. Because of this law all institutions of cultural heritage must have an emergency management plan. However, in 2000 the Cultural Heritage Inspectorate found that only a few national museums and galleries could claim a detailed disaster plan. The situation in the library and archive world was not much better, if not actually worse, hence the Dutch prevention pilot organized in 2003 by The Netherlands Institute for Cultural Heritage, in which the Koninklijke Bibliotheek, the National Library of The Netherlands, also participates.

Methods of Risk Analysis

The term "risk" is often confused with "hazard." A high voltage power supply or a toxic chemical may present a hazard, meaning that it presents the potential for harm. A risk is the probability or chance that a particular hazard will lead to injury. In general, uncertainty about a situation can often indicate risk, which is defined as *the possibility of loss, damage, or any other undesirable event* (Goldman 2000). Most people desire low risk, which would translate to a high probability of success, profit, or some form of gain. The first approach to 'risk' dates back nearly 350 years (Bernstein 1998). Blaise Pascal, a Parisian who was one of the most famous mathematicians and philosophers of his time, first propounded the principles of probability in 1654. Scribbled in the manuscript of his autobiography, Pascal set forth what has come to be known as *le pari de Pascal*, or Pascal's wager (Pascal 2003). He began by daring to ask: "God is, or he is not. Which way should we incline? Reason cannot answer." The point the philosopher (and converted) Pascal was to make was the fact that the *probability* that God is or God is not, is irrelevant.

Blaise Pascal.

Photo courtesy Smithsonian Institution Libraries.

About 50 years later, Jacob Bernoulli wrote a letter to his friend Gottfried von Leibniz, the famous German philosopher and scientist, in which he observed: "It is strange that we know the odds of throwing a seven instead of an eight with a pair of dice, but we do not know the probability that a man of 20 will outlive a man of 60" (Leibniz 1962). Bernoulli proposed an experiment in which he would compare a large number of pairs of men of various ages to see if he could deduce the probabilities from that evidence (Speiser 1955). His message rings true across the centuries. You cannot escape uncertainty. No mathematical model works to perfection. Statisticians are satisfied when they can demonstrate that a model works with only a 5 percent probability. No event is without cause, so ascribing a probability to chance, or luck, is merely assigning a number to our ignorance (Bernstein 1998).

Ever since, philosophers and businessmen alike have tried to comprehend and analyze risk. Today risk assessment is a very common tool.

Generically, risk analysis involves the identification of risk, risk assessment, risk management, and risk communication. There are a number of distinct approaches to risk analysis. These habitually break down into two types: quantitative and qualitative. Quantitative risk analysis, also called probabilistic analysis, is one of several tools that may be chosen by the decision maker when assessing risk. It employs two fundamental elements: the probability of an event occurring and the likely loss should it occur. It makes use of a single figure produced from these elements. This is calculated for an event by simply multiplying the potential loss by the probability. It is thus possible to rank events in order of risk and to make decisions based upon this.

The problems with this type of risk analysis are usually associated with the unreliability and inaccuracy of the data. There are a great number of quantifying models to assess risks, especially in engineering and related disciplines. Providing a suitable model can be constructed and its data inputs realistically quantified, this method can provide insight into problems surrounded by uncertainty. The trend in the 21st century is toward more quantitative methods (Vose 2001). The dominance of rational models of human behavior has led to the notion that some form of quantification of variables can guarantee safety against risk. Already a long time ago, Leibniz took a dim view of the suggestion. "Nature", he wrote, "has established patterns originating in the turn of events, but only for the most part." As patterns repeat themselves only for the most part, we must use the tools of risk management – the art of survival when our forecasts of the unknown future turn out to be wrong. In reaction to this observation, some have argued that risk is not only inevitable but also valuable and that a predictable world would be the most dangerous of all.

Qualitative risk analysis is by far the most widely used approach in business risk assessment. Probability data is not required and only estimated potential loss is used. Most qualitative risk analysis methodologies make use of a number of interrelated elements like threats, vulnerabilities and controls, and put them in a highly rational model. This tool was developed largely in recognition of the rapid changing nature of many businesses.

David Vose, writing on pest risk analysis, gives an interesting third possibility: a qualitative/semi-quantitative risk analysis with a subjective scoring system. A common approach, according to Vose, is to "mix and match," using quantitative data where available and qualitative assessment where not. As there is often uncertainty in the use of subjective estimates, it is advisable to consult experts. (Vose 2001). The Koninklijke Bibliotheek chose this third option for its risk analysis.

The Koninklijke Bibliotheek

Two Emergency Plans

In 2001 the Koninklijke Bibliotheek outsourced development of the emergency management plan. This plan provides response and emergency procedures for the staff and visitors. A year later, library managers realized that the plan did not contain sufficient actions for the collections, so they sought advice from an outsider to "adjust" this plan for the collections housed in the Koninklijke Bibliotheek. During the process a number of unexpected stumbling blocks and problems occurred.

The first concern was to redefine the plan following the advice of The Netherlands Institute for Cultural Heritage. The existing plan was classified as the *company* emergency assistance plan, and the additional plan was classified as the *collection* emergency assistance plan. In the end, the two plans were to be joined together to form the final disaster preparedness plan. This would allow the staff and consultant to pay special attention to emergency procedures for the collections. Since most of the emergency plans in institutions for cultural heritage focused on people and buildings, they directed little attention to the collections, in spite of the fact that the principal task of these institutions is to protect, preserve and secure access to that heritage (Teygeler 2001). Just the same, the Koninklijke Bibliotheek pursues a strict policy that under all circumstances people take precedence over collections.

One could wonder whether the separation of the plan into a *company* emergency assistance and a *collection* emergency assistance plan was a good idea or not. The answer is yes and no.

It is yes, because the division allowed the consultant to concentrate fully on the collection, since the company emergency assistance plan was already finished. This way the consultant could even give some time to desk research, especially on issues that urgently required clarification, such as best freezing methods, best practices in packaging procedures for freezing purposes, methods to remove soot from fire-damaged books, and means to fight the pungent odor after a fire. Furthermore, there was time to pay extra attention to damage and salvage of modern media like optical disks, magnetic audio-visual tapes and computer disks. Last, but not least, there was sufficient time to complete the emergency plan down to the smallest detail. This might sound insignificant, but it was an exceptional opportunity to make contact with many members of the staff from the top floor to the vault. After a while most of the Koninklijke Bibliotheek workers knew that a collection emergency plan was being prepared. Steadily their interest and backing grew, which is, of course, essential to the success of any plan.

However, the development of separate emergency plans also had a disadvantage. Once the layout of the collection plan was established, it was necessary to draw more and more on the company plan for details. Certain crucial matters could not be prepared without the details of the company emergency plan, for which Building and Facilities, the department in charge of the safety and security of the staff, the visitors and the building, was responsible.

In retrospect, it remained a good idea to separate the two emergency plans. It left ample room to focus on the collection, the core business of any cultural heritage institution. Still, we under-estimated the interdependency of the two plans.

Qualifying and Quantifying Risk

Risk assessment is a must for every safety officer. The first step in planning disaster preparedness is to identify the risks. As the consequences of a calamity are entirely different for the collection than for people or buildings, it was necessary to conduct an independent risk analysis for the collections. The problem was which model to adopt. For our purposes, the third model, the qualitative/semi-quantitative risk analysis, seemed to be the most appropriate. This method fit for the purpose for which it is intended: it may include numeric data, but in technical parlance it would be considered to be qualitative.

While the Koninklijke Bibliotheek is a highly modern organization, unlike the information technology business, it is not a super commercial organization that is totally dependent on its high flexibility. The changes in the library world are not that quick, and not all the risk factors are known. They vary from library to library. This made a pure qualitative analysis less suitable. On the other hand, a pure quantitative risk analysis dud not fit our purposes either, since there were no statistics available. The Koninklijke Bibliotheek did not keep any record of calamities and incidents. That is why a combination of qualitative and quantitative risk analyses was chosen.

First, key personnel at the Koninklijke Bibliotheek were asked to identify the main risks, and, at the same time, to indicate the chance of an expected incident and the estimated impact (both on a scale from 1 to 5), as well as to propose ways to prevent the calamities. Multiplying chance by impact provided a concrete number that allowed a comparison of the identified risks with one another (See Figure 1). The outcome had no significance for any rational model; it merely was an opportunity to order the identified risks. To meet the criticism of subjectivity, the results were weighed against the outcome of a brief desk study on risks in cultural heritage institutions in general. There were no disturbing deviations from the general pattern.

Risk Analysis (example) *5 – 1 = high – low

Calamity (cause and effect)	Chance (5 – 1)*	Effect (5 – 1)	Total (chance x effect)	Prevention	Comments
Leakage ***Water damage to objects in depot*** - Frozen water pipes when there is a sharp frost - Building activities from staff outside KB	2 3	2 2	4 6	a) isolate water pipes b) isolate building c) move pipes d) water detector e) regular control f) emergency response kit	The water pipes are directly situated below the ceiling in the depots; the books on the top shelves will suffer the most

Figure 1: Example of Qualitative/ Quantitative Risk Analysis for KB Collections

The general "calamity" picture of the Koninklijke Bibliotheek is a very positive one. Except for a few small-scale incidents in the past and an occasional theft, the library has been spared major disasters. The building seems to function properly, the visitors are not aggressive, and the staff is alert. Still, the library is not totally without risk. The risk assessment shows first that the depots run a comparatively great risk of flooding caused by the continuous renovation activities, by hidden flaws in the building structure, by heavy storms, or by condensation from the air-conditioning system. Second, there is a general fire risk caused by illegal smoking and again by the continuous renovation activities. Third is a medium-to-small risk of theft by library users and non-library personnel. Finally, there is a small risk of pollution with sand, dust and debris produced by the activities of our own technical maintenance staff, as well as by staff from outside the library and by malfunctions in the air-conditioning system.

Flood

From the risk analysis and also from experience, it was clear that the main risk to the Koninklijke Bibliotheek is flooding. The causes can differ widely: a leaking glass pyramid in the ceiling, an ill-closed fire hose, a hidden crack in the outer wall of the underground depot, or condensation of the air-conditioning system. Some of these problems have to do with the construction of the building and others with neglect. Because recurrent or hidden structural faults are difficult to tackle, management decided to increase the monitoring system in the most vulnerable depots by installing extra water detectors and by more closely controlling temperature and relative humidity. As an inundation often occurs during non-office hours and is not discovered until the next morning, an adjustment in the surveillance schedule of the security guards is under consideration.

To be better prepared for a flood, the majority of the items that compose our disaster bin (or emergency response kit) now consist of equipment and materials to counter or absorb water and to prevent the collection from getting wet. Neglect is dealt with by raising employee awareness and increasing formal responsibility for all personnel, both insiders and outsiders.

Fire

Every room in the Koninklijke Bibliotheek is fitted out with smoke detectors, and regular fire drills are held. Nonetheless, the Koninklijke Bibliotheek runs a medium fire risk. The biggest potential danger is the ineradicable smoking habit. A few decades ago, the Dutch government started an anti-smoking campaign. Today smoking is prohibited in public buildings. In private buildings, separate smoking areas are required. The Koninklijke Bibliotheek follows a strict no smoking policy. The whole building is off limits to smokers except for the two designated areas. Even so, a number of cigarette butts have been found in the repositories, the toilets, private offices and the hallways. Needless to say, smoking is a serious fire threat. Because we suspect that the illegal smokers are for the most part outside workers, special attention will be given to the strict smoking policy in all new contracts. Those contracts will also reflect the potential fire hazard of reconstruction activities. Plumbers, welders, electricians and other workmen must always carry their own fire extinguishers on the job.

Another problem is the illegal use of often-insecure household appliances. Some employees are very persistent in making their own hot drinks and do not realize that these machines easily short-circuit and thus can cause a fire. This issue is approached by raising awareness and making clear that all employees bear responsibility for disaster prevention. A stricter monitoring system of the depots will, of course, also reduce the fire risk.

Theft

In general, theft is not a major problem at the Koninklijke Bibliotheek. Nevertheless, the library is occasionally subject to visits of often international operating thieves, who apply highly sophisticated techniques to illegally acquire some of our treasures. The Koninklijke Bibliotheek is seldom confronted with staff members who steal. To counter the undesirable visits requires a number of steps. Most of them concern the Special Collections Department. Access to the reading room has been slightly rerouted, a closed circuit security system has been installed, and access to the vault has become even more restricted. To prevent theft of illustrated single pages, a precision scale has been introduced that can register the slightest change in weight of a book. Other security measures will be introduced during the reconstruction of the reading room of the Special Collections Department and the new Exposition Hall. The library has hired a security expert to look over the reconstruction plans.

Pollution

In such a large building as the Koninklijke Bibliotheek-complex, which also houses several other institutes, the library's technical staff and external workers are always repairing or constructing something. In practice, cleaning rules are not strictly followed. It is not a serious problem, but there is room for improvement. Awareness training is needed for the library's own maintenance crew, who must be shown over and over again the negative effects of debris that attracts all kinds of insects and rodents. Tight housekeeping rules will be added to new maintenance contracts.

Every now and then the heating, ventilating, and air-conditioning (HVAC) system seems to leave a slight layer of black powder on a small area around certain outlet points. As the cause is unknown, extra monitoring is suggested for the time being. The installation of a whole new set of filters for the planned high-rise depot is presently under consideration.

Monitoring

The most striking result from the risk analysis is the fact that almost all the threats are in some way or other caused by security, in particular, minimal monitoring of non-library personnel who access the facilities. As the depots are in constant need of engineering, frequently outside technical staff must enter the depots. Yet, the library did not follow a clear course of action. There was no standard requirement that non-library employees be accompanied, even in the high security depot. Outsiders were not required to sign a code of conduct before starting jobs at the library, nor was such a clause built into their contracts. A complicating factor is that some of the high-tech tasks are outsourced, and these companies send their staff on secondment to the Koninklijke Bibliotheek. They familiarize themselves with the building and the workers and, as a result, often consider themselves part of the library staff. The same goes for the private security service. The risk assessment clearly demonstrates that monitoring non-library workers is not only a security problem; it is also an important safety problem. In short, monitoring greatly contributes to the library's flood and fire safety. Yet that is easier said than done.

At present, the Koninklijke Bibliotheek faces a period of heavy building pressure: a new reading room for the special collections section, a new exposition hall, continuous work on the HVAC-system, groundwork for the new high-rise depot and groundwork for new construction in the neighboring National Archives. For the ongoing work, contracts cannot be changed. Neither is it the right moment to introduce a new monitoring system with everybody constantly running around and just about to collapse under his or her workload. The monitoring system has to be carefully planned. From that moment on, all new contracts with non-library personnel will include clear-cut guidelines on the behavior of contractors and service providers, and all outside personnel will be monitored. Already, the days are over when someone in the library is trusted on his good looks only.

Discipline

Another cause for concern is the undisciplined behavior of the in-house staff. Risk analysis unmistakably shows that the Koninklijke Bibliotheek workers themselves constitute a potential fire and flood risk. Illegal smoking, undesirable consumption of foodstuff (including the use of rickety household machines), and unadvisable houseplants have been detected. Overzealous employees buy their lunch at the cafeteria but consume their meals in their offices and forget to return the dishes, thus attracting insects and rodents. In one repository a refrigerator was discovered. It seemed that a small department makes their own lunch, and, as they did not have room for a fridge, they found a depot employee willing to help them out. Others feel so much at home at the library that they turn their (second) home into their castle, decorating the place with all kinds of plant life. They do not comprehend that they disrupt the pest management policy.

Fortunately, eating, drinking and smoking on the shop floor have not become established practices. Yet measures are necessary to show personnel the consequences on the collections of their risky behavior. It is necessary to raise their awareness at the beginning of their careers. Therefore, all new employees will now receive a new code of conduct stressing hygiene and good housekeeping in their orientation packages.

Writing Disaster, Taking a Risk

In commencing to write a disaster preparedness plan, one undoubtedly will meet with many unexpected problems. At the start it often looks as if nothing is right anymore, and the whole organization needs to change drastically. Naturally this is a general phenomenon for all change processes. Still, the process of writing an emergency plan can be become a risky business in itself. There is always the danger of losing oneself in the many proposed alterations and forgetting the fact that any change must be taken step-by-step.

Some of the problems encountered in the process could not be solved immediately. For example, should the plan also include the digital collections? If so, should it take both hardware and software into consideration? Should it be the main focus of the continuity plan?

The Koninklijke Bibliotheek's computer-based library lending system works fine. Yet the shelf register does not allow searchers to trace a specific title to its exact spot of the bookshelf; it is not that explicit. If an emergency evacuation of the repository occurred, a more specific list would certainly help speed the process. But should we invest a great deal of money to adjust a very complicated software program, or should we accept this limitation?

One result of the recent reorganization of the library was the creation of the Collection Care Department. Up to that time the Building and Facilities Department assumed the responsibility for the contingency plan. But with the new Collection Care Department this situation changed. At the beginning of the planning process, the division of responsibilities, competences and authorities between the two departments had not taken their final shape. This affected the planning process, since some decisions had to be postponed. At the same time, it was evident that both departments would be indispensable to the success of the disaster preparedness plan.

A vital part of any disaster response plan is the initial and continuing survey of the library facility, service areas and collections. The audit or survey is necessary because it provides an overall view of conditions governing the safety and long-term preservation of the collection. Often, action taken as a result of this survey may actually prevent a disaster from occurring. Yet how ambitious should the survey be and where does a quality management program commence? Whatever the case may be, the disaster preparedness plan is a significant step toward a total quality management program.

These problems were discussed at length at different levels in the organization. Some of the problems could be solved; others have been postponed for later resolution. In a rapidly changing society, preparation for the worst is never finished nor is a disaster response plan ever completed.

Conclusion

Disaster strikes anytime, anywhere. It is not subject to time and does not know any boundaries. Disasters must be managed in order to control them, or at least mitigate the effects, and risk management is a vital part in that process. However, life is not without risk. Our cultural heritage will likewise always be exposed to some form of danger, be it small or big. The only thing that can be done is to prepare for the worst and plan for the best. It should be realized that each collection, each building, and each situation is unique and that every institute has to prepare for disasters with its own unique plan.

The Koninklijke Bibliotheek put a lot of effort and resources into the development of a sound disaster response plan. It is rich in detail and will enable the library to respond effectively in time of emergency. Today, the Dutch national treasures housed in the vaults of the Koninklijke Bibliotheek are better protected than ever before.

References

Leibniz, G. 1962. *Mathematische Schriften.* Hildesheim: G. Olms. 77.

Bernstein, P. 1998. Risk at the roots. *Balance Sheet* 7(1):18-20.

Goldman, L. 2000. *Risk analysis and Monte Carlo simulation.* Decisioneering Inc. http://www.pmboulevard.com/expert_column/archives/reg/risk_analysis_and_monte_carlo_goldman.pdf

MacLeod, A, Baker, RHA, 2002 (*unpublished*). Describing scores used in the EPPO Pest risk assessment scheme: Descriptions of scores for Entry and Establishment.

Pascal, B. 2003. *Pensées*, translated by W. F. Trotter. Mineola, N.Y.: Dover Publications.

Speiser, D. (ed.), 1955. *Der Briefwechsel von Johann I. Bernoulli.* Basel, Berlin: Birkhäuser.

Teygeler, R. 2001. *Preservation of archives in tropical climates. An annotated bibliography.* Paris, The Hague, Jakarta: International Council on Archives, National Archives of The Netherlands, National Archives of the Republic of Indonesia.

Vose, D. 2001. *Risk analysis: a quantitative guide.* 2nd ed. Chichester: Wiley & Sons.

The Author

René Teygeler started his academic career in 1970 with his study in Sociology and Social Psychology at Utrecht University. As he developed a taste for books he started studying bookbinding, and book and paper conservation. In 1993, after finishing his education as a conservator at the State School for Conservators, he was appointed as a conservator at the Koninklijke Bibliotheek. He continued his academic training in Anthropology and obtained an honorary degree in 1996. In 1997, he started the consultancy firm Paper in Development and has since advised many institutions in The Netherlands and abroad.

SESSION 6: OPTIONS FOR COLLECTIONS RECOVERY

In this session, specialists discussed options for treating various types of collection materials following a disaster. What are the options – their benefits and risks? What are the proven treatments reported in the literature? What are the promising new technologies? What commercial services are available?

COMPARISON OF DRYING METHODS

Hilary A. Kaplan[1]

Senior Conservator, Document Conservation Laboratory, National Archives and Records Administration, Washington, D.C., USA

Kathleen A. Ludwig

Senior Conservator, Document Conservation Laboratory, National Archives and Records Administration, Washington, D.C., USA

Abstract

The effects of four methods for drying large quantities of water-damaged records were examined. Similar groupings of expendable paper records were assembled to represent the eclectic nature of materials typically found in archives. Records were: 1) air-dried following guidelines consistently found in the literature; 2) dehumidified on-site by staff and off-site by a vendor; 3) vacuum freeze-dried; and 4) vacuum freeze-dried using a patented proprietary process. Evaluation criteria were established based on observations of the successes and drawbacks of each approach. Specific concerns include: expeditious packing and shipping of records; need for record-keeping; potential loss of intellectual control; security; unanticipated costs; and realistic expectations in evaluating the final product. Clearly communicating goals and accurately estimating human or financial resources at the outset of any recovery project underscore a project's ultimate success. Decisions to treat items in-house or negotiate services with outside vendors may be based, not only on quantity of materials affected, available resources, and efficacy of the drying method, but also on security and privacy requirements. The results of this study can help staff in selecting among commonly available options for recovering water-damaged paper-based archives and library materials.

Background

In our efforts to be prepared for water emergencies, the Document Conservation Laboratory at the United States National Archives and Records Administration (NARA) periodically augments and re-evaluates its emergency preparedness, response, and recovery plans. To date, most emergencies have been small and opportunities to observe and evaluate drying methods from available vendor services have been limited. This project was designed to provide a closer look at drying recommendations offered in the literature and compare these approaches to what would approximate real-life circumstances. A deliberate decision was made at the outset of this project to avoid identifying the vendors used in this study to allow for complete objectivity in assessing the results. All participating vendors were aware of our study, but we do not know whether this knowledge had any influence on how our materials were handled.

Conservation staff at NARA strive to keep current with available resources on recovery. Most recovery guides convey the bottom line, recommending one drying method over another based on a specific type of material and degree of wetness. Archives holdings

---

1 We would like to express our appreciation to Doris Hamburg, Director, Preservation Programs, and Mary Lynn Ritzenthaler, Chief, Document Conservation Laboratory for mentoring and support as we embarked on the activities associated with this study. We are also indebted to the assistance and encouragement we received from Supervisory Conservator, Catherine Nicholson, and our colleagues in the Document Conservation Laboratory and in Research and Testing. Special thanks to National Archives staff who donated testing materials and assisted with this project.

represent a wide variety of formats and media that are often contained in one box. If an emergency affects a moderate-to-large quantity of holdings, sorting and culling disparate materials from wet records is not practical or even possible. Databases that identify record formats in a given location and pinpoint available space for re-locating materials from damaged areas promise to greatly assist in future recovery efforts. Knowing more about the quantity and composition of affected records will help to set priorities and minimize potential damage during response and recovery.

When Materials Get Wet

Protective efforts to prevent water from coming into direct contact with archives materials are imperative when we consider the potential damage that may otherwise occur. When exposed to water, papers and books absorb moisture. Hygroscopic materials like papers, boards, and skins increase both in size and weight. Because books are composite structures, their components – boards, cloth or leather, sewing, adhesives, and text paper – may expand or contract at different rates. This differential expansion can cause damage to the structure of a book.

Upon drying, leather and parchment may shrink if not restrained. Wet parchment leaves can adhere if dried in contact with one another. Water can also cause metal fasteners to corrode. Corrosion from iron and copper weakens paper and often results in physical damage. Exposure to moisture can prompt image media to become soluble. The dissolution of media may transfer or bleed to adjacent sheets, move horizontally or vertically within the sheet, or completely obliterate information. Water may make components of paper soluble, such as dyes, sizings, fillers, surface coatings, and degradation products of aged papers. Formerly wet sheets may show characteristic dark tide lines formed by impurities in the water or dissolved degradation byproducts that have moved within a sheet.

Mold is always a potential consequence of water damage when the drying process is delayed beyond a two-day period. The elevated moisture content of organic materials, such as the papers, leathers, parchments, and cloths found in libraries and archives, provides an environment conducive for mold to flourish.

The Project

In order to better understand how various drying methods would affect a sampling of archives materials, the effects of four drying approaches were observed and compared on sets of similar materials. Our study was performed using expendable items donated by a number of the Archives' custodial units. These disposable paper-based records were diverse, although they did not represent the entire universe of media and supports found within the Archives. Sufficient examples were available to create seven sets of paper records, each filling two records storage boxes and measuring .06796 cubic meters.

The four processes compared were air-drying, dehumidification-drying, vacuum freeze-drying, and a vacuum thermal freeze-drying proprietary process. The following paper conveys how we carried out this study; observations made; and what we have learned along the way.

Air-drying

Air-drying involves drying records at room temperature, in-house. Typically, materials are dried in a prepared workspace and spread out on, or interleaved with, absorbent papers. In some instances, materials may be dried under restraint in a stack of weighted blotters.

Dehumidification-drying

In dehumidification-drying, also referred to as desiccant-drying, materials are dried by introducing dried (dehumidified) air at very low relative humidities, often below 15 percent, and circulating that dried air with fans in and around the drying chamber. Air temperatures vary throughout the drying process, but usually are in the range of 26-37° C (79-99° F).

Vacuum Freeze-drying

Vacuum freeze-drying is generally recommended for large quantities of wet or damp materials. Materials must be in a frozen state when entering the vacuum freeze-drying chamber and remain frozen throughout the drying process. Items are placed within a high vacuum at temperatures below freezing, while cycles of controlled heat are applied. This process causes frozen water to sublimate to a vapor without passing through a liquid stage – advantageous in minimizing feathering and bleeding of soluble media. It allows coated materials to dry without blocking, and results in minimal distortion. The process can be performed on-site by vendors equipped with mobile vacuum chambers, or items may be sent to a drying facility. Drying time depends on the wetness of the materials but can usually be accomplished in less than two weeks.

Vacuum Thermal Drying

The fourth method we set out to investigate was vacuum thermal drying, which has been recommended for wet or damp materials. Materials can be placed into the chamber, either frozen or thawed, and are dried above 0°C (32°F). Materials are dried in a chamber under a vacuum with heated air. Generally recommended for un-coated papers, vacuum thermal drying is often cited as a cost-effective option for materials of low intrinsic value. This procedure is known to distort paper, causes coated records to block, and exacerbates the feathering and bleeding of soluble inks. Drying time is usually shorter than vacuum freeze-drying, but this will depend on initial wetness.

We did not, in fact, investigate this process as described, though this was indeed the service we intended to purchase. An absence of clearly understood terminology resulted in obtaining *thermal vacuum freeze-drying*, not *thermal vacuum-drying*. This discrepancy only became obvious once materials were returned and did not display the characteristic effects anticipated: blocking of coated paper, feathering and bleeding of soluble inks.

The results from thermal vacuum freeze-drying, however, provided a useful sampling for comparison with other methods evaluated. Thermal vacuum freeze-drying is similar to vacuum freeze-drying in using reduced pressure and controlled heat to vaporize water, but it also employs a patented procedure to compress subjected materials into shape. Such proprietary processes may not be universally available, and like other technologies, may be specific to particular locales.

Methodology

Seven sets, made up of two boxes each, were carefully packed with expendable materials. Special care was taken to place all items in the same order within the boxes. Six sets were wetted and dried; the seventh set remained as an untreated control.

To approximate a real-life situation, we attempted to simulate two levels of wetness. All of the boxes were allowed to absorb standing water for a 24-hour period. An additional eight liters of water were poured over half of the box tops to simulate a sprinkler discharge or burst pipe. After 24 hours, water was released from the sink in which the boxes stood, and the records were left to drain for two hours prior to freezing.

We observed that the boxes absorbed varying amounts of water. The boxes, we concluded, played a decided role in how well their contents became saturated. Papers with high ground wood content, such as newsprint, were also seen to saturate while adjacent sheets wet up only to the immersion water line. This "sponge-like" property of groundwood was most visible where water- soluble green felt-tip pen lines were marked in the same locations on three experimental sheets. Pen lines feathered on newsprint papers, but remained unaltered on the non-newsprint samples.

Specific directions from the selected vendors were then followed to prepare the wet records for shipping. All twelve wet boxes were wrapped twice in a layer of 4-mil polyethylene sheeting, each layer sealed with packing tape. The boxes were then placed in manual defrost chest freezers with .7 cubic meter capacity.

It is critical to communicate with commercial drying facilities about how boxes containing records are to be packed. This will have a large impact on how well materials will survive transit and dry. Wet records can readily damage a cardboard box if precautions are not taken – such as wrapping the interior in plastic. Doing so will preserve label information on the exterior of the box, but means that records will be manipulated if the vendor requests that the plastic be removed to achieve optimal drying. It is, in fact, possible to leave the plastic lining in place by opening the top of the box to expose the records and allow the moisture to sublimate. Not removing the plastic at all, however, prolongs the length of time needed for drying. The care exercised in the packing stage inevitably pays off in the condition of the final product.

While efforts were made to provide similar samples for our study, a number of variables could have contributed to the final results observed. In examining the donated expendable records, it was clear that not all like groupings of records were identical. The number of pages within bound volumes, pamphlets, and folders varied, as did media. The composition and condition of record substrates were also different. Efforts were made to make the sample sets as similar as possible, but they were not identical.

Differential wetting may have occurred as uneven water absorption of the original corrugated cardboard boxes was observed. Boxes varied in board composition and age, though all appeared in good condition and sufficiently supported the records when dry.

All wet boxes were handled in the same manner prior to leaving the Archives, but we do not know the environmental conditions or duration of the overnight transport to the vendor. We also do not know how the boxes were handled once they arrived at the vendor's facility. Had the materials thoroughly thawed? Were the boxes crushed or misshapen during transit? Were boxes immediately placed into a freezer or did they sit for a period of time thawed and wrapped in their plastic? These unknowns may have contributed to item damage prior to the commercial drying process.

In-house Drying

Air-drying

Air-drying has been the method of choice for small water-related incidents at the National Archives. In this study, we departed from our customary response so that all boxes would be handled in a similar manner – materials to be air-dried were frozen just like those materials to be sent off-site for commercial processes. Freezing might be a necessary step following a large-scale disaster. Since air-drying can require vast surface areas not readily available, materials may be frozen and thawed in manageable amounts as drying space becomes available. A frozen water-saturated records storage box (.0339 cubic meters) can take up to 24 or more hours to completely thaw at room temperature.

Archives staff has had a great deal of experience air-drying records. Air-drying offers us the security and privacy controls that are often required for our holdings. It allows us to isolate materials that may need special handling, such as coated papers, parchment, or photographic materials, and provides direct monitoring of original order, allowing us to maintain intellectual control.

Air-drying pre-supposes that ample space and trained personnel are available for carrying out this labor-intensive activity. Other drying methods may be preferable when the quantity of damaged materials is great and there is a lack of available space or personnel.

After the records in our study completely thawed, items were set onto tables lined with absorbent blotting paper. Bound materials that could not be safely supported upright were laid flat on blotting paper for drying. Pages were turned periodically during the two days of air-drying. Stacks of cards or groupings of papers were turned to expose wet surfaces throughout the process.

During the air-drying process, attention was focused on maintaining original order of the folders and their contents. When possible, it is very helpful to have the same individual unpack wet and reassemble the same dried materials to maintain close control over original order. Items with coated paper were individually interleaved with sheets of a polyester non-woven fabric, Holytex™ or Remay™, to prevent blocking of the pages upon drying.

Dupont Clysar™ EHC shrink-wrap (a stable industrial plastic film adapted for preservation packaging and transport) and Mylar™D, and Melinex™ 516 polyester films (used in protective L-sleeves and encapsulations) are typically found in records at the National Archives. For effective air-drying, completely remove plastic films from water-damaged sheets and volumes.

The ambient conditions within the air-drying area were monitored with a Rotronic™ Data Logger and air-drying was successfully completed in two days. The temperature readings were just above 21°C (70°F). The relative humidity fluctuated between 20-30 percent.

Dehumidification-drying

Dehumidification-drying is often cited in the literature for its excellent results in drying *damp* collections. It allows access to the materials during the drying process, if desired or required. Dehumidification can be performed on-site with equipment rented from a vendor. Drying procedures can be carried out in-house by institutional staff or by professionals from the drying service. Items may also be sent directly to the vendor's location for the same services. Drying is completed within several days, depending on the initial degree of wetness of materials.

Dehumidification in an on-site drying chamber is an attractive option when dealing with large quantities of content-sensitive materials. As a chamber was already up and running at a NARA facility, we included dehumidification as a drying method to be examined. The results of drying conducted by our staff were then compared to those carried out by a vendor off-site using the same method. To confine requisite dry air, a chamber had been constructed in a loading dock bay. Dehumidification equipment was rented and installed by the contractor and drying procedures were carried out by Archives staff.

Records were placed upright on plastic shelving, supported by vertical polyvinyl chloride (PVC) pipes inserted at regular intervals. Bound materials could be opened and supported upright by the poles of the drying rack. Corrugated boards and blotter paper were inserted to support the drying materials, but proved inadequate. As the records dried, distortion occurred. Though holdings originally filled two boxes, four boxes were required to accommodate the size of cockled dried materials following dehumidification-drying.

Dehumidification-drying has been successfully employed *in situ* for slightly damp materials where items are dried in place, without removing them from their shelves or from their box. Though our experimental records were *wet*, not damp, we were anxious to see how well the dehumidification system already set up on-site could successfully dry wet items *in situ*. Would they eventually dry? How long would it take? Would mold grow under such dry ambient conditions?

An archivist at the NARA facility took daily measurements of the materials being dried *in situ* and recorded the data using a Delmhorst™ P-2000 moisture meter. This instrument works optimally when the papers to be measured are between 21-32°C (70-90°F). It measures the relationship between moisture content and electrical resistance using a scale of 4.3-18 percent moisture content. Five to seven percent (5-7) moisture content is considered dry. The Rotronic™ data logger was placed next to the boxes being dried *in situ* to record environmental conditions. Moisture content percentage was recorded daily to track the drying progression.

The *in situ* dehumidification-drying trial ended on the 13th day of the project when the rented drying equipment was returned to the vendor. Wet boxes did not dry during this period. A core area of the box measured initially exceeded the upper range of the moisture meter's 18.2 percent moisture content and remained at that level for the duration of the project's test period. Only the sides and outer ends of the boxes were beginning to dry by day 13. The least wet box diminished from 16.0 to 15.3 percent moisture content.

The temperature in the drying chamber fluctuated from 21-37°C (70-99°F) and the humidity was within 5-20 percent throughout the thirteen-day period. The data-logger corroborated our impression that working conditions for staff within the chamber were oppressive. Staff found the hot, dry conditions too uncomfortable for productivity and often turned off the equipment and raised the loading-dock doors when actively loading and unloading the chamber. The system was, however, consistently turned back on at night when staff presence was not required.

Ideally, this system is designed to be loaded, sealed, turned on, and completed before personnel would need to spend time within the chamber. But the circumstances of this situation dictated the process be completed as quickly as possible due to administrative concerns that materials be readily available and financial constraints – such as fuel to run the freezer trucks and personnel. As a result, the cycles were modified from the original plan design recommended by the equipment vendor.

Our attempt at dehumidification *in situ* was not successful and confirmed recommendations found in the literature; dehumidification *in situ* is not a suitable approach for drying *wet* materials. Mold grew on a variety of substrates. These wet samples were eliminated from further comparison, bagged and discarded.

Commercial Off-site Drying: Issues of Intellectual Control

Drying records on-site repeatedly demonstrates a level of intellectual control that does not always appear attainable when items leave the repository. The use of labeled plastic "milk crates" is one means to safely transport many small volumes to an area prepared for drying. Though space-consuming to store, these crates are sturdy, can be used again and again, and are not terribly susceptible to damage from water or weight. If necessary, crates with damaged materials can be placed directly into a freezer for drying.

Maintaining intellectual control is a far greater challenge when items leave the repository. Be sure to ask contractors to keep original boxes or labels. Only one of a group of four boxes contained a label fragment from its original box. File trace numbers were written on the outside of the box, but no original label information was preserved. We did not explicitly instruct the vendors to save all label information, but erroneously assumed that they would. Was documentation for these samples not preserved because boxes were understood to be test materials? We did explicitly request that our test records be handled in the same manner as true collection items. No subsequent data for lost descriptive information was forthcoming – we did not learn if it had been misplaced or discarded.

Although each box had been identically packed prior to wetting, the order in some boxes was disrupted when they were returned. Sides of original boxes containing information were inserted into new boxes of dried records. While this ensured that all label information was retained, staff needed to open each new box and copy pertinent information to it. In one instance, a pocket-folder filled with documents was returned with items removed from a pocket and inserted as a single grouping within the folder. Original order was disrupted and lost.

It is best to negotiate box quality if dried records cannot be returned in original boxes. Vendors returned our items in new boxes of unknown chemical quality that had been covered with pressure sensitive tape and mailing labels. These boxes were supplied at an additional charge that had not been specified at the outset of the project. One vendor charged $8.00 (US) per box, or approximately €7.00 (euros). A less expensive transport box is preferred if records are to be transferred upon return to a permanent quality records storage box.

Comparing Physical Results

Equal numbers of printed forms consisting of 1960s machine-made card stock with pen and pencil entries were set side by side to evaluate the increase in volume and degree of cockling. Vacuum freeze-drying produced the least distortion followed by air-drying. Dehumidification-drying performed by a vendor off-site and on-site yielded records with the greatest increase in volume and cockling.

Bound volumes behaved much like unrestrained loose pages when dried. The patented vacuum freeze-dry process produced results most like the control. In general, if volumes are misshapen when packed for freeze-drying, they remain in that shape when dry. The patented vacuum freeze-dry process is specifically designed to press volumes back into shape through a compression system in its drying cycle, and often obviates the need for rebinding. Volumes fit back on the shelves as they once were.

The patented process developers have also introduced a Rare Book Drying method in which a volume's text block is dried without desiccating its leather covers, diminishing the likelihood of broken hinges and need for subsequent repair. This approach is, however, more than four times the cost of traditional vacuum freeze-drying – approximately $250 (US) or €230 (euros) per cubic foot.

Not all books exhibited the same ability to open flat once dried. Both vacuum freeze-dried samples felt stiff and exhibited a slight resistance to opening flat. This may be the binding structure's response to mechanical stress placed on it, and its adhesives during the wetting and drying processes.

Books bound with metal fasteners dried satisfactorily. The air-dried volume exhibited the most pronounced distortion. Because of the absence of a hard cover, the book could not be dried vertically and pages were forced to flex across the fastener in a flat open format used for drying.

All pamphlet-style volumes dried acceptably, though the dehumidification samples show the greatest distortion. The patented vacuum-freeze dried sample is thought to have suffered from the size limitations of the compression plates, or its placement next to smaller volumes and folders within a box.

We surmise that the heat used in the patented vacuum freeze-dry process is sufficient to accelerate the movement of the binder's vinyl plasticizers, causing toner from the adjacent photocopies to fuse to the vinyl. Photocopies inserted into the cover's clear vinyl pocket and in contact with the title page blocked to the vinyl and transferred its text to the binder. Photocopied pages within the binder did not, however, block at all.

Because plastic film retards drying, shrink-wrapping needs to be removed from bound volumes for drying by all methods except vacuum freeze-drying. Mold growth resulted before the volume dried.

Coated paper magazines were dried using the same methods as other materials. In almost all instances, coated paper sheets left in direct contact with one another during the drying process adhered. Only vacuum freeze-dried materials were successfully recovered without interleaving. Once an item is blocked, it is seldom separated without incurring damage. Only coated papers dried by vacuum freeze-drying process did not adhere, even though their pages were in direct contact with one another during the drying process.

Rolled items present special challenges because there is often little space available to unroll long items for drying. While efforts have been made to re-house many rolled materials flat or around rigid wide-diameter cores, many rolled items remain unsupported. Curious to see how well rolled items could dry in their existing format, we subjected them to the same methods as volumes and documents. Depending on the length and thickness of paper, most rolled items in our study successfully dried within their rolled formats.

It is not possible to know if the creases and physical damage seen in the patented freeze-dry process resulted from the process itself, or from the thawing and shipment of the items. Though the equipment used to compress materials into shape by the patented process may be ultimately inappropriate for unique archival holdings of disparate sizes or formats, we believe that the process holds great promise for published uniformly bound structures in circulating collections.

Non-water-soluble coatings, such as cellulose nitrate, frequently found on mid-to-late 20th-century architectural linens bubbled and delaminated in areas where water was trapped under the film. Damage was apparent in all test samples but seemed to be exacerbated in vacuum freeze-drying processes.

Groupings of polyester-sleeved items were placed within sample boxes for wetting and drying to see if they could be successfully vacuum-dried. Would the vacuum process sublimate water out of openings of the sleeves? Would water be effectively removed from encapsulation where corners were clipped? Would water be removed from an ultrasonic- or heat-welded item?

Vacuum freeze-dried sleeved and encapsulated records dried successfully within their sleeves. A moisture meter reading was slightly below the "dry" range of five to seven percent (5-7 percent). Large quantities of water-damaged collections that are sleeved or encapsulated may therefore be effectively vacuum freeze-dried.

Wet or damp sheets left within the sleeves did not dry at the same rate as the non-sleeved records. All of the records set out to air-dry did so within 48 hours. Yet a reading taken of a polyester-sleeved sheet after the same period of time showed moisture content of 14.5 percent. We note that paper needs to be removed from its sleeve to dry.

Most metal fasteners showed signs of corrosion in the short period of time in which they had been exposed to water. Staples, paper clips, and other metal fasteners all exhibited rust. Items that were air-dried or vacuum freeze-dried displayed the least amount of corrosion.

Contracting with Commercial Services: A Summary

In summary, we learned a number of lessons in dealing with commercial drying facilities:

- Contact vendors to become acquainted with their services and drying technologies *before* an event strikes.
- Gain an understanding of the particular process available.
- Check references and evaluate carefully.
- Specify the exact treatment desired.
  - Request no alternative treatments be performed without express permission.
  - Make sure terminology is clear.
- Obtain a listing of fees for services and
  - Determine if there is a minimum charge for small jobs or cost breaks for large quantities.
  - Ask if there are additional fees for boxes, labeling or other special services.
  - Ask if there are costs for return shipping.

  One records storage box does not equal .028 cubic meters or one cubic foot. From the vendor's perspective, this box is equivalent to .034 cubic meters. This increase will be reflected in final charges. Each set of two records storage boxes, equivalent to .057 cubic meters, was billed as 2.4 cubic feet, or .0679 cubic meters, by all vendors.
- Be aware that intellectual control and original order may not be preserved unless specified.
  - Indicate how groupings of records are to be re-associated if the fasteners, folders, or adhesive attachments cannot be preserved and retained with records.
  - Specify how label information is to be preserved.
  - Negotiate the quality and design of replacement boxes.

- Recognize that records may be exposed to undesirable conditions, processes, and treatments.
  - Keep in mind that shipping may contribute to records' distortion and length of exposure to moisture.
  - Despite all efforts, records may be lost.

Selecting an Appropriate Drying Method: Conclusions

Preparations for all drying activities involve staff time, whether in direct recovery, or in administering activities associated with an off-site commercial process. For security purposes, records may need to remain on-site or be handled only by staff before being sent for vendor services. If housings no longer maintain adequate structural support, water-saturated records may need to be handled for re-boxing and re-labeling before freezing and shipping.

Air-drying is useful for small numbers of damp materials. It is attractive because records do not need to leave the repository, and it allows for item by item retrieval or inspection for special handling needs – optimal control during manipulation if necessary, provided that expertise is available. Air-drying is best for plastic coated materials.

Air-drying also has drawbacks. It is very labor-intensive. Time is needed to lay out and re-assemble records and remove damp or wet papers from plastic enclosures. Air-drying requires large areas of surface space. While potentially less expensive than commercial drying services, costs for air-drying include supplies such as absorbent and interleaving materials, security charges, and energy expenses for de-humidifiers and fans. Costs associated with staff time carrying out recovery actions in place of regular work cannot be underestimated. Even if routine tasks are not interrupted, staff may be displaced as workspaces are occupied by drying activities.

Though air-dried items are treated in-house, there is still a chance for disruption of original order. The possibility for mold is ever-present, and cockling without restraint during drying results in an increase in volume of dried materials, and potential need for re-boxing or rebinding. Coated papers will irreversibly block without interleaving and extensive handling may exacerbate damage.

Dehumidification-drying is suitable for *damp*, not wet materials. Like air-drying, on-site dehumidification-drying is advantageous from an access and security standpoint, but results in a distorted product with greater corrosion from metal fasteners. Dehumidification-drying may be more suitable than air-drying for large quantities of damp materials. This process also holds promise for drying slightly damp items *in situ*, i.e., without removing them from their housings or locations.

Vacuum freeze-drying is the drying method of choice for large quantities of wet materials. It results in the least amount of distortion, precluding the need to re-house or re-label most materials. Freezing immobilizes water to minimize corrosion from metal fasteners. Soluble media will not move once the document is frozen or during subsequent drying, and coated papers do not stick. Even items enclosed in plastic need not be removed from their original housings or enclosures, minimizing disruption of original order or potential loss. Existing labels are preserved.

While advantages generally outweigh disadvantages, vacuum freeze-drying also has downsides. No access to materials during the frozen state or drying process is available.

Your materials may be included with other records in the drying chamber. While the cost for freeze-drying appears comparable to other processes, materials must be kept frozen, and the logistics of keeping materials frozen during transport is an additional cost factor. This may make freeze-drying small quantities of materials expensive. Increased delamination in cellulose nitrate coated architectural drawings was noted.

Being an informed consumer about the recovery services purchased will help make the best value of limited resources and ultimately yield the most satisfying results from a water-related incident. As a result of our experiences, we have learned how important it is to be as precise as possible at the outset of a project about expectations for a final product. Proprietary processes may offer outstanding final products, but caution is best exercised to ensure that your needs and specifications for what are acceptable and unacceptable methods and materials are assiduously followed. Regardless of technique used, many of the issues raised will be useful in the decision-making process so critical in determining the most appropriate action for a particular group of materials. While the information we accumulated in our review of drying processes has repeatedly proved fruitful, we wish to emphasize that there is no substitute for a building-wide risk assessment and preparedness plan.

The commercial drying industry continues to be responsive to the preservation community, tailoring, improving, and expanding their products and services. We are grateful for their steadfast cooperation in working to minimize loss to cultural property from water-related disasters.

References

Technical data for polyester films is available at http://www.dupontteijinfilms.com. Such materials are slowly permeable to moisture over time. Their rates of water vapor transmission are dependent on film thickness and the environmental conditions to which they are exposed. After 24 hours of immersion, we witnessed moisture inside both shrink-wrap and polyester film. This effect is less likely the result of moisture permeability than a disruption in the integrity of the seal, or a flaw in the film, such as a small hole.

A PowerPoint version of this paper is available online at the United States National Archives and Records Administration Website at http://www.archives.gov/preservation/conferences/lessons_learned.html

List of Suppliers

Hygrolog with LC Display available from Rotronic Instrument Corp., 160 E. Main Street, Huntington, New York 11743, USA, Telephone: 631-427-3898.

Delmhorst™ P-2000 Paper Moisture Meter with 12-inch blade electrode available from Delmhorst Instrument Company, 51 Indian Lane East P.O. Box 68 Towaco, New Jersey 07082, USA, Telephone: 800-222-0638.

The Authors

Hilary A. Kaplan is a senior conservator at the United States National Archives and Records Administration in College Park, Maryland. From 1989 to 2002, she was conservator and preservation services manager at the Georgia Department of Archives and

History. In 1990, she became a professional associate of the American Institute for Conservation (AIC), and has served as secretary of the AIC Board, and advisor for the AIC Archives Project since 2000. Hilary holds degrees in music from Hunter College and The University of Chicago, and received her M.S. and Certificate in Library and Archives Conservation from Columbia University School of Library Service Conservation Education Program. She has taught several workshops on emergency preparedness, response, and recovery on local, regional, and national levels.

Kathleen A. Ludwig is a senior conservator at the United States National Archives and Records Administration in College Park, Maryland. From 1984 to 1997, she was an archives conservator at the Minnesota Historical Society. She is a professional associate of the American Institute for Conservation (AIC), and received her M.S. and Certificate in Library and Archives Conservation from Columbia University School of Library Service Conservation Education Program.

Comparison of Drying Methods: Paper-Based Records

All photos courtesy National Archives and Records Administration except where noted.

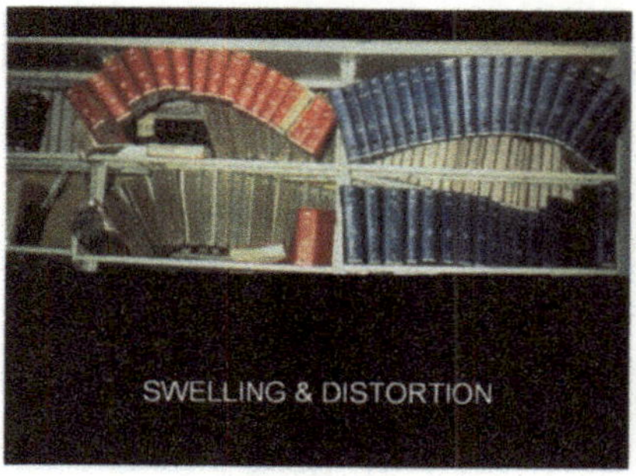

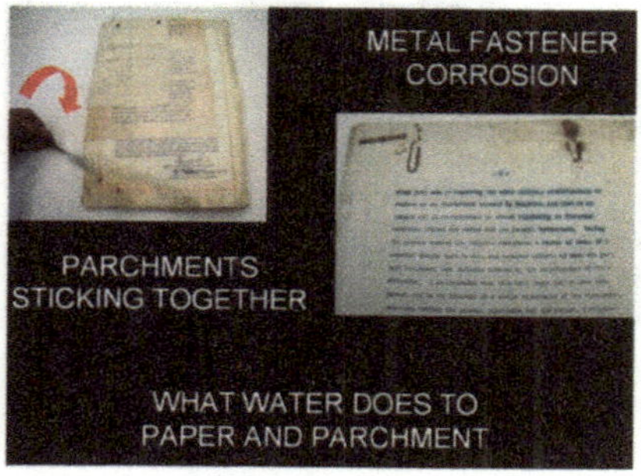

Photo courtesy Randy Silverman.

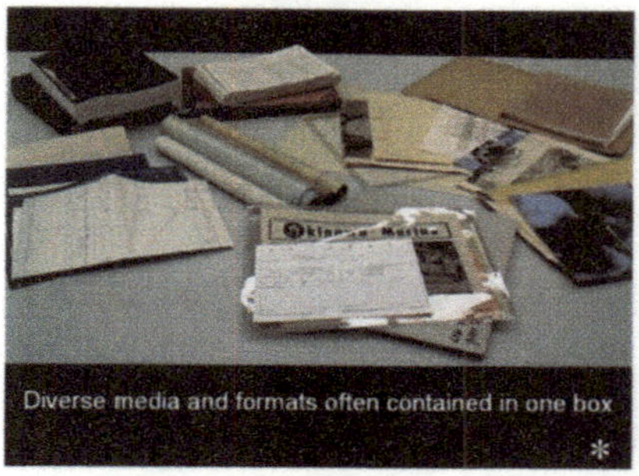

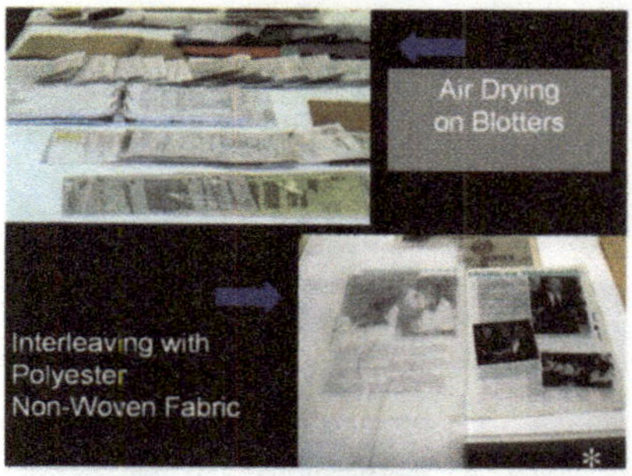

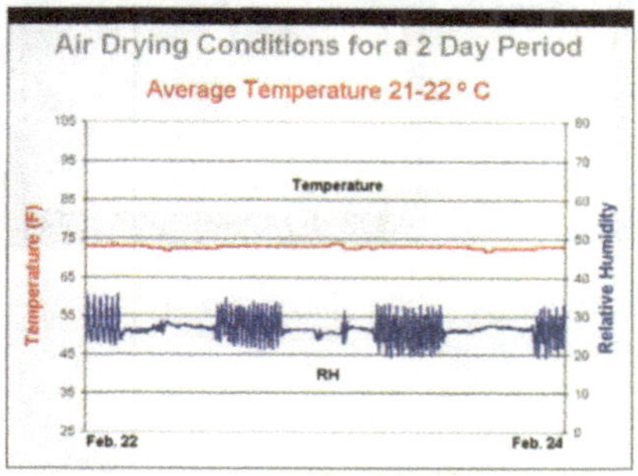

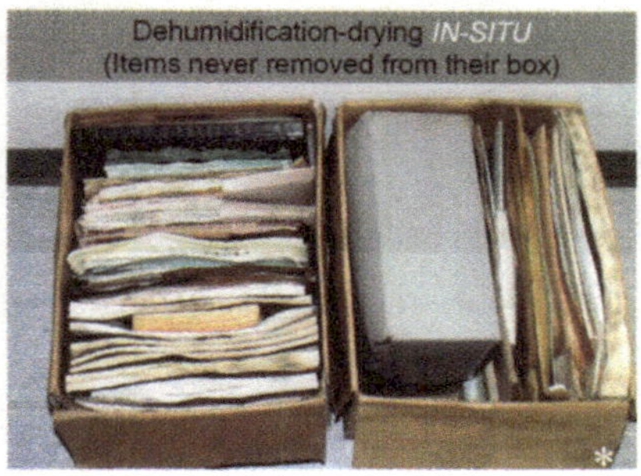

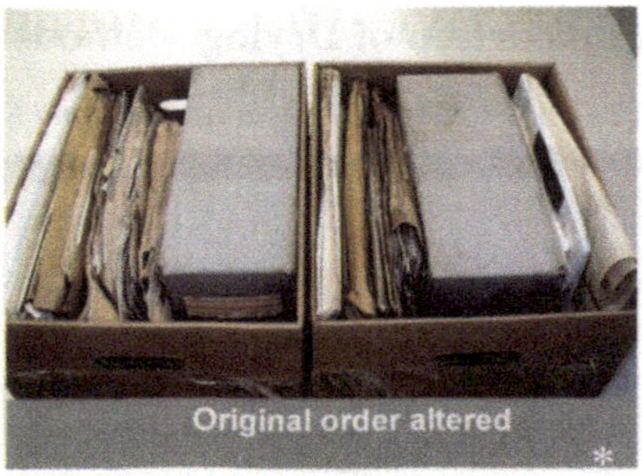

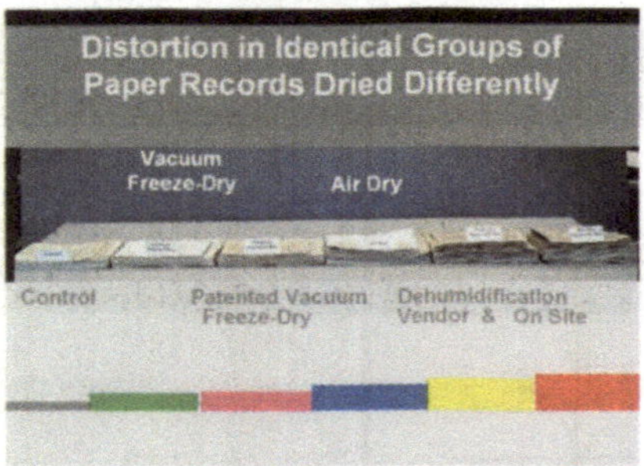

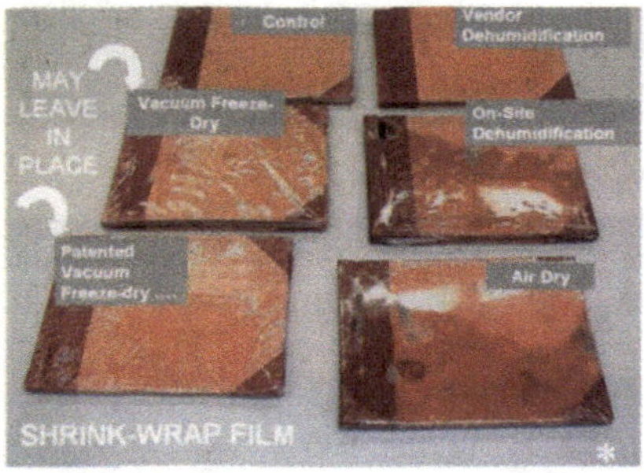

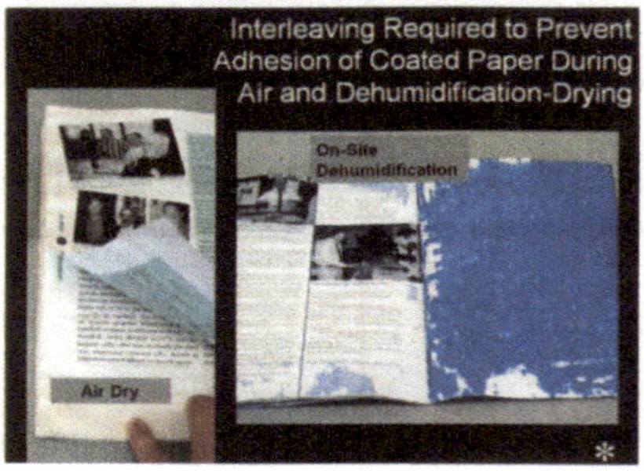

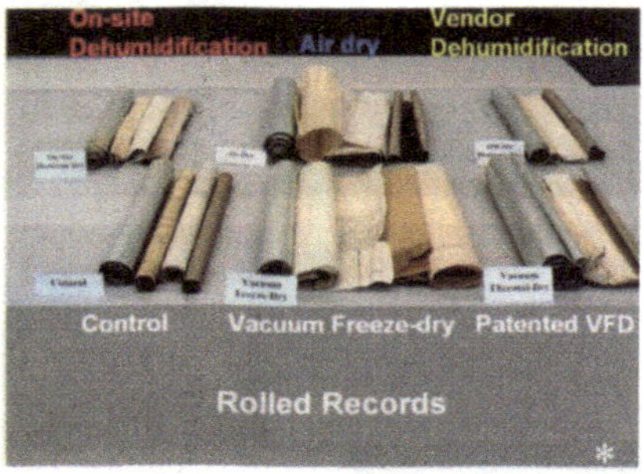

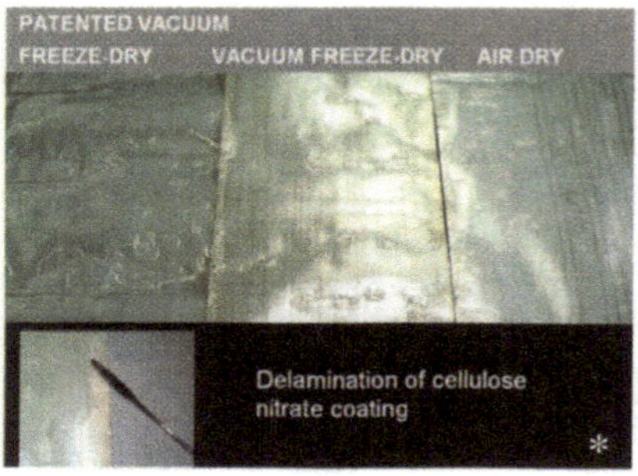

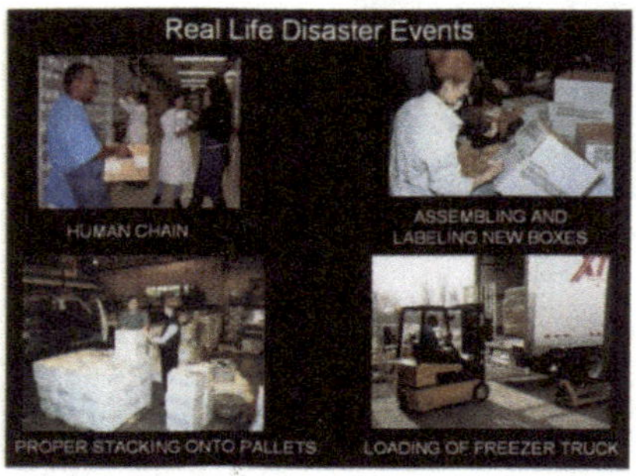

* *Note: These are sample materials NOT actual records materials.*

RECOVERY OF A WATER-SOAKED PHOTOGRAPHIC COLLECTION IN THE NETHERLANDS

Clara C. von Waldthausen[1]

Conservator in Private Practice, Amsterdam, The Netherlands

Abstract

On the night of October 17, 2002, ground water flooded the storage facility and reading room of the Regional Archives of Wijk bij Duurstede, The Netherlands. The ground water reached a height of 1.8 meters (5.9 feet), soaking and soiling the entire collection and sparing only collection materials that were stored on the top boards of the shelving. Firemen, volunteers and archive employees spent three long days bagging, boxing and transporting the collection to a cold vault in the neighbouring town. This paper reviews drying techniques used for the recovery of the water-soaked photographic collections of the Regional Archives and provides an overview of the drying operations and decision-making process surrounding the drying of the wet photographs. The paper also examines air-drying techniques used and discusses the results from tests with freeze-drying, as well as the advantages and disadvantages of each process.

Introduction

On the night of October 17, 2002, ground water flooded the storage facility and reading room of the Regional Archives of Wijk bij Duurstede, The Netherlands. The archives are housed in the basement of the City Hall of Wijk bij Duurstede, and construction was under way for the building of a new wing when the flood occurred. The hired contracting firm used pumps to purify and remove ground water from the construction site. A technical problem with the pumps caused water to gush into the basement of the archives at a high rate, flooding it almost to the ceiling in a matter of hours.

During the three-day salvage operation, most collection materials were packaged and transported to a nearby cold storage vault. The author was asked to consult on drying the photograph collection five days after the flooding. Prior to contact with the author, the regional archivist received advice that slides and glass plate negatives should not be placed into cold storage. One thousand framed 35 mm slides and approximately 115 glass plate negatives had not been frozen and were stored on the main floor of the archive in sealed black trash bags. Plans had to be made immediately to limit physical and biological deterioration of these collection materials. The budget for recovery was extremely limited due to confusion and lack of information surrounding the cause of the flooding. The discussions, research and indecision between insurance companies are still ongoing more than a year after the flood occurred.

A laboratory space was installed in an office building halfway between the Regional Archives and the cold storage vault. The rooms were equipped with shelving, tables and chairs. The space had central heat and large glass windows facing north that could be opened. The National Archives and several municipal archives were extremely accom-

---

1 The author would like to thank Ria van der Eerden-Vonk for support and collaboration on the drying of the photographs of Wijk bij Duurstede. Many thanks also to Douglas Nishimura and Scott Williams for the time they took to discuss recovery issues. Finally, the author would like to acknowledge Hadassa Koning and Marie Beutter for their help during recovery and Lyzanne Gann, Martin Jürgens and Anja Lorenz for their support in reviewing this paper.

modating and donated blotting paper, trays and other materials necessary for air-drying. Volunteers, who had been working on housing and registering the photograph collection prior to the disaster and who had a reputation at the archives for high-quality work, offered their services and were asked to assist the conservators in recovering the photograph collection and re-housing the photographs after drying.

Most volunteers had good hand skills and were extremely precise in their actions. Others were asked to help in other ways that accommodated their personalities and skills. Four volunteers were present at least twice a week during the six-month recovery project; it is largely through their efforts that the recovery of the collection succeeded within the constraints of time and budget.

The Collection

The photograph collection of the Regional Archives Wijk Bij Duurstede is made up of approximately 20,000 photographs, slides, negatives and microfiches. The collection holds approximately 5,500 photographs adhered to secondary supports and 11,000 microfiche. There are approximately 200 contemporary albums made of synthetic, four-ring binders that house polypropylene sleeves with pockets of varying sizes to accommodate the various photograph formats. In addition, there are roughly 35 historic albums distributed throughout the collection. Some of these were cased, sewn albums covered in a synthetic leather material; others were loose-leaf albums, side sewn with paper covers. (Primanis 2000)

The collection was stored in a one-room depository in the basement of the archives. The contemporary albums were stored vertically on shelving. Other photographs were mounted to secondary supports using local application of adhesive or a single hinge of Filmoplast P90™ pressure-sensitive adhesive tape along the top edge of the photograph. These were stored vertically in file cabinets standing in one corner of the storage room. Glass plate negatives were stored in their original boxes and other non-archival storage boxes. The 35mm slides were framed in paper and plastic slide mounts, some of which were glazed, and housed in projection trays that slide into grey plastic storage containers two columns wide and five trays high. The microfiches were housed in paper enclosures and stored in metal drawers in the reading room that had also been flooded completely.

Cold Storage

During the initial salvage, almost all of the photographs and photograph albums were placed into blue plastic crates that had been used as wastepaper baskets by archive employees. The paper collection materials, on the other hand, were bagged and placed into brown corrugated cardboard storage boxes in order to distinguish them from the photograph collection. The filled crates were then transported to the cold storage vault in the neighbouring town. Here, they were stacked onto wooden pallets, wrapped in plastic foil and blast frozen at -30°C (-22°F). After 48 hours they were moved to a warmer storage space held at -20°C (-4°F). The collection remained in this vault until recovery operations were launched, and a calculated number of objects could be removed for drying.

The Conservation Space

The two-room conservation laboratory situated on the second floor of an office building proved to be very accommodating, especially when drying various collections simultaneously. The rooms could be locked, a kitchen and bathroom were next door, and a separate space was created for the consumption of food and drink. The photographs could be divided between rooms and separated according to material and drying method. Another advantage was the additional wall space where shelving could be placed and more photographs could be laid out to dry.

The relative humidity and temperature in the conservation space was regulated by the central heating system and by opening or closing the windows. A hygrograph was placed in the rooms to monitor the relative humidity. Readings were taken in the beginning, in the middle and at the end of the day to establish the peaks and the length of time of high humidity. The humidity averaged 35 percent in the beginning of the day and at the end of the day often more than doubled to a maximum of 75 percent. By the next morning the humidity usually had decreased to 40 percent or 45 percent. It gradually decreased throughout the second-day drying period. On the third day, when the dried photographs were re-housed, the relative humidity decreased to an average of 35 percent. Had this not been the case, dehumidifiers would have been needed to prevent the possibility of mold growth, which would have burdened the restricted budget.

Drying Water-Soaked Slides and Glass Plate Negatives

Not Placed into Cold Storage

On the sixth day after the flooding, the laboratory space was installed, materials were compiled and a group of dedicated volunteers convened. Attention was first given to the materials that had not been placed into cold storage. The danger of mold growth inside the bags was considerable after storage at high relative humidity for five days. After thorough instructions and brief training, the volunteers with good hand skills were chosen to assist in opening the slide mounts and drying the slides. The glass plate negatives were treated solely by a photograph conservator.

Chromogenic Slides

The color slides were first surveyed for condition and mold damage. Because water had entered the plastic storage containers and could not completely drain out of the containers, the slides housed in the lower two rows of projection trays were completely water-soaked. The emulsion of some slides was locally dissolved in the form of small spots equivalent in size to water droplets. The emulsion of the slides in the bottom rows, on the other hand, had completely disintegrated and run off the cellulose acetate film base; puddles of mottled dyes flowed out of the storage boxes upon opening. Mold was not visible on any slide materials.

The slides in the upper trays had dried during the six days of storage. The emulsions were delicate and slightly tacky, but appeared to be stable. These were removed from the slide mounts, rinsed in deionised water for a few seconds to remove eventual impurities from the floodwater, and hung by their sprocket holes on paper clips opened to form an "S"-shape to dry on lines strung through the room. The corresponding slide mounts were hung next to each slide so as not to lose the relevant documentation that was written in permanent ink or pencil. When dry, the slides were remounted into new plastic slide mounts and the inscription on the old mounts was copied onto the new mounts using permanent fine-pointed markers. Trays with wet slides were placed onto blotting paper to air-dry before removal. These were not rinsed but were removed and hung to dry completely as described above. Most of these slides were lost due to local or complete loss of the image. Slides with minor loss, in which the image had been preserved, were dried and re-mounted as described above. The storage containers and slide trays were thoroughly cleaned. Once dry, the slides were replaced in their original order into the trays, which in turn were placed in the newly labelled storage containers, which were then returned to the archives.

Silver Gelatine Glass Plate Negatives

The silver gelatine glass plate negatives, all dating from the twentieth century, were separated in each box by individual blue-lined white notebook paper wrappers. In some cases a descriptive inscription had been written on the notebook paper in blue ink. Local mold growth in the shape of small grey clusters was visually identified on the outside of only two of the more than twelve boxes and was not visually identified on any of the glass plate negatives or the notebook paper. As it was completely saturated with water, the notebook paper did not adhere to the emulsion. It was easily removed from the negatives, although minor delamination of the emulsion along the edges of the negative was visible in three instances. The main damage to the glass plate negatives was caused by the migration of the ink into the gelatine emulsion, which resulted in a reversed blue inscription in the emulsion. This damage only occurred where the ink was in direct contact with the emulsion. A second form of damage was visible on the negative emulsions that were coated with clear varnish. The varnish on these negatives had cracked, flaked and partially or completely delaminated from the surface.

The glass plate negatives were removed from their boxes, and the notebook paper was carefully separated from them. The glass plate negatives were dried flat, emulsion side up, on blotting paper. Retouching dyes or pigments were not visible on either recto or verso of any of the glass plate negatives. The emulsions of varnished negatives appeared more stable, and they were rinsed in deionised water to remove the loose, scattered varnish fragments, and then dried as described above. Once dry, each glass plate negative was housed in a four-flap envelope (PAT).[2] The inscriptions and registration numbers were transferred onto the four-flap envelope prior to housing, using a soft lead pencil. The negatives were stored in glass plate negative boxes made out of corrugated cardboard and returned to the archives. The original boxes for the glass plate negatives were cleaned, dried and stored in larger separate boxes.

Drying Methods for Frozen Photographic Materials

For drying the frozen photographs, two methods were explored: air-drying and freeze-drying. Literature research shows a preference for air-drying photographs. Since the budget was limited and working with volunteers appeared viable, a pilot project was launched to determine the stability of the photographs and explore air-drying procedures. The same literature also describes freeze-drying procedures, but cautions against possible visual changes in the surface of the photograph after treatment (Norris 1998 and Lavédrine 2003). Since images depicting these surface changes are rare, testing was performed on water-soaked photographs in the collection that had a lower priority due to historical value or content, with the aim of examining the effects that freeze-drying techniques available in The Netherlands would have on the photographs.

2 The Photographic Activity Test (ISO 18916) tests materials that come into contact with photographic materials for chemical interaction with the image silver and the gelatine emulsion.

Logistics for Air-drying

The photographs were removed from cold storage a day prior to drying and were thawed at approximately 15-18°C (59-64°F). The average thawing time of a crate of photographic materials measuring approximately 50 x 25 cm (roughly 20 x 10 inches) was between 17 and 24 hours. Thawing time depended on the mass and density of the material and on the amount of water present in and surrounding the material. Contemporary albums could be thawed in a matter of hours, while a crate of large format photographs hinged to museum board could take as long as 24 to 30 hours before the core had thawed.

Careful planning regarding the amount and type of material that was removed from cold storage and allowed to thaw proved crucial to the project. This was also dependant upon the number of workers present to dry the photographs and on the amount of available space.

Air-drying

The pilot project revealed that the binders or emulsions of almost all thawed color and monochrome photographs (except Polaroid™ peel-apart. See Figure 1) were stable enough to allow immersion in a bath of cold, clean deionised water for about 5 to 20 minutes. Soiled photographs were first rinsed in baths of tap water. Deionised water was chosen for the final rinsing baths because of its aggressive nature and affinity to bond with residual impurities in the photograph due to the flooding. However, discussion ensued concerning the influence of deionised water on the chemistry of the photograph. After communication with conservation scientists, it was decided to pour the cold, deionised water into the baths while holding a clean, un-gloved hand under the stream.[3] In this way the water would bond with the salts on the skin, and its reactivity would be decreased.

Rinsing was performed using two trays of deionised water in which the prints were consecutively immersed. The baths were regularly agitated and cleaned at the first signs of contamination in the form of fibers, discoloration or sediment. On occasion, the emulsion was lightly stroked, while under water, with a clean bare hand to reduce surface grime. Care was taken to interleave photographs with ink inscriptions so that the inks would not migrate to the emulsion of the underlying photograph. Photographs with ink stamps were rinsed only briefly to hinder the ink from the stamp from migrating through the photograph paper to the emulsion.

After rinsing, excess water was allowed to drip off the photograph, and it was placed emulsion side up on blotting paper to dry. After the water droplets had evaporated from the surface, fiber-based photographs were turned emulsion side down in order to reduce curling. Occasionally, a clean piece of blotting paper was placed on the drying prints to function as a slight weight for the same reason. Photographs that were adhered to contemporary museum board were removed from their soiled supports and, when possible, pressure-sensitive adhesive tapes were removed from the verso of the photographs by a photograph conservator. Inscriptions on the secondary supports were cut out and kept with the photographs, and the order of the photographs in the collection was retained.

There were very few photographs mounted to original early 19th- or 20th-century supports. Tests performed during the pilot project demonstrated that the adhesives used to

---

3 Communication with Doug Nishimura from the Image Permanence Institute, Rochester, N.Y., USA, and with Scott Williams, Canadian Conservation Institute, Ottawa, Canada.

attach the photograph and, in some cases, the facing paper, to the original cardboard support were weakened and sometimes dissolved as a result of prolonged exposure to water during the flood. The facing paper and photograph of these objects detached from the cardboard support during drying. For this reason, these photographs were dried under weight between blotting paper and non-woven polyester tissue. Blotters were changed regularly. The drying time reached up to four weeks depending on the thickness of the secondary support.

Air-drying Negatives and Microfiches on Flexible Supports

Negatives and microfiches on film supports were first freed from envelopes or housings. Plastic housings were cut open along their seams using scalpel blades and the plastic was pulled back from the film so that the negative or microfiche could be freed without friction and risk of delamination of the emulsion. These materials were also rinsed in the baths described above and hung to dry using clothespins or open paper clips depending on the format and type of material.

Air-drying Photograph Albums

Photographs in the contemporary albums were removed from the plastic album leaves in the same manner as the negatives and microfiches. Inscriptions that were present in the album pockets were dried with the photographs, and the order of the photographs in the album was maintained. After air-drying, the photographs were housed in new polyethylene sleeves. Tests were performed to see if curled fiber-based photographs could be carefully inserted into the polyethylene sleeves without causing damage to the gelatine emulsion. It was anticipated that the photographs would be flattened solely through the pressure and weight of the album pages. Examination of the photographs after three months confirmed that fiber-based prints had indeed flattened and the emulsion was not damaged. The slight curl in resin coated (RC) prints was also reduced.

The adhesives used for the album bindings were often partially or completely dissolved. Some album covers were very swollen and partially dissolved (gummy). Another major form of damage was the migration of dyes from black album pages to the photographs. Ink inscriptions also bled into adjacent photograph emulsions. The photographs in all albums were mounted with corners, slits or a water-soluble adhesive. It was decided to have the photographs removed from the albums by a photograph conservator and to dry them as described above. The albums were then dried by interleaving the pages with blotter and non-woven polyester tissue. In a second phase, conservation treatment might be performed to stabilize the albums and reinsert the photographs.

Freeze-drying

Freeze-drying was performed at two venues in The Netherlands. Although the apparatus varied according to venue, the mechanisms of freeze-drying are similar. Freeze-drying allows wet photographs and other materials to be dried while in a frozen state. Frozen objects are placed in the freeze-drying chamber and a vacuum is established that ensures that the chamber is devoid of air and operating at a very low absolute pressure (less than 5 mbar), which is necessary to keep the materials frozen. When the proper pressure is reached the moisture in the frozen materials begins to sublimate, i.e., the ice is directly converted to vapour.

The emitted vapour is reduced back to ice on a condensing surface outside the chamber, which is typically cooled to between -50°C and -60°C (-58°F and -76°F). This mechanism protects the high-grade vacuum pump from potentially damaging water, oils and fats that might be part of the composition of the object being dried. Finally, a controlled gradual temperature rise completes the process by driving off more vapour and promoting the release of bound water from the product. It is interesting to note that 90 percent of the drying is achieved at temperatures below freezing.[4]

Evaluation

Cold Storage

Considering the amount of damage that occurred to the slide collection because it had been wet for such a long time, it would have been better to place the collection into cold storage with the other collection materials. Examination of the frozen negatives and microfiche demonstrates that these materials, similar in composition to slides, could be safely frozen without any visual adverse effects.

Glass plate negatives that were *not* frozen were freed from their housing and paper wrappers and air-dried without visually compromising the stability of the emulsion. However, another 250 gelatine silver glass plate negatives were later discovered frozen in the cold storage vault. These negatives were packed in stacks of thirty or more plates in plastic bags without interleaving, housing or boxes. It is interesting to note that none of these negatives were physically damaged during the salvage, freezing, thawing and drying operation. Emulsions appeared to be more stable than those of the negatives that had *not* been frozen, and, unlike the *not*-frozen plates, these negatives could be rinsed in water and horizontally air-dried on shelving. Some negatives were wrapped in paper with an ink inscription, and just as with the *not*-frozen glass plate negatives, the ink had migrated into the emulsion. Ink migration may have taken place while the collection was immersed in water or during thawing.

Interleaving

Most publications specify that photographs must be interleaved before freezing to prevent their sticking together. However, because of time and logistical constraints, none of the photographs were interleaved prior to freezing. For this reason, the author was very apprehensive of the state of the photographs after thawing and anticipated that most gelatine photographs would be found adhered to each other. However, only photographs that were partially dry showed a tendency to adhere to adjacent materials. In a few instances, for example, the emulsions of the outermost photographs were in contact with the blue crates. These images had partially dried during thawing before they could be removed from the crate for treatment. The emulsion was extremely tacky and adhered locally to the sides of the crates. The photographs could be separated and removed from the crate without damage to the emulsion using a fine water mister.

Volunteers

The volunteers were an indispensable asset to the salvage process. They provided assistance in handling and rinsing photographs, and they collected and housed the photographs after drying. They were also able to re-establish the lost order and sequencing,

---

4 Written communication with John van Dorsten, Managing Director, Preservation Technologies, The Netherlands.

because they were familiar with the photographs and also with the buildings and citizens of surrounding towns that were depicted in the photographs. Due to the limited budget, the project could not have been finished in the same amount of time without the assistance of volunteers. Consideration must always be given to the background, loyalty and honesty of the volunteer and his or her affiliation with the archive prior to any salvage operation. Security is an important aspect and should be dealt with on an institutional level.

It is important to emphasize that volunteers must always be carefully evaluated and given projects that complement their abilities. In no way should a volunteer be confronted with tasks that may jeopardize their health, the health of others or the condition of the photographs. Volunteers with lesser hand skills, for example, should not be given a scalpel or have to deal with separating any fragile images from enclosures. However, they can be very helpful in preparing fresh water trays, placing the photographs on shelves, or turning over fiber-based photographs over to hinder curling. It is crucial that all members feel they are contributing and performing important tasks that together will save the collection.

Another important consideration when discussing the role of volunteers is the length of the project. The drying of the photograph collection lasted seven months, and it was apparent that interest in the project began to decline after three months. The hand skills, familiarity and the general experience gained by volunteers that assist on a regular basis are crucial for the success of the project.

Air-drying

The main advantage to air-drying the collection is that, depending on the stability and the photographic process, the photographs can be rinsed in clean, deionised water. Rinsing can help reduce the grime, impurities and salts on and in the swollen photograph emulsion and thereby reduces the chance of image fading or discoloration.[5] However, before rinsing, the stability of the photograph must always be evaluated on a single-item basis. Experience demonstrated that the photographic emulsions were too fragile to withstand thawing, refreezing and re-thawing.[6] Therefore it is crucial that the logistics surrounding air-drying are planned carefully prior to launching a recovery project.

A second advantage is that each photograph can be assessed and that special treatment can be given to a particular photograph or collection if necessary. For example pressure-sensitive adhesive films were removed from the verso of photographs (by a photograph conservator) prior to air-drying. Also, photographs were removed from their soiled, contemporary mounts, reducing the drying time and future treatment during a second conservation phase.[7]

No visual indication of gloss reduction could be observed after air-drying the photographs. The surface gloss after air-drying was even in all cases, except when glassine in-

---

5 Salvage operations, time and a lack of clean space and water may not permit rinsing prior to placing the wet photographs into cold storage.

6 Refreezing occurred accidentally once during the drying operation due to miscommunication as to which day treatment would occur. Most of the photographs that were refrozen and thawed again suffered from partial delamination of the emulsion onto adjacent materials. In some cases, parts of the emulsion appeared to have dissolved.

7 It is interesting to note that the removal of the Filmoplast™ P90 from the verso of Resin Coated prints varied greatly depending on the photographic paper. The Filmoplast™ P90 was easily lifted from Kodak papers and was sometimes extremely difficult to remove from papers that were not stamped with the manufacturer's name.

Process	Size of collection	Cold vault	Percent recovered[8]	Damage
Silver gelatine glass plate negatives	± 375	50% in cold vault	± 99.4%	- Local delamination of the emulsion. - Local migration of inks into the emulsion - Local or complete delamination of varnish
Slides 35 mm	± 1000	No	± 50%	Partial or complete loss of emulsion
Negatives on flexible supports (cellulose acetate rolls: 35mm & 120 mm)	±100	Yes	100%	- In ± 70% of the cases anti-halo dyes from negatives migrated into the paper enclosures. Dye was not visible in the negative - did not discolor the support or emulsion.
Silver dye bleach (Cibachrome)	± 10	Yes	± 99%[9]	Partial migration of image dyes into adjacent mat board
Silver dye diffusion (Polaroid™ peel-apart)	± 45	Yes	± 1%	Non reversible swelling and dissolving of emulsion
Silver dye diffusion (Polaroid ™ SX-70 type)	± 70	Yes	At least 14%	Local cracking of the image forming substance
Chromogenic and silver gelatine prints[10]	± 7000 (5500 on museum board)	Yes	± 98.5%	- Local ink migration into image & binder - Curling of fiber -based photographs - Partial loss of emulsion
Silver Gelatine, Chromogenic and Polaroid™ photographs in Contemporary albums	± 200	Yes	± 99%	- Peel-apart Polaroid™ prints were lost - Metal parts of albums rusted - Polypropylene album pages were soiled
Historic albums holding Silver Gelatine photographs	± 35	Yes	± 60%	- All water-soluble adhesives used in the construction of the album dissolved - Glassine interleaving caused local non- reversible deformation of photograph emulsion - Starch impregnated cloth album covers dissolved
Microfiches	± 11,000	Yes	± 98%	- Formation of small bubbles between emulsion and support

Table 1. A list of photographic process and the main types of damage observed with air-drying

terleaving from photograph albums had been in contact with the wet photograph emulsion. In this case, a slight change of surface texture in the photograph could be noticed corresponding to creases in the glassine interleaving (formed by water absorption). The change in surface gloss could not be reduced by immersing the print for up to twenty minutes in a cold bath of deionised water.[8,9,10]

---

8 Photographs were included in "percent recovered" if the visual information in the image was maintained after salvage.

9 It is difficult to assess the percentage of loss of image dyes. The photograph and the component dyes were visually in good condition. Calculations could not be made as to the amount of dye migration that had occurred since data of dye density prior to flooding is not available.

10 The percentage of photographs that were damaged by local migration of inks from adjacent text into the emulsion was very high (±60 percent). Only one blue crate contained chromogenic and silver gelatine photographs that exhibited partial loss of emulsion. This was due to the fact that this crate had accidentally been thawed and refrozen.

Air-drying of the historical albums was the most time consuming and compromising. It was found that the blotting paper had to be changed at least once every day to ensure drying, and that flattening of the album pages and the photographs would be extremely difficult without removing the photographs from the albums. The texture of the non-woven polyester interleaving was transferred onto the emulsion during drying so that the use of pressure, at least initially, was not an option. A photograph conservator would be needed daily to perform drying, because evaluation of the drying of the photographs and the album and the control needed for drying were essential. This was not an option. However, the photographs that were removed from the albums for air-drying, can be reinserted into the albums after the necessary conservation treatment on these is performed.

The main forms of damage observed on photographs while air-drying are listed in Table 1. Whether these forms of damage occurred during the initial flooding or thawing is difficult to establish.[11] Since some of the same forms of damage are also visible in freeze-dried photographs, it can be assumed that at least some of the damage listed in Table 1 was caused during the initial flooding and immersion.

Effects of Freeze-drying

Freeze-drying has the advantage that large amounts of collection materials can be dried without continuous supervision of a photograph conservator and without the need for a separate drying space. The test materials that were freeze-dried were visually examined under normal and raking light and under magnification using a stereomicroscope at 6, 10, 20, and 40x magnification. As the literature indicates, photographs that were freeze-dried showed various types of visual change in the surface of the emulsion.

Firstly, local change in the surface gloss was observed. The areas of change were locally distributed throughout the image of the photograph and were glossier than the original gloss (See Figures 2 & 3). Secondly, a local micro cracking (See Figure 4-7) and a local texture change similar to an ice crystal formation on a windowpane were discerned. These areas of change exhibited a decrease in gloss and the texture could not be reduced during local treatment using a cotton swab moistened with a mixture of ethanol and deionised water. White powdery crystals soluble in deionised water were also observed on some photographs and may be caused by impurities present in the ground water (See Figure 8). Spot testing confirms large concentrations of surface grime left on the photograph surface after freeze-drying. The risk of enclosing impurities in the swollen emulsion during freeze-drying seems very large and the possibility to reduce these impurities after freeze-drying seems very slight.

Forms of damage found both on air-dried and freeze-dried photographs were local cracking of Polaroid™ SX-70 prints and ink migration from materials that were in contact with the photograph emulsion. Interestingly, the emulsion of Polaroid™ peel-apart photographs was not lost after freeze-drying as it was by air-drying. However, as can be seen in Figure 9, image dyes migrated into adjacent materials. Table 2 lists the main types of damage found on the photograph surface after freeze-drying.[12]

11 The materials not frozen were damaged due to prolonged contact with water.
12 Other processes were not included in the freeze-drying tests.

Effects of Drying on Photographs

All photos courtesy Clara von Waldthausen.

Figure 1. Polaroid ™ peel-apart after air-drying. Normal light.

Figure 2. Photograph mounted to secondary support. Secondary support is soiled. Normal light.

Figure 3. Gloss differences in the surface are visible under raking light. See Figure 2.

Figure 4. Dye migration is locally visible throughout the image. Normal light.

Figure 5. Detail of figure 4. Local micro cracking is visible throughout the image (within the black border). Ink migration from the verso to the recto is visible. Raking light.

Figure 6. Freeze-dried photograph. Normal light.

Figure 7. Detail of Figure 6 exhibiting a surface change after freeze-drying, which is similar in structure to ice crystals.

Figure 8. Detail depicting local crystallization in upper left corner of image. Normal light.

Figure 9. Polaroid ™ peel-apart after freeze-drying. Dye migration is visible on the secondary support in contact with the image (top). Normal light.

Process	Damage
Silver dye diffusion (Polaroid™ SX-70 type)	- Local cracking and crystal formation on the surface of the photograph
Chromogenic and silver gelatine prints	- Local ink migration into image and binder - Surface grime deposits - Crystallization on the emulsion - Change in texture and surface gloss
Silver Gelatine, Chromogenic and Polaroid™ photographs in contemporary albums	- Some ink migration into image & binder - Change in texture and surface gloss - Album and polypropylene album pages were soiled

Table 2. Main types of damage observed after freeze-drying

Conclusion

The success of recovery projects depends largely upon the source of the water, the immersion time, the stability of the photographic materials and the decision-making surrounding salvage and recovery efforts. Differences in the physical and chemical composition and the discrepancy in the stability of the various photographic materials make the presence of a photograph conservator essential during recovery operations. The logistics and space must also be considered. Careful planning is needed to calculate the amount of material thawed and the number of workers and space needed for recovery.

The possibility of using loyal volunteers may be reviewed. The health, ability, hand skills, and security for the volunteer and the objects must be examined and carefully considered. Attention must also be paid to ensure thorough training and supervision of the activities performed by non-experts. Working with volunteers during the recovery of the flooded collection at Wijk bij Duurstede proved successful in that the photographs were safely dried within a relatively short amount of time and within the financial budget that was available.

The wet photographic emulsions did not adhere to one another after thawing. The photographs were easily separated and the emulsions were stable enough, even after three days prior to being frozen, to allow rinsing in cold-water baths. Refreezing thawed photographs proved detrimental and emulsions were delaminated and partially dissolved. If it is not possible to clean and interleave photographic materials before freezing, it is important to thoroughly wet all photographs and mounts to prevent their adhesion.

Testing by means of freeze-drying showed alterations in the image gloss and surface texture. The surface of the emulsion exhibited crystallization, soil and grime. These results probably stemmed from impurities in the groundwater that were not rinsed off prior to freezing. Primarily for these reasons, decisions were made to air-dry the photographs in the collection. Finally, additional research is needed to gain a clearer view of the effects of freeze-drying on the emulsion and compositions of photographs.

The main form of damage to the photograph collection was the migration of inks into the photographic emulsion. The source of these inks was felt-tipped and ball-point pens, permanent markers, ink stamps, typewriter inks and others. The damage could have been prevented by using pencil or by interleaving photographs with cardboard, paper or plastic onto which no inscriptions or labels were placed in direct contact with the photograph emulsion. Other damage occurred due to misleading conceptions surrounding the freezing of 35 mm slides. The accidentally frozen silver gelatine glass plate negatives were not physically damaged during freezing and the emulsion appeared to be more stable than those of the silver gelatine glass plate negatives that were not frozen. Rinsing the photographs in deionised water reduced surface grime and soil. However, more investigation is necessary to examine the effects of deionised water on the stability of photographs and also to determine the immersion time needed for proper rinsing.

References

Hendriks, Klaus. 2002. *A Life Remembered.* Denmark: L.P. Nielsen Bogtryk. 99-104.

Jovic, Kara, assoc. ed. *Water damage restoration using freeze-drying equipment, techniques.* Brochure from Freeze dry Specialists, Inc. http://www.freezedry.com/r_Luther.htm.

Lavédrine, Bertrand. 2003. *A guide to the preventive conservation of photograph collections.* Los Angeles: Getty Conservation Institute. 128-132.

Hess Norris, Debbie. 1996. Air-drying of water-soaked photographic materials: Observations and recommendations. In Bridgeland, Janet (ed)., *ICOM Committee for Conservation 11th Triennial meeting, Edinburgh, Scotland, 1–6 September 1996. Preprints.* London: James and James Ltd. 601-608.

Primanis, Olivia. 1999. Interim report on the HRHRC photograph album survey. 1. Nineteenth-century photograph albums: Structures, condition, and treatments. In Zachary, Shannon (compiler), *Conservation of Scrapbooks and Albums. Post prints of the Book and Paper Group / Photographic Materials Group Joint Session at the 27th Annual Meeting of the American Institute for Conservation of Historic and Artistic Works, June 11, 1999, St. Louis, Missouri.* Washington, D.C.: AIC. 69-79.

Walsh, Betty. 1997. Salvage operations for water-damaged archival collections: A second glance. *WAAC Newsletter* 19(2):12-23.

The Author

Clara von Waldthausen is a photographic conservator in private practice. She received an undergraduate degree from DePauw University in Indiana and a degree in the conservation of photographic materials from The Netherlands Institute for Cultural Heritage in 2000. She is an active member of the American Institute of Conservation, the International Council of Museums – Conservation Committee working group on photography conservation and the national association for conservators (VAR) in The Netherlands. In her private practice, she treats photographs and consults about conservation of photographs, as well as teaching and organizing workshops nationally and internationally.

AUDIOVISUAL AND MODERN INFORMATION MEDIA: DISASTER MITIGATION & RECOVERY

Léon-Bavi Vilmont

Research Engineer, Audiovisual Materials and New Media, Centre de Recherches sur la Conservation des Documents Graphiques (CRCDG), Paris, France

Abstract

Water damage is by far the most frequently encountered disaster that affects library collections, but water is often accompanied by mud or other debris. This causes physical problems with media and prevents the information from being read correctly. Audiovisual and modern information media collections can be categorized in ways that will facilitate further preservation procedures. The author reviews practical aspects of disaster mitigation and recovery, taking into account specific and diverse media collections, with an emphasis on magnetic media.

Introduction

Disasters are generally dramatic events causing damage to collections and buildings and disruption to professional activities. Audiovisual and modern information media can be seriously endangered, particularly when exposed to the intense heat of fire. In this case, they can not be recovered, as they are either burnt or completely deformed. Water damage is by far the most frequently encountered disaster that affects library collections, but flooding may bring with it mud or other debris. This causes physical problems with the media and prevents the information from being read correctly. Therefore, recovery of carriers may include dealing with issues such as deterioration. As a matter of interest, disasters due to technological failure may occur if nothing is done to anticipate it by making certain there are redundant backups of data. Massive hardware failures are a specific case. This paper will not extend to the issue of logical data recovery. Dealing with audiovisual and modern information media is not easy due to the diversity of the materials and their specific issues. Recovery of magnetic tapes is emphasized, because of its "spooled" aspect.

Categorizing Media

What do we mean exactly by audiovisual (AV) media and modern information media? Are they all discs or all tapes? Or perhaps magnetic media and optical media? Which one is analogue and which one is digital? Depending on the chosen criteria, there are diverse ways of classifying media. The classification chosen in this paper is based on the recording and/or playback technology of the media, which allows media to be put into three categories by carrier: *mechanical*, *magnetic* and *optical*.

The main feature of the documents supported by these carriers is that they are machine-readable and therefore require specific and dedicated playback equipment. The carriers should not only match and correspond perfectly with the equipment from a physical or mechanical point of view, but they also have to be readable. This means, for instance, that magnetic media and optical media should through the years retain respectively their magnetic and optical properties.

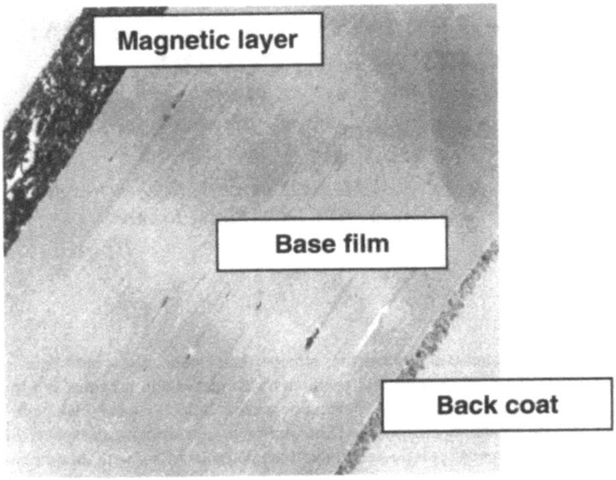

Agfa U-matic ¾ Video Tape Cross Section (TEM).
Photo courtesy CRCDG.

Mechanical Group

"Mechanical" carriers cover a wide range of materials from early sound recordings, such as cylinders made of wax or celluloid, Berliner's vulcanite discs, shellac discs, acetate discs to vinyl records. Shellac discs contain a large quantity of fillers that render them rather heavy and susceptible to breakage if they are accidentally shocked or dropped. Acetate discs consist of an aluminium base covered with a thin lacquer of cellulose-acetate or nitro-cellulose plasticized with castor oil. Nowadays, even if vinyl records have vanished almost totally from the consumer's shelves, they are still part of numerous library collections.

Magnetic Group

The magnetic media group includes tapes (reel-to-reel tapes or open-reel tapes), audio and video cassettes, and computer tapes and data discs. Tape formats are numerous and vary by size, width, thickness, composition, etc. As shown below, a typical cross section of a tape consists of three layers. The large middle part is the base film, also called a substrate. It is coated with a magnetic, recording layer (left) and an optional back coat on the opposite side.

Paper, then polymer, was used for the base film material for earlier tapes. The polymer first used was cellulose acetate, then PVC (polyvinylchloride), and finally a polyester called polyethylene-terephthalate or Mylar™. More recently, alternative polymers have been tried in order to improve the mechanical properties.

The recording layer composition is made of a magnetic coating of particle media, which is used in the majority of magnetic carriers. In this type of coating, the magnetic particles – metal oxides or pure metal particles – are mixed with a polymeric binder, lubricants and other additives. The typical damage encountered is the breakdown of the binder, which leads to "sticky shed" syndrome and head clogging. Gummy deposits are left on tape path guides and heads after the tape has been played. The binder's polymeric material is quite vulnerable to water hydrolysis.

A more recent type of recording layer is described as Metal Evaporated (abbreviated ME). The recording layer is the result of the controlled deposition of vapour evaporated from the metal target. In this case, water can be also harmful and leads to corrosion of the metal layer, which then becomes unreadable.

All the information and data stored on magnetic media are susceptible to erasure if a stray magnetic field is higher than a specific limit value determined for each magnetic media. According to a recommended practice proposed by the Society of Motion Picture and Television Engineers (SMPTE), the stray magnetic field at any point on the surface of the tape shall not exceed a field strength of 800 A/m (10 oersteds).

Optical Group

Following the earlier Laser discs, videodiscs and other proprietary digital optical discs, *compact discs* (CDs) and now *digital versatile discs* (DVDs) are by far the most significant optical media used in libraries. Compact discs include both moulded CDs, such as CD-ROMs or CD-audio, and recordable CDs such as CD-R, which is recordable one time, and the CD-RW that is re-writable. The laser accessing the data must be able to pass through the polymer substrate that is typically polycarbonate. The laser reflects or scatters off the data bits on the information layer. For compact discs (CD-ROMs and audio CD), this information is made up of a spiral of pits moulded on the polymer surface. For a CD-R, it results from "burning" the dye layer.

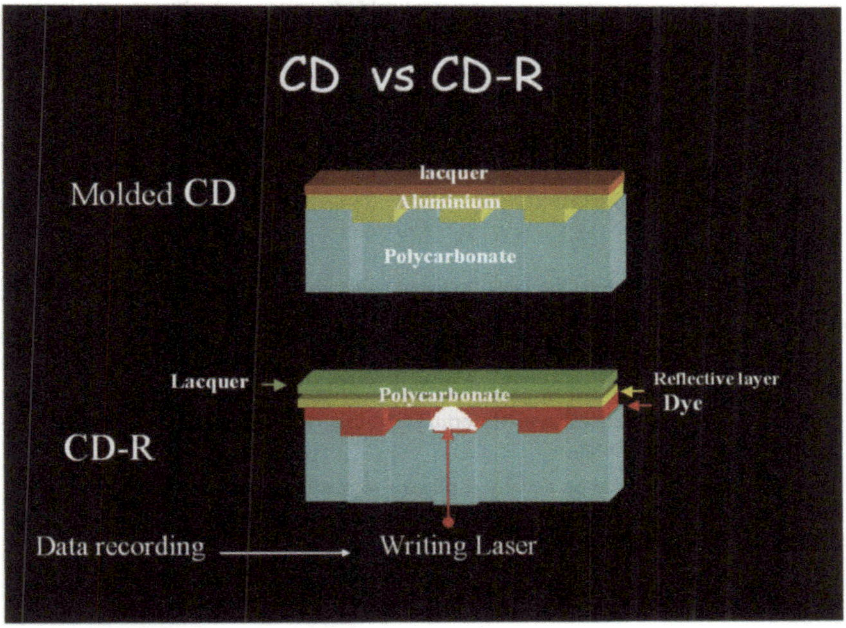

Photo courtesy CRCDG.

Typical Damage

Some types of media are susceptible to typical types of damage, which will render them illegible. Thus,

- Cylinders and shellac discs may be broken by shock.
- Lacquer may flake off from the acetate discs.
- Vinyl records are susceptible to distortion and warping when exposed to heat.

All types are easily scratched and are dramatically endangered when exposed to fire and flood.

Information stored on magnetic media may be erased by exposure to stray magnetic fields. For optical discs, loss of layer integrity and changes in reflectivity render the information unreadable. The metal reflecting layer is considered to be the most susceptible of the components, largely because of the vulnerability of the metal to oxidation. Over time, oxidation leads to corrosion and the data becomes unreadable.

The upper layers of a CD – lacquer, reflective layer – are very thin (several microns) in comparison to the overall thickness of the CD (1.2 mm). Consequently, simple scratches on the label surface would severely affect the information layer and therefore the data becomes unreadable.

Types of Disaster

Broadly speaking, three categories of disaster could affect any institution or organization:

1. Natural disasters – dramatic events, such as

- hurricanes that periodically threaten coastal regions,
- terrible earthquakes,
- devastating heavy rains and floods, and
- fire (maybe the worst).

2. Accidental disasters

Among accidental disasters, the most frequently encountered are caused by breakdowns in the physical plant, such as burst pipes or a broken water main.

3. Human-related disasters

Human-related disasters can be caused by inappropriate or careless handling; they can also result from bad management. Unfortunately, this type of disaster may also include military and terrorist attacks.

Environmental factors can be equally damaging to media carriers and corrupt the information on them. Most common among them are debris and airborne contaminants such as dust and high humidity leading to mold growth.

Disaster Response

When an emergency occurs, the damage to the materials must be assessed rapidly and immediate steps to stabilize their condition taken to prevent further damage. In 1996, the National Archives and Records Administration in the United States issued guidelines useful for mitigation and recovery from disasters, which cover the following steps:

- assessing the situation
- organizing and prioritizing efforts

- establishing a command post
- eliminating hazards
- controlling the environment
- dealing with the media
- obtaining emergency supplies
- providing security
- providing human comforts
- training for salvage techniques on-site

It may also be useful to consult with contractors that provide disaster recovery services, if the assessment indicates the need for their expertise.

Assessing the Situation

After a disaster, the sooner staff get to the collections to initiate salvage, the better the chance of recovery. But be aware that disaster areas are not secure and may contain hidden hazards. Safety and security precautions must already be in place when staff enters the disaster site.

The types of media present will determine the appropriate response, but the type and extent of damage are also important considerations. If water-damaged collections include mixed media, staff should give priority to paper-based, parchment, or leather materials, which are more susceptible to fungal attack and to decay. AV collections, with the exception of the early sound media, are relatively less time susceptible to water action.

Recovery Team

It is important to assemble the recovery team designated in the disaster preparedness manual as soon as possible and follow the chain of command with appropriate flexibility. Do not hesitate to assign someone who can take over if an employee becomes unable to his or her job. If there is no disaster preparedness plan, rapidly set up a team with the staff members present on the site.

Clearly identify one person who has both the responsibility and the authority to act immediately or assign a backup person if this person is not available.

Assign one person to make an inventory of the salvage effort. Note what was completely destroyed and what is being removed for salvage – types of document, normal location, names, etc. This person will catalogue and label or mark removed boxes or packed crates.

Train any volunteers on site.

Recovery Area

As a disaster site can be wet, humid, dusty, and hazardous, salvage must be undertaken elsewhere. The whole collection should be removed from the disaster area.

The ideal location for recovery purposes is a clean, dry and secure area with a temperature below 21°C (70°F) and an RH of 40%. This space should be large enough to allow both transitory storage and recovery processing of affected materials.

Don't forget to keep the magnetic media away from magnetic fields.

Steps in Salvage and Recovery for Water-Damaged Items

Recovery procedures must be appropriate to the types of materials damaged. As first steps,

- Remove collections from the disaster area and transfer them to the recovery area;
- Separate damaged from undamaged material;
- Separate materials from their containers for specific recover; and then,
- Implement the recovery treatment and copy.

Priorities for Recovery

Give priority to

- Unique, rare materials and masters, as well as older materials.
- Organic materials (wax cylinders, paper-backed magnetic tapes, etc.) that are more susceptible to water damage.

Wax Cylinders

- Remove the cylinders from their containers, but handle them carefully because cylinders could drop and break.
- Blot them dry as completely as possible, making sure to remove dirt and debris.
- Set the cylinders on end and allow them to air dry completely.

Phonodiscs

- Remove the discs from their sleeves and jackets. If the labels have separated, mark the centre of the disc with a wax pen and keep track of the label.
- If dirt has been deposited on the discs, wash them in a solution of non-ionic surfactant in cold distilled water, and then rinse thoroughly with cold distilled water.
- Blot excess water with a lint-free cloth, and then air-dry the discs vertically on a support that permits the free circulation of air.
- Air-dry the jackets, sleeves and labels.

Magnetic Tapes

Priority for the recovery of tapes depends on the tape substrate composition and the magnetic metals corrosion. Thus, older tapes must be salvaged before newer ones, paper-backed tapes before cellulose, acetate before polyester. On the other hand, master and unique tapes must be salvaged before those for which copies exist.

The quality of winding is essential for a tape. When spooled properly, the tape pack surface is smooth and has no contact with the tape flanges, which play a protective role. A tape pack is the structure that is formed when a tape is wound onto a hub. Magnetic tapes should be rewound at a controlled tension and speed. If gaps appear between the windings, the tape has been wound too loosely. The distortions of the tape backing are minimized by a tape that is wound tightly. In the event of a disaster, tightly wound tapes prevent water, mud and other debris from penetrating between the windings and causing damage in the core of the tape.

Disaster mitigation procedures involve a series of preliminary actions:

- Separate the wet from the dry tapes.
- Empty water from the tape containers.
- Check the labels for legibility and replace if necessary.
- Allow the tapes to dry without heating in an area with a high circulation of air.
- Once dried, run tapes on a tape-cleaner or winder to remove the debris.
- Copy tapes before checking the data; verify the data from the new tape.

If tapes are just contaminated by water, rinse them in cold water at room temperature, then air dry or dehumidify them at room temperature. It is more complicated when contamination is caused by dirty or salty water, which contains diverse corrosive agents. In these cases, rinse off tapes as soon as possible with clean, cold water.

Remove mud debris from the tape with a detergent solution in water and rinse it with distilled water. If sea water is involved, immerse the tape in tap water, then remove the debris with a mild acidic solution and rinse it thoroughly first with tap water, then distilled water. In all cases, air- dry the tapes at room temperature.

Freeze-drying wet tapes is not recommended. Furthermore, better recovery results are obtained when restoration experts can begin working on tapes while they are still wet. All paper inserts and wet cardboard should be removed to reduce the possibility of fungal growth.

Keep the tapes in a cool and well ventilated area.

Wax crayon may be used to identify the tapes temporarily while being cleaned and dried. Shake off excess water. Do not separate the tape labels from the appropriate tapes.

Tapes on Open Reels (for example, reel-to-reel audio, open-reel computer tape)

- Remove the tapes from canisters and remove the wrap around.
- Rinse the tapes as soon as possible in clean, cold water. If necessary, add a non-aggressive detergent agent to help remove mud or sewage.
- For tapes exposed to clean water, just rinse in distilled water.
- Blot the tapes carefully with a lint-free towel only if the tape is wound properly (if it is not, water got inside the tape pack), and air-dry vertically at room temperature.

Cassettes or Cartridges

If water has not penetrated inside the cassette or cartridge, let it air-dry on absorbent materials. If water has penetrated inside the cassette or cartridge, dismantle it and treat it as open reel tape.

Tapes Damaged by Shock

Recovery of a tape from mild shock requires rewinding the tape properly by re-tensioning and re-spooling it. Severe shocks can break tapes into pieces. If this happens, replace the broken pieces (cassette, reel) and/or re-splice with a high quality tape.

Computer Diskettes

The same procedures used for recovery of tapes can be adopted for computer diskettes. Store diskettes upright, without crowding, in cool distilled water. Do not leave them for more than 72 hours, because water causes leaching of chemicals from the support.

Optical Discs

Undamaged discs with surface deposits can be washed in a one percent solution of a non-ionic solution using a soft brush to carefully dislodge particles. Thoroughly rinse off the solution with plain distilled water and place the discs vertically in a rack, leaving to dry slowly at room temperature.

Note that even if the recovery procedures are similar, shellac, acetate and vinyl discs should be washed in separate containers.

If they have no artifactual value, record jackets or paper protective sleeves should be discarded as they can trap moisture and may develop mold.

The Problem of Mold

Mold growth is a direct consequence of damage caused by water. Recovery from mold requires proper equipment to protect personnel during their work. Moldy materials should be isolated and kept at a relative humidity less than 50 percent.

Mold can be removed by gently wiping the surface with a nonabrasive cloth, a cotton bud or vacuuming with a HEPA (high efficiency particulate air) filter. In some critical cases, alternative sterilization treatment (fumigation) may be necessary.

Conclusion

In conclusion, while it is possible successfully to rescue audiovisual and modern information media, the process can be made more efficient and severe damage mitigated if great attention is given to setting up and implementing preventive conservation programs and disaster preparedness planning.

But all must be accompanied by an ounce of flexibility.

References

Iraci, Joe. 2002. *La récupération des supports d'information modernes, disques compacts, et bandes et disques magnétiques. Bulletin technique n°25.* Ottawa, Canada: Institut canadien de conservation.. Also available in English.

National Archives and Records Administration. 1996. *Vital records and records disaster, mitigation and recovery; an instructional guide.* Washington, D.C., USA. http://palimpsest.stanford.edu/bytopic/disasters/misc/vitalrec/

Society of Motion Picture and Television Engineers. *Care, Storage, Operation, Handling and Shipping of Video Tape for Television.* RP 103-1995. Proposed update, RP 103-1999, is not yet published.

Utah Division of State Archives. 2004. *Disaster preparedness for archives and records centers: A selected bibliography.* http://www.archives.utah.gov/preserv/disprfoa.htm

Van Bogart, John. 1995. *Emergency preparedness and disaster recovery of audio, film and video materials, the Library of Congress Symposium on "Recovery from Disasters," Washington, D.C., USA, September 21, 1995.*

Zacker, Craig and Paul Doyle et al. 1996. Disaster planning for networks. In *Upgrading and Repairing Networks*. Indianapolis: Que.

Author

Léon-Bavi Vilmont is a research scientist at the CRCDG, a joint research laboratory of the French Ministry of Culture and the National Science Research Council. His activities focus on the study of collection materials, characterizing their properties and setting up safeguarding and long-term preservation methods. He is currently conducting a project on the stabilization of audio and video tapes for INA, the organization in charge of the French Broadcasting Archives.

APPENDIX 1
SPEAKERS CONTACT LIST

John Aarons
Government Archivist of Jamaica
Jamaica Archives and Records Department
Office of the Prime Minister
Spanish Town
Jamaica
Tel: 876 984 2581 Fax: 876 984 8254
Email: jard@cwjamaica.com

Chu Tuyet Lan
Director, Department of Documentation and Information
The Institute of Han-Nom Studies
183 Dang Tien Dong
Dong Da
Hanoi
Vietnam
Tel: 844 857 4641 Fax: 844 857 0940
Email: manh@netnam.org.vn

Nevra Erturk
Research Assistant
Faculty of Art and Design
Museum Studies Graduate Program, Art Management Program
Yildiz Technical University
Yildiz Kampusu, 34349
Bestiktas, Istanbul
Turkey
Tel: 00 90 212 259 70 70-2317 Fax: 00 90 212 260 42 59
Email: nerturk@yildiz.edu.tr

Dr. Annette Gerlach
Head of Historical Collections
Zentral- und Landesbibliothek Berlin
Histroische Sondersammlungen
Breite Str. 30-36
10178 Berlin
Germany
Tel: 49 30 90226 717 Fax: 49 30 90226 718
Email: gerlach@zlb.de

Hilary Kaplan
Senior Conservator
National Archives and Records Administration
National Archives at College Park
8601 Adelphi Road
College Park, Maryland 20740-6001
USA
Tel: 1 301 837 0998 Fax: 1 301 837 3615
Email: hilary.kaplan@nara.gov

Dr. Maj Klasson
Professor
Library and Information Science
University College of Borås
Hamngatan 21
58226 Linköping, Sweden
Tel: 0708 164275 Fax (home): 4613 358955
Email: maj.klasson@hb.se

Kathleen Ludwig
Senior Conservator
National Archives and Records Administration
National Archives at College Park
8601 Adelphi Road
College Park, Maryland 20740-6001, USA
Tel: 1 301 837 0998 Fax: 1 301 837 3615
Email: kathleen.ludwig@nara.gov

Graham Matthews
Professor of Information and Library Management
School of Business Information
Faculty of Business and Law
Liverpool John Moores University
John Foster Building
98 Mount Pleasant
Liverpool
United Kingdom L3 5UZ
Tel: 0151 231 3861 Fax: 0151 707 0423
Email: G.Matthews@livjm.ac.uk

Marja Peek
Consultant
Netherlands Institute for Cultural Heritage
PO Box 76709
1070 KA Amsterdam
The Netherlands
Tel: 31 20 3054721 Fax: 31 20 3054633
Email: marja.peek@icn.nl

Lawrence L. Reger
President
Heritage Preservation
Suite 1200
1012 14th Street, NW
Washington, D.C., USA
Tel: 202 233 0815 Fax: 202 233 0807
Email: lreger@heritagepreservation.org

Ross Shimmon
7 Nobel Court
Faversham
Kent ME13 7SD, United Kingdom
Tel: +44 (0)1795 533137
Email: pandrshimmon@btinternet.com

René Teygeler
Consultant
J. van Effenstraat 23 bis
3511 HJ Utrecht, The Netherlands
Tel: 030 2322071 Fax: 030 23282170
Email: rene.teygeler@wxs.nl

Léon-Bavi Vilmont
Research Engineer, Audiovisual Materials and New Media
Centre de Recherches sur la Conservation des Documents Graphiques (CRCDG)
36, rue Geoffroy Saint-Hilaire
F-75005 Paris, France
Tel: 33 1 44 08 69 98 Fax: 33 1 47 07 62 95
Email: vilmont@mnhn.fr

Jiří Vnouček
Head of Conservation Department
National Library of the Czech Republic
Klementinum 190
11001, Praha 1, Czech Republic
Tel: 00 420 2810 13 232 Fax: 0 420 2810 13 107
Email: Jiri.Vnoucek@cdh.nkp.cz

Clara von Waldthausen
Photograph Conservator in Private Practice
Fotorestauratie Atelier C.C. von Waldthausen
Kromme Palmstraat 5
HH Amsterdam, The Netherlands
Tel: 31 20 528 79 74 Fax: 31 20 528 78 4
Email: c.waldthausen@planet.nl

R. Robert Waller
Chief, Conservation
Canadian Museum of Nature
Box 3443, Station D
Ottawa, Ontario K1P 6P4, Canada
Tel: 1 613 566 4797 Fax: 1 613 364 4027
Email: rwaller@mus-nature.ca

Celia Ribeiro Zaher
Director
National Library of Brazil
Av. Rio Branco, 219-40
20040-008 RJ, Rio de Janeiro, Brazil
Tel: 55 21 25448596 Fax: Same
Email: czaher@bn.br

APPENDIX 2

PREPARING FOR THE WORST, PLANNING FOR THE BEST: PROTECTING OUR CULTURAL HERITAGE FROM DISASTER

Akademie der Wissenschaften – Berlin, Germany
July 30-August 1, 2003

TRADE FAIR

The conference on disaster management benefited greatly from the support of several companies who participated in a trade fair. Conferees were able to visit the tables of the companies during breaks and before and after each day's program. The planning committee also set aside time for vendors to make presentations to the audience, if they chose to do so. Company representatives heard the papers and contributed greatly to the overall success of the event. Below is a list of those who participated.

Ashgate Publishing, Ltd.
Gower House, Croft Road
Aldershot, Hampshire GU11 3HR
United Kingdom
http://www.ashgate.com
Represented by:
Suzie Duke, Commissioning Editor
Library & Information Management

Ashgate is a leading international academic publisher in the social sciences and humanities and in professional practice. Two titles of interest are *Disaster Management in Libraries and Archives*, edited by Graham Matthews and John Feather (2003), and *Managing Preservation in Libraries and Archives*, edited by John Feather (2004).

BELFOR International GmbH
Fran-Haniel-Platz 6-8
47119 Duisburg, Germany
http://www.belfor.com/flash/index_select_country.cfm
Represented by:
Dr. Rupert Pentenrieder, BELFOR International GmbH
Christophe Brodhag, BELFOR France S.A.
Cornelia Meyer von Bremen, International Marketing

BELFOR is the world's leading provider of fire, water and storm damage repair services. BELFOR restores damage in private homes, offices and commercial enterprises, as well as in all kinds of large-scale industrial situations, mostly in close cooperation with insurers. Services include drying and restoration of buildings, machines and electronic equipment; restoration of documents; and damage repair in private homes and high-tech areas. BELFOR was involved in clean-up work following the terrorist attacks on the World Trade Center in New York City and in repairing extensive damage caused by the flood disaster in eastern Europe.

Council on Library and Information Resources, Inc.
1755 Massachusetts Ave., NW, Suite 500
Washington, DC 20036 USA
http://www.clir.org/
Represented by:
Alice Bishop, Special Projects Associate

The Council on Library and Information Resources (CLIR) is an independent, nonprofit organization that works to expand access to information, however recorded and preserved, as a public good. In partnership with other organizations, CLIR helps create services that expand the concept of "library" and supports the providers and preservers of information. Through projects, programs, and publications, CLIR works to maintain and improve access to information for generations to come.

Krah & Grote Measurement Solutions
Fichtenstrasse 23
85649 Hofolding, Germany
http://www.krah-grote.com.de
Represented by:
Andreas Reiter

Krah & Grote is engaged in the development of high precision sensors and measurement systems for museums, restoration, industry, science and research. The company provides calibration services for relative humidity and temperature.

PAL Preservation Academy GmbH
Kreuzstrasse 4
04103 Leipzig, Germany
http://www.bestandserhaltung.com/
Represented by:
Eva Fischer, Restorer
Dr. Alexander Geschke

PAL's principal activity is preservation of paper, including conservation treatments such as wet treatment, deacidification and stabilization by paper splitting, microfilming and digitization. The Academy is engaged in research and development as well as in education for all customers in libraries, archives, and other collections.

Preservation Technologies, B.V. (Europe)
Pluim-es 18
2925 CM Krimpen a/d ljssel
The Netherlands
http://www.ptlp.com/contact.html
Represented by:
John van Dorsten, Managing Director

Preservation Technologies provides deacidification products and services, freeze-drying services, packing and re-boxing in acid-free packing material. In cases of disaster, the company arranges for transport of wet materials to cold stores for freeze-drying, repacking and boxing.

Bei Fragen zur Produktsicherheit wenden Sie sich bitte an:
If you have any questions regarding product safety,
please contact:

Walter de Gruyter GmbH
Genthiner Straße 13
10785 Berlin
productsafety@degruyterbrill.com